ACCOUNTING FOR SOCIAL VALUE

Edited by Laurie Mook

When organizations use social accounting practices, they are able to measure their performance in terms of benefits accrued to key stakeholders such as their communities, human resources, and those investing in the organization. The application of social accounting practices can lead to a fundamentally different perspective on the value of an organization. Through case studies of organizations that have implemented social accounting in the United States, Canada, India, and Scotland, *Accounting for Social Value* sheds light on key issues in this growing field.

Building on two related titles, *Researching the Social Economy* (2010) and *Businesses with a Difference* (2012), *Accounting for Social Value* offers academics, accountants, policy-developers, and members of non-profit, co-operative, and for-profit organizations tools and insights to explore the connections between economic, social, and environmental dimensions. The lessons learned are valuable not only for other social economy organizations, but also for organizations in the public and for-profit sectors.

LAURIE MOOK is an assistant professor in the School of Community Resources and Development at Arizona State University.

Accounting for Social Value

EDITED BY LAURIE MOOK

UNIVERSITY OF TORONTO PRESS
Toronto Buffalo London

© University of Toronto Press 2013
Toronto Buffalo London
www.utppublishing.com
Printed in Canada

ISBN 978-1-4426-4263-8 (cloth)
ISBN 978-1-4426-1146-7 (paper)

∞

Printed on acid-free, 100% post-consumer recycled paper with vegetable-based inks.

Library and Archives Canada Cataloguing in Publication

Accounting for social value / edited by Laurie Mook

Includes bibliographical references.

ISBN 978-1-4426-4263-8 (bound). — ISBN 978-1-4426-1146-7 (pbk.)

1. Social accounting. 2. Economies — Sociological aspects. 3. Environmental economics. 4. Social entrepreneurship. I. Mook, Laurie.

HD60.A33 2012   658.4'08   C2012-908099-3

University of Toronto Press acknowledges the financial assistance to its publishing program of the Canada Council for the Arts and the Ontario Arts Council.

 Canada Council   Conseil des Arts
for the Arts   du Canada

ONTARIO ARTS COUNCIL
CONSEIL DES ARTS DE L'ONTARIO
50 YEARS OF ONTARIO GOVERNMENT SUPPORT OF THE ARTS
50 ANS DE SOUTIEN DU GOUVERNEMENT DE L'ONTARIO AUX ARTS

University of Toronto Press acknowledges the financial support of the Government of Canada through the Canada Book Fund for its publishing activities.

Contents

Preface

In Canada and throughout the world, there is a myriad of organizations that have both social and economic objectives. Among them are social economy organizations (non-profit organizations, co-operatives, social enterprises), for-profits with environmental and social mandates, and public sector enterprises.

The initial impetus for this book is that the traditional accounting statements (i.e., income statements and balance sheets) for socially minded organizations fall short in two important areas. First, traditional accounting is incomplete as it ignores several significant sources of input, for instance, volunteer labour. Second, it ignores a significant part of its output, particularly social and environmental outputs that do not involve market exchange. Because of these two features, traditional accounting leaves much to be desired in terms of helping socially minded organizations to measure their performance according to their combined social and economic objectives.

Indeed, traditional accounting primarily reflects the needs of owners and managers of profit-oriented businesses. However, there is nothing inherent in accounting that limits it to this set of interests. Social accounting reorients accounting to a broader set of social variables and social interests.

The general purpose of this book is to provide an understanding of key issues and areas of activity in social accounting, especially as it relates to social economy organizations today.

There are varying definitions of social accounting; however, all share the common goal of expanding the range of criteria that are taken into consideration when measuring performance and looking at an organization in relation to its surrounding environment. Additionally, they stress that the audience for social accounting is broader and may differ from that for other forms of accounting. Social accounting can be conceptualized as a systematic analysis of the effects of an organization on its communities of interest or stakeholders.

Much of the research on which these chapters are based was funded through a Social Sciences and Humanities Research Council of Canada (SSHRC) grant for work on the social economy, which ran from 2005 to 2010, and for which we are grateful. It is exciting to see the resulting rise in knowledge dissemination and the multiple new approaches to exploring issues relevant to both practice and theory in the social economy. This book is the latest of a series of books on the social economy that we have published recently: *What Counts: Social Accounting for Nonprofits and Co-operatives* (2007); *Understanding the Social Economy* (2010); *Researching the Social Economy* (2010); and *Businesses with a Difference* (2012).

Overall, the chapters in this book, which include case studies from Canada, the U.S., India, and Scotland, offer academics, accountants, policy developers, members of organizations, and society at large the tools and insights to explore the connections between economic, social, and environmental dimensions, as well as the inter-relationships between organizations in different sectors of society. They provide an alternate way of thinking about how economic, social, and environmental issues coincide – and also collide. We believe that this book will make a valuable contribution to the understanding of social economy organizations, and we hope that the lessons learned from these organizations will be useful for the public and for-profit sectors as well.

There are many to thank for making this volume possible. First are the authors and organizations who created the innovative and thoughtful social accounting frameworks presented in this book. Jack Quarter at the University of Toronto provided unfailing leadership in securing the SSHRC grant that led to many of these chapters. Mikulas Pstross provided exceptional assistance in carefully reviewing the manuscript and in co-writing the concluding chapter with me. I would also like to acknowledge the invaluable support of Jennifer DiDomenico, editor of Business and Economics at the University of Toronto Press. Finally, thank you to all our families and friends, and we hope this book inspires a new generation of social accountants throughout the world.

Laurie Mook

Contributors

Jan Bebbington holds a chair in Accounting and Sustainable Development in the School of Management at the University of St Andrews and is the director of the St Andrews Sustainability Institute, which was formed in 2006 to co-ordinate interdisciplinary research and to develop post-graduate degrees in sustainable development. Her research interests focus around the dual themes of corporate reporting on sustainable development and full-cost accounting and modelling. Professor Bebbington was also vice-chair (Scotland) of the UK's Sustainable Development Commission from 2006–11 and has an interest in furthering governance for sustainable development within governments.

Leslie Brown is a professor in the Department of Sociology and Anthropology at Mount Saint Vincent University. She was the director of the SSHRC-funded Social Economy and Sustainability Research Network (SESRN) and is Atlantic Cluster Co-lead in the Measuring the Co-operative Difference Research Network (MCDRN). She has written and published extensively in the areas of organizational democracy, co-operatives, and community development. Most recently she co-edited, with S. Novkovic, *Social Economy: Communities, Economies and Solidarity in Atlantic Canada*, published by Cape Breton University Press (Sydney, NS, 2012).

Manjula Cherkil is a senior executive at the Centre for Corporate Governance and Citizenship, Indian Institute of Management, Bangalore, India, and a research associate for the Five College Women's Studies

Research Center (FCWSRC), Mount Holyoke College, South Hadley. She is actively involved with leading women's movements in India, with a view to providing knowledge and skills in the application of the principles of the UN Convention on the Elimination of All Forms of Discrimination against Women (CEDAW). Her research focuses on disadvantaged women workers who have been displaced from the agrarian sector and forced into informal employment. She holds a Master of Economics (University of Madras, India).

Massimo Contrafatto is a lecturer in the Department of Management, Accounting and Quantitative Methods at the University of Bergamo (Italy), and lecturer and assistant professor in social and environmental reporting and management accounting. His research interests are primarily in social and environmental reporting, sustainability reporting, institutional theory, and organizational change. He has conducted several pieces of research adopting methodologies based on field case studies and action research.

Elizabeth Hicks is a chartered accountant and an associate professor in the Business and Tourism Department at Mount Saint Vincent University where she teaches courses in accounting and taxation. She is a board member of both the Centre of Excellence in Accounting and Reporting for Co-operatives (CEAEC) and the Association of Nonprofit and Social Economy Research (ANSER). Her research interests are in the area of financial, environmental, social, and ethical accounting and reporting for co-operatives.

Edward T. Jackson is a faculty member in the School of Public Policy and Administration at Carleton University, where he is also cross-appointed to the Norman Paterson School of International Affairs and the Institute of African Studies. In addition, he serves as a senior research fellow in the Carleton Centre for Community Innovation. A former associate dean (research) in Carleton's Faculty of Public Affairs, and co-founder of the Carleton University-World Bank International Program for Development Evaluation Training, he is an authority on participatory evaluation, results-based management, social enterprise, social finance, and community-university partnerships. He has directed major projects financed by CIDA, the McConnell Foundation, the Ontario Trillium Foundation, the Rockefeller Foundation, and SSHRC.

Robert J. Johnston is the director of the George Perkins Marsh Institute and a professor of economics at Clark University. He is an environmental economist with extensive publications on nonmarket valuation, benefit transfer, and tourism economics. He is past president of the Northeastern Agricultural and Resource Economics Association, vice-president of the Marine Resource Economics Foundation, and is on the Program Committee for the Charles Darwin Foundation, the Science Advisory Board for the Communication Partnership for Science and the Sea, and the Gulf of Maine Regional Ocean Science Council. He is also on the advisory boards of the Connecticut and New York Sea Grant programs.

J.J. McMurtry is an associate professor in the Business and Society Program at York University. His teaching and research focus on the theory and practice of the social economy.

Jacqueline Medalye is a PhD candidate in political science at York University and currently serves as the climate justice research fellow at the York Institute for Research and Innovation in Sustainability (IRIS). Her dissertation explores the politics of climate change adaptation in the Global South.

Laurie Mook is an assistant professor in the Nonprofit Leadership and Management program in the School of Community Resources and Development, Arizona State University, and research associate at the Lodestar Center for Nonprofit Innovation and Philanthropy, also at Arizona State University. Prior to moving to Arizona, Laurie was co-director of the Social Economy Centre of the University of Toronto in Canada. Among other books, she is co-author of *What Counts: Social Accounting for Nonprofits and Cooperatives*, now in its second edition from Sigel Press. Her areas of interest are the social economy (non-profits, co-operatives, and social enterprises), volunteerism, and social accounting.

Ananya Mukherjee is a professor of political science and development studies at York University, Toronto. She is the founding director of the International Secretariat of Human Development (ISHD) at York University. Ananya's latest book, *Human Development and Social Power: Perspectives from South Asia*, was published by Routledge (New York, 2008).

Mikulas Pstross is a doctoral student in the School of Community Resources and Development at Arizona State University. His research is anchored in community development, specifically in the topic of youth civic engagement.

Darryl Reed teaches in the Business and Society program at York University. While he has a wide range of academic interests including business ethics, corporate social responsibility, and development ethics, his primary focus is on the social economy in the context of development, with a special emphasis on co-operatives and fair trade movements.

Katherine Ruff is a researcher at Charity Intelligence Canada where she is responsible for the ongoing development of methodologies to assess the social results of charities. Her work on intermediaries and transparency systems is an extension of her master's thesis at the London School of Economics.

Bryn Sadownik is the program manager of evaluation and community impact at Vancity Community Foundation. She works to enhance the capacity of Vancity and a number of community-based organizations to strategically plan, manage, and communicate the value of their work, and in particular the measurement of their social and environmental impact. Bryn has over fifteen years of experience working in impact assessment and cost-effectiveness analysis. Bryn previously worked as a consultant and researcher at Simon Fraser University, leading numerous projects for government, private sector, and non-profit organizations. Bryn holds a BA from Carleton University and a Master of Resource and Environmental Management from SFU.

Michele Tarsilla is an evaluation advisor at Social Impact Inc. (Washington, DC). Michele has designed and managed over twenty participatory evaluations of World Bank and United Nations projects in a variety of sectors (including health, social protection, and food security) in sub-Saharan Africa and Latin America over the last ten years. He also has undertaken evaluations of microfinance initiatives and corporate social responsibility programs for foundations and credit unions in North America. As a Fulbright Scholar, Michele received his master's degree in Foreign Service at Georgetown University. After completing his graduate diploma in public policy and program evaluation at Carleton University (Ottawa), he received his PhD in interdisciplinary evaluation at Western Michigan University.

Timothy J. Tyrrell, director of the Center for Sustainable Tourism at Arizona State University, earned a PhD from Cornell University in agricultural economics after an MA in economics from the University of Tennessee and a BA in mathematics from the University of South Florida. He served as professor of environmental economics at the University of Rhode Island from 1978 until 2005, and is currently professor of tourism development and management at ASU. He has conducted market research, sustainable development, and economic impact studies of tourism in many parts of the world and has published numerous articles.

ACCOUNTING FOR SOCIAL VALUE

PART I

Introduction

1 Social Accounting for the Social Economy

LAURIE MOOK

Social accounting expands the range of criteria taken into consideration when measuring performance in the context of an organization's environment, both social and natural. It typically highlights economic, social, and environmental factors, and is intended for a broad audience. Accounting in general has an influence on behaviour, and for organizations that have a social purpose as their primary raison d'être, social accounting has the potential to be a driver of social change (Mook, 2007).

This chapter provides an overview of social accounting for organizations that have a social purpose or mission – for instance, non-profit organizations, co-operatives, and social enterprises. It begins with the critique of traditional accounting from which social accounting rose, followed by an examination of the emergence of the social accounting model in three waves: during the 1970s, the 1990s, and from the 2000s on. It continues with an overview of the remaining chapters in this book.

Approaches to Accounting

Accounting is typically defined as the process of identifying, gathering, measuring, summarizing, and analysing financial data in order to support economic decision-making (American Accounting Association, 1990, 1992). This approach to accounting is reflected in teaching and professional development, which treats the discipline as a neutral, technical, and value-free activity and focuses on technique acquisition (Gray, Bebbington, & McPhail, 1994; Hopwood, 1990; Lewis, Humphrey, & Owen, 1992; Roslender & Dillard, 2003).

Criticisms to traditional accounting emerged in the 1960s and 1970s and gave birth to a second approach known as critical accounting. Critical accounting scholars systematically questioned the assumptions underlying traditional accounting, arguing that accounting practices are not objective, neutral, or value-free, and that they create, sustain, and may even change social reality (Cooper & Neu, 1997; Craig & Amernic, 2004; Gray, 2002; Hines, 1988; Hopper, Storey, & Willmott, 1987; Llewellyn, 1994; Lodh & Gaffikin, 1997; Morgan, 1988; Tinker, 1985). For instance, critical accountants argue that, by the very act of counting certain things and excluding others, accounting shapes a particular interpretation of social reality. This interpretation, which corresponds to particular assumptions about how society functions and should function, in turn has implications for decision-making and policy (Hines, 1988; Tinker, Merino, & Neimark, 1982).

Critical accounting also urges us to reflect upon the conditions and consequences of accounting – especially as they lead to alienation, oppression, and emancipation – and to consider accounting within a broad societal context (Lodh & Gaffikin, 1997; Roslender & Dillard, 2003). Critical accounting asserts that organizations have an impact on a wide group of stakeholders and that accountability to these groups is desirable as a democratic mechanism (Gray et al., 1997).

At its best, critical accounting seeks not only to understand the world but also to change it. Indeed, in theory, critical accounting aims to "engender progressive change within the conceptual, institutional, practical, and political territories of accounting" through all evaluative forms of social praxis (Tinker, 2005, p. 100). Yet this goal is hypothetical, as most often critical accounting theorists develop critiques without suggesting alternative models to address issues of economic, social, and ecological justice in everyday life (Cooper, 2002; Cooper & Hopper, 2006; Dey, 2000, 2002; Gray, 1998; Gray, Owen, & Adams, 2010). This emphasis on theoretical critique is not meant to detract from the merits of critical accounting. In fact, its contributions have raised important insights that are helpful for understanding accounting frameworks and practices from a critical perspective. However, for the most part, this approach does not provide accountants with working strategies and tools that challenge traditional accounting practices. This is precisely the intent of the third approach, social accounting.

Social accounting shares most of the critiques of traditional accounting that are raised by critical accounting, but attempts to provide a working framework that takes into consideration a broader range of factors and actors in the accounting process. Social accounting is a broad term that includes a variety of alternative accounting models, including expanded value added accounting, environmental accounting, and sustainability accounting.

Social accounting has been criticized by supporters of both traditional accounting and critical accounting. The traditional response relates to Friedman's frequently quoted statement on corporate orientation:

> There is one and only one social responsibility of business – to use its resources and engage in activities designed to increase its profits so long as it stays within the rules of the game, which is to say, engages in open and free competition without deception or fraud. (Friedman, 1970, p. 32)

From this perspective, social responsibility is narrowly constructed to mean the maximization of profits, and thus any focus outside of this is not considered to be in the best interest of the firm.

From a critical accounting standpoint, social accounting is sometimes seen as a discourse that legitimizes the status quo; that does not question the role that capitalism plays in perpetuating unequal and exploitive social relations; and that actually creates the illusion that progress can be made by corporations (Everett & Neu, 2000). Lehman (1999, p. 220) goes even further and states: "The procedural and instrumental tendencies within reform accounting models can stall the construction of more critical and interpretive models." Indeed, it is becoming more apparent that the current form of capitalism, "based on private property rights, growth and expansion, competition, maximizing consumption of non-essentials, maximizing returns to shareholders and directors and so on," is not sustainable and cannot be sustainable (Gore, 2006; Gray, 2005; Gray & Milne, 2004, p. 73).

The problem with this critique is that it does not give accountants or anyone else the agency to change accounting frameworks and practices. This book argues instead that, while accountants have the option of continuing with the current accounting systems that sustain the status quo, they also have the ability to create more democratic, transparent, and participatory accounting practices in the context of a broader strategy for social change. Moreover, social accounting can be applied to any social system; it is not strictly a capitalist project. The idea of looking at multiple bottom lines from a stakeholder perspective is a useful way of understanding the interconnections between the economic, social, and environmental dimensions of any society. Indeed, it provides processes necessary to understand and take simultaneous action on economic, social, and ecological justice issues.

Social Accounting Models

It is pertinent to note that social accounting projects can fall into two broad categories. One of them, which we call supplemental social accounting, uses qualitative data and descriptive statistics to assess the extent to which an organization is meeting the expectations of its stakeholders in executing its mission (New Economics Foundation, 1998; Sillanpää, 1998; Zadek, 1998). Such qualitative social accounting is frequently supplemental to the organization's financial accounts, and as such often receives secondary status (Coupland, 2006). It may also be difficult with supplemental reports to judge the relative materiality of social and environmental actions with respect to economic performance. As a result, social and environmental reports published by an increasing number of corporations are frequently dismissed as "greenwashing" or "specious gloss" (Laufer, 2003; Owen & Swift, 2001, p. 5).

Other models integrate social, environmental, and economic data. In other words, in these models the social and environmental dimensions are not supplemental to the financial accounts; rather, the three together are integral. We use the term "integrated social accounting" to refer to this approach. These models expand the range of items considered when measuring performance and present them in one statement. They assign a monetary value to non-monetary social and environmental items in order to include items not exchanged on the market within an accounting statement. In addition, many are driven by a vision of justice, take a stakeholder approach, and thus make visible the concept of social relations.

As can be seen in Table 1.1, there have been three waves of integrated social accounting. The first was in the 1970s and was characterized by bold experimentation with alternative accounting models for for-profit organizations, as well as bold claims about what they could measure and represent. This experimentation all but disappeared in the 1980s, and in the 1990s a second wave re-emerged – albeit with a more cautious approach that was more realistic about what these models could measure (Gray, 1998, 2001). This second wave also saw several models applied to organizations outside the for-profit sector, such as nonprofits and co-operatives. The third wave, which began in the 2000s and has continued until today, takes a more holistic view of the organization, including a broader view of accountability. It incorporates both

Table 1.1. Integrated Social Accounting in Three Waves

First Wave (1970s) • Bold experimentation • Bold expectations		Second Wave (1990s on) • Cautious experimentation • More realistic expectations		Third Wave (2000s on) • Holistic approach • Accountability & strategic planning • Approaching mainstream	
Applied to for-profit organizations	Applied to other organizations	Applied to for-profit organizations	Applied to other organizations	Applied to for-profit organizations	Applied to other organizations
Social and Financial Income Statement (1971, Abt & Associates)		Triple Bottom Line (1994, Elkington)	Social Impact Statement (1996, Land)	GRI Guidelines & Supplements (2003)	Balanced Scorecard approach (2001 Kaplan; 2004 Somers; 2007, Bull; 2008, Martello, Watson, & Fischer; 2007, Manville)
Socio-economic Operating Statement (1972, Linowes)		Bottomline[3] (2006, Weidmann & Lenzen)	Co-operative Social Balance (1997, Vaccari)		Global Reporting Initiative NGO Sector Supplement (2010, GRI)
Statement of Fund Flows for Socially Relevant Activities (1973, Dilley & Weygandt)		Sustainable Cost Calculation (1990s, Bebbington & Gray)	Community Social Return on Investment (1999, Richmond)		
Social Impact Statement (1976, Estes)		Sustainability Assessment Model (late 1990s, Baxter, Bebbington, & Cutteridge)	Expanded Value Added Statement (1999, 2002, 2007, Mook)		
Goal-Oriented Profit-and-Loss Statement (1977, Gröjer & Stark)		Financial Sustainability Accounting (2002, Bent & Richardson)	Socio-economic Impact Statement (2002, 2006, Mook)		
			Socio-economic Resource Statement (2002, Mook)		

qualitative and quantitative measures while integrating financial, social, and environmental factors.

The First Wave

The 1970s saw a growing public demand for information related to expenditures and associated social impacts (Dilley & Weygandt, 1973). As
a result, there was also increased experimentation with different accounting statements. Predictions were made that social audits would be
required for business organizations within the next ten years (Linowes,
1972). However, as we know now, this was not to be.

It was in this period that David Linowes (1972) created the Socio-
economic Operating Statement, designed to include "expenditures
made voluntarily by a business aimed at the improvement of the welfare of the employees and public, safety of the product, and/or conditions of the environment" (Linowes, 1973, p. 40). In this statement,
Linowes highlighted improvements and detriments, taking the difference between the two as the total socio-economic contribution or deficit
for the year. Examples of improvements included the cost of pollution
abatement equipment required by law; tangible benefits for employees
not specified in collective agreements; and cash and in-kind donations
made by the organization. Detriments were those items that had been
brought to the attention of management but had not been acted upon,
such as safety devices or pollution-reduction devices that management
had neglected to install.

Linowes's call to identify and include elements that had been brought
to the attention of management but ignored, or "social nonactions,"
was controversial (Burton, 1973; Linowes, 1973, p. 41; Mobley, 1973), as
was the monetization of social actions (Bauer, 1973; Burton, 1973; Lewis,
1973; Mobley, 1973). Linowes's goal to come up with a firm's total yearly
socio-economic contribution or deficit that could be comparable with
others in the same industry was clearly fraught with a great range of
complexities. These complexities led most commentators to dismiss
this form of accounting. However, the criticism did not stop other experiments from emerging. A similar statement was proposed by Estes
(1976), which he called the Social Impact Statement. In this case, he used
the terminology "social benefit" and "social costs," with a resulting
"social surplus" or "social deficit."

Dilley and Weygandt (1973) presented a Social Responsibility Annual Report for a publicly owned Midwest gas and electric utility and

included with it a Statement of Funds Flow for socially relevant activities. Although they saw a benefit-cost approach as the most promising, they proposed the cost outlay approach as a first step because of the difficulty in measuring benefits. The Dilley and Weygandt statement highlighted expenditures related to environmental and social activities, and also showed these expenditures as a percentage of operating revenues in order to indicate the portion of sales revenues applied to social concerns. It also showed environmental and social expenditures as a percentage of advertising expenses to illustrate "the emphasis placed on solving social problems versus creating future sales" (p. 70). Items under the category "environmental" related to pollution control and environmental research, while the category "social" included items such as charitable contributions and employee educational and recreational expenditures. The Statement of Funds Flow highlighted the additional expenditures that the company incurred by taking social and environmental considerations into account.

The Abt model was another early attempt at social accounting (Abt & Associates, 1971, as cited in Butcher, 1973). Unlike other accounting innovators of this period who created new accounting statements to supplement traditional ones, the Abt model attempted to modify existing statements by rearranging them and adding items that broadened the issues included. For example, the Abt group produced a balance sheet that attempted to estimate an organization's impact on staff, clients, owners, the neighbouring community, and the general public. They also produced a Social and Financial Income Statement using the same principles as for the balance sheet – a broader array of variables, including those for which market values have to be estimated, and a breakdown by stakeholder groups. For example, the stakeholder "community" was shown to receive benefits through local taxes paid by the company, environmental improvements, and reduced parking space. Layoffs and involuntary terminations were treated as a social cost, as was the difference of earnings between a minority or female staff member and a non-minority or male staff member. Staff overtime "worked but not paid" was considered a subsidy to society and clients, and environmental resources used through pollution were treated as a cost to society because these were effects of production for which the company did not pay. However, Abt's approach was seen as too abstract and complicated to be viable for traditional accounting (Bauer & Fenn, 1973).

In Sweden, Gröjer and Stark (1977) undertook a social accounting experiment with a major Swedish company called Fortia Group, responding to what they saw as changes in social values towards a greater emphasis on quality of life. They sought to develop a social accounting framework founded on a theoretical base, and they started by defining their understanding of the purpose of accounting: "accounting is seen as providing a description in both monetary and non-monetary terms of the positive and negative effects which human beings or groups of human beings perceive as stemming from a company's operations" (Gröjer & Stark, 1977, p. 350). They rejected the idea that financial accounting was a subset of social accounting, instead positing that it was neither possible nor desirable to separate economic from social factors. They attempted to answer three questions: "(1) Accounting by whom? (2) Accounting for whom? (3) Accounting of what?" (Gröjer & Stark, 1977, p. 351). Using a goal-oriented approach, they determined the goal fulfillment criteria of the company's different groups of participants – employees, local authorities (municipalities), county councils, national authorities, the external environment, foreign participants, shareholders, and the firm – and constructed a profit and loss account for each group. The goals were translated into indicators at the micro level, and the accounting entity thus became defined through an identification of the effects of the company's operations on the goals of each of the different participants. Theoretically, the totality of these individual profit-and-loss statements would give the total profit and loss of the company; practically, however, the model provided a surrogate measure rather than a real measure of welfare. Nevertheless, the researchers felt that this was still better than the measure of performance expressed through traditional financial statements.

The Second Wave

After the first wave of the 1970s, integrated approaches to social accounting all but disappeared for a decade. They reappeared with the triple bottom line approach proposed by John Elkington in the early 1990s (Elkington, 2004), signalling the start of the second wave. The three bottoms lines he referred to were: people (social equity), planet (environmental quality), and profit (economic prosperity) (Elkington, 2004). This was a conscious effort to develop language that would resonate with business, as business organizations were his main clients (Elkington, 2004). And resonate it did.

   The triple-bottom-line concept was taken up by researchers at the University of Sydney in the Centre for Integrated Sustainability Analysis (out of the School of Physics) to develop a framework for measuring corporate performance against economic, social, and environmental sector benchmarks (Weidmann & Lenzen, 2006). They applied the framework to dozens of organizations including companies, government departments, and non-profits. One clear finding from the applications of this model was that the data collection burden had to be small if the framework was to be taken up at all. As a result, they developed a software tool called *Bottomline*[3] that would create a comprehensive sustainability report based on existing financial information only. An interesting output of this program was the generation of a benchmark "spider diagram," which showed how the key financial, social, and environmental indicators of the organization measured against the average triple-bottom-line performance of the sector that the organization was based in.

The second wave of integrated social accounting also saw the emergence of a derivative of social and environmental accounting called sustainability accounting. Sustainability is a term that has a long history and many definitions, but its public and policy consciousness is most often linked to the 1987 United Nations report, *Our Common Future*, also known as the Brundtland Report (Bebbington & Gray, 2006). The report calls for "a form of sustainable development which meets the needs of the present without compromising the ability of future generations to meet their own needs" (UNWCED, 1987, p. 8). In other words, there was a call for both inter- and intra-generational equity and development that was not about increasing profits and the standard of living for a few, but about efficient, profitable, and fair production to make life better for everyone while also protecting the environment (Gray & Milne, 2004).

Sustainability accounting supports and monitors an organization's contribution towards or away from sustainability (Gray & Milne, 2004; Schaltegger, Bennett, & Burritt, 2006). Whereas the concept of the triple bottom line is often thought of as the pillar of economic, social, and environmental bottom lines, sustainability accounting addresses the integration of these three facets while taking efficiency and effectiveness into consideration. It tries to move away from the approach of "making the wrong things less bad," focusing instead on doing the right thing in the first place (McDonough & Braungart, 2002, p. 76). Sustainability accounting is thought to be most useful in considering the impacts of a range of organizations as opposed to the impact of individual organizations. In this way it is a systems concept rather than an organizational concept (Gray & Milne, 2004).

Another experiment with integrated accounting in the 1990s was done by Bebbington and Gray (2001), who attempted to develop a "sustainable cost calculation" for a New Zealand company that specialized in conducting research into the sustainable management of land ecosystems. Although the researchers and the organization did not have any detailed idea about how to put together a sustainable cost calculation, they did initially have some expectations about the magnitude of the figures that would be produced. As a first stage, they set out to get an idea of the organization's scope of operations. Based on factors they thought would have a significant environmental impact and which were quantifiable, they decided to focus on four areas: energy, transport, core operations, and a recently completed building project. The first three of these areas related to revenue-generating activities, and the last to a capital project.

They developed a costing method over the next seven years, showing in incremental steps what it would cost to become fully sustainable. However, when all the numbers were put together they were much smaller than anticipated, and this caused uncertainties about the relevance of the project. In practical terms, there were several issues, first of all in terms of the completeness of the data and the availability of reliable cost data. Second, it was found that there was only so much a firm could do to move towards sustainability by changing its operating and purchasing habits to target more sustainable goods and services. Finally, one issue that no one had fully anticipated was the organization's reluctance to significantly change its way from "business-as-usual." Nevertheless, key lessons from this experiment included the central importance of undertaking new accounting experiments in actual organizations, reflecting on the process and results, and re-conceptualizing as needed.

An example from the late 1990s was that of British Petroleum, in collaboration with the University of Aberdeen and Genesis Oil and Gas Consultants, who took the concept of sustainability accounting and developed the Sustainability Assessment Model (SAM). This model quantified the social, environmental, economic, and resource usage impacts of infrastructure projects over their full life cycle, from "cradle to grave" (Baxter, Bebbington, & Cutteridge, 2004; Brown & Frame, 2005). Impacts were measured through twenty-two performance indicators and then monetized. The result was a project-specific, graphical "SAM signature" showing both the positive and negative impacts of changes in economic, environmental, and social capital. The SAM signature presented performance in four categories: social impacts (positive and negative), environmental impacts (primarily damage), resource usages, and financial flows to the economic entity and its stakeholders (e.g., shareholders, employees, suppliers, government). The developers of the Sustainability Assessment Model explicitly maintain that the SAM does not make a definitive statement of an organization's impact on sustainable development. Rather, they advocate the use of the model as a starting point for discussions and decision-making.

Another group of researchers, Bent and Richardson (2002), started with the main traditional accounting statements and modified them along three dimensions: timing, location, and type of impact. Their model involved restating the profit-and-loss statement to show the internal flow of goods and services through a Value Added Statement, an Environmental Financial Statement, and a Social Financial Statement. They also proposed an extended balance sheet to include a fuller account of an organization's range of assets (manufacturing, financial, human, social, and natural capital) and "shadow" liabilities (liabilities relating to sustainability risks).

Social Accounting for Social Economy Organizations

The second wave of integrated social accounting also saw the beginning of experimentation with models for organizations outside of the for-profit sector. For non-profits, Land (1996) developed a Social Impact Statement that distinguished between three components: output, outcome, and side-effect indicators. He used the example of a Meals on Wheels program to show how these indicators could be measured. For instance, output indicators included the number of meals delivered and people served; outcome indicators focused on client satisfaction; and side-effect indicators looked at the impact of the delivery of meals on the clients' nutritional or health status.

Based on this framework, Richmond (1999) created the Community Social Return on Investment model in order to look at how social organizations create value from the perspective of the community. Using a case study of a community-based employment training agency serving persons with disabilities and other severe barriers to employment, the model analysed the organization's primary, secondary, and tertiary outputs in order to reflect the organization's social return-on-investment. In order to do so, it developed a comparative economic value for social outputs and also included a value for volunteer contributions.

Vaccari (1997) developed a Co-operative Social Balance Statement to reflect the extent to which co-operatives achieve their social mission. This statement is organized by stakeholder groups: members, consumers, employees, civil society, and the co-operative movement. One unique feature of this statement is a section that highlights the co-operative's investment in member participation in committees, in the board of directors, and in annual general meetings.

The Expanded Value Added Statement (EVAS), which was developed by Mook starting in the late 1990s (Mook, 2007), is based on the Value Added Statement and is expanded to include social and environmental factors. The Value Added Statement assumes that the purpose of an organization, in addition to profitability, is to contribute to a broader community (Suojanen, 1954). The measure of this contribution is called "value added." The groups that are typically considered in the creation and distribution of value added are employees, creditors, the government, and the organization.

The EVAS also assumes that the purpose of organizations is to contribute to a broader community, but it includes both paid and unpaid labour as well as physical and natural capital. For example, unpaid labour such as volunteer contributions and natural capital such as the environment are considered in the EVAS (Mook, 2007; Mook et al., 2007). In addition, the EVAS has been applied in other settings, for instance with community economic development organizations in Canada (Babcock, 2007; Jackson, Babcock, Cholich, & Harji, 2007), and in the annual report of a large non-profit organization in the Netherlands under the guidance of a major accounting firm (KNRM, 2012; van der Meer, 2007). The EVAS was also used in a major study of the value added from literacy volunteers in Ontario (Community Literacy of Ontario, 2005).

By making explicit the distribution of wealth that goes to stakeholder groups, the Expanded Value Added Statement makes issues of equity visible, providing an opportunity to evaluate the fairness of these distributions. A more challenging issue is found in shifting the paradigm of accounting from focusing on profits for owners and shareholders to focusing on wealth for a larger group of stakeholders, including sustaining the planet for future generations. The value-added approach is useful in this regard as it asks us to look at the value added or subtracted in the transformation by labour and capital of externally purchased goods and services. It is a way of focusing on the implications of our actions that can be easily understood by those outside the accounting profession. It attempts to answer the question, *what difference do our actions make in economic, social, and environmental terms?* This is in sharp contrast to the question asked by traditional accounting, *how can we maximize profit for our owners?*

Two additional social accounting frameworks developed by Mook in the early 2000s were the Socio-economic Impact Statement and the Socio-economic Resource Statement (Mook & Quarter, 2006; Mook et al., 2007). The first of these considers the flow of monetary and social resources to and from stakeholders, while the latter examines the resources and obligations of an organization at a specific point in time. In this statement, value-creating resources include both economic (financial and physical) resources and intellectual resources, with the latter being broken down into three components: human capital (including volunteers), organizational capital, and relational capital.

The Third Wave

Starting at the beginning of the 2000s and continuing to the present, a more holistic approach to social accounting was advanced to encompass issues of accountability, performance, and strategic planning. Two notable social accounting models that have emerged during this phase are the Balanced Scorecard and the Global Reporting Initiative.

The Balanced Scorecard has been used in the for-profit sector as a performance measurement and management tool for strategic planning since the 1980s, however it was only adapted by non-profit and other social organizations starting in the 2000s (e.g., Bull, 2007; Kaplan, 2001; Manville, 2007; Martello et al., 2008; Somers, 2004). The Balanced Scorecard was originally developed to address the failure of the financial accounting model to account for intangible items such as information technology and employee skills and knowledge. In order to provide a more "balanced" view of an organization's performance and creation of value, it brought together four perspectives: financial, customer, internal management processes, and organization learning and growth (Mook, 2010). In the social economy sector, the Balanced Scorecard has been modified to reflect a focus on mission instead of profit, as well as multiple bottom lines and accountabilities that are indicative of these organizations.

Another social accounting framework used primarily by for-profit organizations and subsequently modified for non-profit organizations is the Global Reporting Initiative. The Global Reporting Initiative (GRI) published its first guidelines in 2000 with the purpose of helping organizations disclose their economic, social, and environmental performance. The latest iteration of these guidelines, the GRI G3 Guidelines, provides protocols for indicators in six dimensions: economic, environment, human rights, labour, product responsibility, and society (GRI, 2005).

In response to increased calls for transparency and accountability in the non-governmental organization (NGO) sector, a process was started to develop a Global Reporting Initiative supplement that would be relevant for NGOs. The NGO Supplement was developed by a multi-stakeholder group of non-profit organizations from all over the world, and was released in 2010 after two years of sector consultations. It follows the G3 guidelines with a few expansions. For instance, it pays additional attention to issues of stakeholder engagement, program effectiveness, gender and diversity, public awareness and advocacy, resource allocation, ethical fundraising, and labour and management relations as they relate to volunteers (GRI, 2010).

The Remainder of the Book

This introductory chapter presented an overview of the way that accounting practices have been reoriented to a broader set of economic, social, and environmental variables and interests over the last forty years or so. The remainder of this book picks up from here and presents some of the latest thinking on social accounting for social economy organizations. *Accounting for Social Value* highlights important insights for organizations wanting to monitor and influence the way they create social value.

Next, we look at several case studies of social accounting models under development to gain insight into the complexities of operationalizing this work. First is an example of how one organization sought to translate a stewardship-centred mission into systems designed to both guide its operations and shape its interactions with its stakeholders. This case is presented in chapter 2 where Massimo Contrafatto and Jan Bebbington, in partnership with the Falkland Centre for Stewardship, seek to understand how to make stewardship of natural, social, financial, and cultural assets a reality and develop an appreciation of how accounting and reporting technologies could assist with that task.

Another case study, conducted by Ananya Mukherjee, Darryl Reed, J.J. McMurtry, and Manjula Cherkil, and presented in chapter 3, examines the business model of a fair trade social enterprise and the challenges that it has faced in competing in the fair trade and organic cotton markets. Fair trade certification of cotton is a relatively recent phenomenon; it began only in 2004. While rules for certifying cotton as fair trade are similar to those for the certification of other fair trade agricultural products, the complexity of garment chains raises new issues as it extends fair trade into the realm of manufacturing. More specifically, it brings labour issues to the fore, as most manufacturing units in fair trade garment chains are traditional for-profit firms. Assisi Organics, the focus of this case, is run by Franciscan nuns in Tirupur, the garment centre of India, and is an exception in this regard. While formally registered as a partnership, Assisi is unique among fair trade garment factories as it functions both as a social purpose business (in that it was established to provide employment to handicapped and vulnerable women) and a social enterprise (in that it uses its surplus to fund charitable enterprises such as hospitals and schools). Particular attention is paid to whether and how Assisi's model promotes more socially and environmentally responsible practices and the viability of their model being extended and scaled up.

Many social accounting models emphasize the importance of involving multiple stakeholders. In order to do so, it is essential both to be very clear about the purpose of stakeholder engagement, and to distinguish between stakeholder management and more profound stakeholder engagement. As shown in chapter 4 by Leslie Brown and Elizabeth Hicks, when done well, stakeholder engagement has the potential to be much more than a means of managing risk. It can contribute to the organization's sustainable performance and help with the integration of social, environmental, and economic issues into its core strategies and business model. Stakeholder engagement is not easy, however, and is definitely not formulaic. The chapter discusses some key aspects of any successful engagement process, including some of the challenges that can emerge and some creative responses to these challenges.

Chapter 5 by Edward Jackson and Michele Tarsilla reports on an evaluation of Alterna Savings, a credit union, and their operation of a micro-loan program serving new Canadians. In this case study, social accounting is shown to be a tool for both social responsibility and core-business growth. Using a mix of methods that include logic-model analysis, social accounting, participatory strategies, and a survey of a sample of the program's 300 borrowers, the findings of this evaluation suggest that not only is the program enabling borrowers to first stabilize and then grow their household income; it is also a platform upon which they can, and do, proceed to access larger loans and other financial products from the credit union. Experience from the study suggests that, while it requires considerable effort and time, a social accounting framework that uses a mixed-methods strategy can enrich the analysis and insights of a performance assessment of a social enterprise.

In chapter 6 by Bryn Sadownik, we take a critical look at a unique community-based initiative, Demonstrating Value. The initiative's goal was to design a framework that could help social enterprise organizations identify, develop, and use data collection and reporting for their day-to-day operations, planning, communications, and accountability needs. The project was developed to assist those who operate and invest in the social economy in addressing community needs, and to bring about desirable social and environmental change. It also sought to understand if and how organizations such as social enterprises, co-operatives, and non-profit organizations are meeting the objectives for which they were created, and to use that information to improve performance. The chapter explores the dynamics of this collaborative development and the degree to which the framework has been successful in meeting both investor and operator interests. It also explores how this experience can relate to other social accounting practices, particularly lessons learned for small- and medium-sized social economy organizations.

As funders, including governments, put more emphasis on social return on investment (ROI), standard business ROI calculations that quantify financial impact are being revised to encompass comprehensive social, economic, and environmental measures. This is exactly the challenge posed to convention and visitors bureaus (CVBs) in the United States, the majority of which are independent non-profit organizations. Chapter 7 by Timothy Tyrrell and Robert Johnston uses the triple bottom line framework introduced in 1994 by John Elkington in order to develop a method for quantifying the values to residents of tourism-induced changes in social, economic, and environmental attributes. Using choice-based survey results, the activities of tourism businesses and their CVBs are weighted in a formula that captures the values held by their community. The chapter also shows how use of this measure provides important information to planners and policy makers about community support for tourism that is not captured by the traditional measures of financial impact.

The last three chapters of the book focus on moving the field of social accounting forward. As a new opportunity for social accounting development, chapter 8 by J.J. McMurtry, Darryl Reed, and Jackie Medalye looks at purchasing policies, specifically those of universities. The authors begin with a background discussion about the history of university purchasing policies and the factors that have led universities to be a key site of activism around sustainability issues. From there, the chapter analyses the sustainable purchasing policies of Canadian universities. More specifically, it investigates issues of social and environmental sustainability by looking at the degree to which university purchasing policies incorporate requirements related to environmental sustainability, labour rights, and fair trade practices. Drawing upon survey data and interviews with purchasing policy managers, the chapter also outlines the origins of the policies (and specific environmental, "no sweat," and fair trade provisions), the content of the policies, issues related to implementation of the policies, and the reception of the policies by different stakeholder groups.

Re-orienting accounting systems and standards is a highly contested territory, as shown in chapter 9 by Katherine Ruff. Katherine presents as a case study the creation of Anglo-American financial accounting, supplemented by recent literature on transparency systems and standard-setting. Through this work, we gain an understanding of how accounting standards and other transparency systems emerged in the past, and what attributes are shared by those that remain. What is interesting here is that many of the same concerns and hindrances that affected traditional accounting in the past can be heard today about social accounting.

Finally, in the concluding chapter by Laurie Mook and Mikulas Pstross, the differences and similarities of the preceding case studies are analysed, and specific emphasis is placed on the educational dimension of moving social accounting forward. What new skills and knowledge will future leaders and managers need to develop in order to integrate a broader set of economic, social, and environmental variables into their operational and strategic thinking?

Conclusion

Social accounting is a tool that can be used in a myriad of ways: as a showcase of an organization's performance story; as a facilitator of learning about sustainability and alternate ways of seeing; and as a driver of behaviour in a variety of settings.

Socially minded organizations such as non-profits, co-operatives, social purpose businesses, and socially responsible businesses already have a portion of their success linked to factors other than economic ones as part of their overall mission. To some extent they may be motivated by profit, but their social values are also ingrained in their ways of operating. This group of organizations subscribes to an (at least somewhat) alternate paradigm of how to run an organization and measure success. However, their traditional accounting statements do not reflect this alternate paradigm; rather they are devised to measure profit and shareholder wealth with the assumption that these are the measures that reflect success.

In each of these chapters, the authors succeed in telling a different performance story than that told by traditional accounting. The relationships between economic, social, and environmental factors are highlighted, as are the relationships between different stakeholder groups. Social accounting opens possibilities for other essential factors to be considered in an accounting framework, and its adaptability and flexibility to different contexts are key features of its relevance.

REFERENCES

Abt & Associates. (1971). *1971 Annual report of Abt Associates.* Cambridge: Abt & Associates.

American Accounting Association (AAA). (1990). Position Statement No. One: *Objectives of education for accountants.* Retrieved May 13, 2007, from: http://aaahq.org/AECC/PositionsandIssues/pos1.htm

American Accounting Association (AAA). (1992). Position Statement No. Two: *The first course in accounting.* Retrieved May 13, 2007, from: http://aaahq.org/AECC/PositionsandIssues/pos2.htm

Babcock, K. (2007). *PARO Centre for Women's Enterprise: Measuring social impact.* Ottawa: Carleton University.

Bauer, R.A. (1973, Winter). Commentary to "Let's get on with the social audit: A specific proposal." *Business and Society Review,* 43–4.

Bauer, R.A., & Fenn, D.H., Jr. (1973, January-February). What *is* a corporate social audit? *Harvard Business Review,* 37–48.

Baxter, T., Bebbington, J., & Cutteridge, D. (2004). Sustainability assessment model: Modelling economic, resource, environmental and social flows of a project. In A. Henriques & J. Richardson (Eds.), *The triple bottom line: Does it all add up?* (pp. 113–20). London: Earthscan.

Bebbington, J., & Gray, R.H. (2001). An account of sustainability: failure, success and a reconceptualisation. *Critical Perspectives on Accounting,* 12(5), 557–88. http://dx.doi.org/10.1006/cpac.2000.0450

Bebbington, J., & Gray, R.H. (2006). A social constructionist analysis of sustainable development disclosures in United Kingdom environmental reports. Paper presented at the Eighth Interdisciplinary Perspectives on Accounting Conference, Cardiff Business School, Cardiff University, July 10–12.

Bent, D., & Richardson, J. (2002). *Sustainability accounting guide*. London: SIGMA Project. Retrieved October 22, 2004, from: http://www.projectsigma. co.uk/Toolkit/SIGMASustainabilityAccounting.pdf

Brown, J., & Frame, B. (2005). *Democratizing accounting technologies: The potential of the sustainability model (SAM)*. Working Paper Series No. 15. Wellington: Centre for Accounting, Governance and Taxation Research, Victoria University of Wellington.

Bull, M. (2007). Balance: The development of a social enterprise business performance analysis tool. *Social Enterprise Journal, 3*(1), 49–66. http://dx.doi. org/10.1108/17508610780000721

Burton, J.C. (1973, Winter). Commentary to "Let's get on with the social audit: A specific proposal." *Business and Society Review*, 42–3.

Butcher, B.L. (1973). The program management approach to the corporate social audit. *California Management Review, 16*(1), 11–16.

Community Literacy of Ontario. (2005). *The literacy volunteers: Value added research report*. Barrie: Community Literacy of Ontario.

Cooper, C. (2002). Critical accounting in Scotland. *Critical Perspectives on Accounting, 13*(4), 451–62. http://dx.doi.org/10.1006/cpac.2002.0544

Cooper, D.J., & Hopper, T.M. (2006). Critical theorizing in strategic management accounting research. Paper presented at the Eighth Interdisciplinary Perspectives on Accounting Conference, Cardiff Business School, Cardiff University, July 10–12.

Cooper, D.J., & Neu, D. (1997). *Accounting interventions*. Retrieved July 4, 2003, from: http://les.man.ac.uk/ipa97/papers/neu14.pdf

Coupland, C. (2006). Corporate social and environmental responsibility in web-based reports: Currency in the banking sector? *Critical Perspectives on Accounting, 17*(7), 865–81. http://dx.doi.org/10.1016/j.cpa.2005.01.001

Craig, R., & Amernic, J. (2004). The deployment of accounting-related rhetoric in the prelude to a privatization. *Accounting, Auditing & Accountability Journal, 17*(1), 41–58. http://dx.doi.org/10.1108/09513570410525201

Dey, C.R. (2000). Bookkeeping and ethnography at Traidcraft plc: A review of an experiment in social accounting. *Social and Environmental Accountability Journal, 20*(2), 16–18. http://dx.doi.org/10.1080/0969160X.2000.9651638

Dey, C.R. (2002). Methodological issues: The use of critical ethnography as an active research methodology. *Accounting, Auditing & Accountability Journal, 15*(1), 106–21. http://dx.doi.org/10.1108/09513570210418923

Dilley, S.C., & Weygandt, J.J. (1973). Measuring social responsibility: An empirical test. *Journal of Accountancy, 136*(3), 62–70.

Elkington, J. (2004). Enter the triple bottom line. In A. Henriques & J. Richardson (Eds.), *The triple bottom line: Does it all add up? Assessing the sustainability of business and CSR* (pp. 1–16). London: Earthscan Publications Ltd.

Estes, R. (1976). *Corporate social accounting.* New York: John Wiley.

Everett, J., & Neu, D. (2000). Ecological modernisation and the limits of environmental accounting. *Accounting Forum, 24*(1), 5–29. http://dx.doi.org/10.1111/1467-6303.00027

Friedman, M. (1970, September 13). Social responsibility of business is to increase its profits. *The New York Times Magazine,* 32–3.

Global Reporting Initiative (GRI). (2005). G3 guidelines. Retrieved June 14, 2006, from: http://www.grig3.org/guidelines/overview.html

Global Reporting Initiative (GRI). (2010). An introduction to the GRI NGO sector supplement. Retrieved January 28, 2011, from: http://www.globalreporting.org/NR/rdonlyres/19B9E00D-299D-4F3C-A5A7-6B9650EDC532/4207/AnIntroductiontotheGRINGOSectorSupplement.pdf

Gore, A. (2006). *An inconvenient truth.* New York: Rodale Inc.

Gray, R. (1998). Imagination, a bowl of petunias and social accounting. *Critical Perspectives on Accounting, 9*(2), 205–16. http://dx.doi.org/10.1006/cpac.1997.0169

Gray, R. (2001). Thirty years of social accounting, reporting and auditing: What (if anything) have we learnt? *Business Ethics (Oxford, England), 10*(1), 9–15. http://dx.doi.org/10.1111/1467-8608.00207

Gray, R. (2002). The social accounting project and *Accounting Organizations and Society:* Privileging engagement, imaginings, new accountings and pragmatism over critique? *Accounting, Organizations and Society, 27*(7), 687–708. http://dx.doi.org/10.1016/S0361-3682(00)00003-9

Gray, R. (2005). Taking a long view on what we now know about social and environmental accountability and reporting. *Electronic Journal of Radical Organisation Theory 9* (1). Retrieved April 27, 2007, from: http://www.mngt.waikato.ac.nz/ejrot/Vol9_1/Gray.pdf

Gray, R.H., Bebbington, J., & McPhail, K. (1994). Teaching ethics in accounting and the ethics of accounting teaching: Educating for immorality and a possible case for social and environmental accounting education. *Accounting Education, 3*(1), 51–75. http://dx.doi.org/10.1080/09639289400000005

Gray, R., Dey, C., Owen, D., Evans, R., & Zadek, S. (1997). Struggling with the praxis of social accounting: Stakeholders, accountability, audits and procedures. *Accounting, Auditing & Accountability Journal, 10*(3), 325–64. http://dx.doi.org/10.1108/09513579710178106

Gray, R., & Milne, M. (2004). Towards reporting on the triple bottom line: Mirages, methods and myths. In A. Henriques & J. Richardson (Eds.), *The triple bottom line: Does it all add up?* (pp. 70–80). London: Earthscan.

Gray, R., Owen, D., & Adams, C. (2010). Some theories for social accounting?: A review essay and a tentative pedagogic categorisation of theorisations around social accounting. In M. Freedman & B. Jaggi (Eds.), *Sustainability, Environmental Performance, and Disclosures* (pp. 1–54). Bingley: Emerald.

Gröjer, J.E., & Stark, A. (1977). Social accounting: A Swedish attempt. *Accounting, Organizations and Society, 2*(4), 349–85. http://dx.doi.org/10.1016/0361-3682(77)90024-1

Hines, R.D. (1988). Financial accounting: In communicating reality, we construct reality. *Accounting, Organizations and Society, 13*(3), 251–61. http://dx.doi.org/10.1016/0361-3682(88)90003-7

Hopper, T., Storey, J., & Willmott, H. (1987). Accounting for accounting: Towards the development of a dialectical view. *Accounting, Organizations and Society, 12*(5), 437–56. http://dx.doi.org/10.1016/0361-3682(87)90030-4

Hopwood, A.G. (1990). Ambiguity, knowledge and territorial claims: Some observations on the doctrine of substance over form: A review essay. *British Accounting Review, 22*(1), 79–87. http://dx.doi.org/10.1016/0890-8389(90)90118-2

Jackson, E.T., Babcock, K., Cholich, M., & Harji, K. (2007). Social return on investment by Canadian social enterprise: Three cases. Panel presented at the Canadian Evaluation Society Conference, Winnipeg, June 4–6.

Kaplan, R.S. (2001). Strategic performance measurement and management in nonprofit organizations. *Nonprofit Management & Leadership, 11*(3), 353–370. http://dx.doi.org/10.1002/nml.11308

KNRM (2012). Jaarverslagen [Annual Reports]. Retrieved January 14, 2012, from: http://www.knrm.nl/downloads/publicaties/jaarverslag/?contentID=65A7B2

Land, K. (1996). Social indicators for assessing the impact of the independent, not-for-profit sector on society. Paper presented at a meeting of the Independent Sector, Washington, DC.

Laufer, W.S. (2003). Social accountability and corporate greenwashing. *Journal of Business Ethics, 43*(3), 253–61. http://dx.doi.org/10.1023/A:1022962719299

Lehman, G. (1999). Disclosing new worlds: A role for social and environmental accounting and auditing. *Accounting, Organizations and Society, 24*(3), 217–41. http://dx.doi.org/10.1016/S0361-3682(98)00044-0

Lewis, R.F. (1973, Winter). Commentary to 'Let's get on with the social audit: A specific proposal'. *Business and Society Review*, 45–46.

Lewis, L., Humphrey, C., & Owen, D. (1992). Accounting and the social: a pedagogic perspective. *British Accounting Review, 24*(3), 219–33. http://dx.doi.org/10.1016/S0890-8389(05)80021-6

Linowes, D. (1972). An approach to socio-economic accounting. *Conference Board Record, 9*(11), 58–61.

Linowes, D. (1973, Winter). Let's get on with the social audit: A specific proposal. *Business and Society Review*, 39–42.

Llewellyn, S. (1994). Managing the boundary: How accounting is implicated in maintaining the organization. *Accounting. Auditing & Accountability, 7*(4), 4–23. http://dx.doi.org/10.1108/09513579410069821

Lodh, S.C., & Gaffikin, M.J.R. (1997). Critical studies in accounting research, rationality and Habermas: A methodological reflection. *Critical Perspectives on Accounting, 8*(5), 433–74. http://dx.doi.org/10.1006/cpac.1996.0108

Manville, G. (2007). Implementing a balanced scorecard framework in a not for profit SME. *International Journal of Productivity and Performance Management, 56*(2), 162–69. http://dx.doi.org/10.1108/17410400710722653

Martello, M., Watson, J.G., & Fischer, M.J. (2008). Implementing a Balanced Scorecard in a not-for-profit organization. *Journal of Business & Economics Research, 6*(9), 67–80.

McDonough, W., & Braungart, M. (2002). *Cradle to cradle: Remaking the way we make things.* New York: North Point Press.

Mobley, S.C. (1973, Winter). Commentary to "Let's get on with the social audit: A specific proposal." *Business and Society Review*, 48–9.

Mook, L. (2010). Social accounting. In R. Taylor (Ed.), *Third sector research* (pp. 171–85). New York: Springer. http://dx.doi.org/10.1007/978-1-4419-5707-8_13

Mook, L. (2007). Social and environmental accounting: The Expanded Value Added Statement. Unpublished doctoral dissertation. Toronto: University of Toronto.

Mook, L. (2006). Integrating and reporting an organisation's economic, social and environmental performance: The Expanded Value Added Statement. In S. Schaltegger, M. Bennett, J. Bouma, & R. Burritt (Eds.), *Sustainability accounting and reporting* (pp. 281–98). Dordrecht: Springer Kluwer Publishers.

Mook, L., & Quarter, J. (2006). Accounting for the social economy: the socioeconomic impact statement. *Annals of Public and Cooperative Economics, 77*(2), 247–69. http://dx.doi.org/10.1111/j.1370-4788.2006.00305.x

Mook, L., Quarter, J., & Richmond, B.J. (2007). *What counts: Social accounting for nonprofits and cooperatives* (2nd ed.). London: Sigel Press.

Morgan, G. (1988). Accounting as reality construction: Towards a new epistemology for accounting practice. *Accounting, Organizations and Society,* 13(5), 477–85. http://dx.doi.org/10.1016/0361-3682(88)90018-9

New Economics Foundation. (1998). *Briefing paper on social auditing.* London: New Economics Foundation.

Owen, D., & Swift, T. (2001). Introduction: Social accounting, reporting and auditing: Beyond the rhetoric? *Business Ethics (Oxford, England), 10*(1), 4–8. http://dx.doi.org/10.1111/1467-8608.00206

Richmond, B.J. (1999). Counting on each other: A social audit model to assess the impact of nonprofit organizations. Unpublished PhD dissertation. Toronto: University of Toronto.

Roslender, R., & Dillard, J.F. (2003). Reflections on the interdisciplinary perspectives on accounting project. *Critical Perspectives on Accounting, 14*(3), 325–51. http://dx.doi.org/10.1006/cpac.2002.0526

Schaltegger, S., Bennett, M., & Burritt, R. (Eds.). (2006). *Sustainability accounting and reporting.* Dordrecht: Springer. http://dx.doi.org/10.1007/978-1-4020-4974-3

Sillanpää, M. (1998). The Body Shop values report: Towards integrated stakeholder auditing. *Journal of Business Ethics, 17*(13), 1443–56. http://dx.doi.org/10.1023/A:1006099731105

Somers, A.B. (2004). *Shaping the Balanced Scorecard for use in UK social enterprises.* London: Social Enterprises London.

Suojanen, W.W. (1954). Accounting theory and the large corporation. *Accounting Review, 29*(3), 391–98.

Tinker, T. (1985). *Paper prophets: A social critique of accounting.* New York: Praeger.

Tinker, T. (2005). The withering of criticism: A review of professional, Foucauldian, ethnographic, and epistemic studies in accounting. *Accounting, Auditing & Accountability Journal, 18*(1), 100–35. http://dx.doi.org/10.1108/09513570510584674

Tinker, A.M., Merino, B.D., & Neimark, M.D. (1982). The normative origins of positive theories: Ideology and accounting thought. *Accounting, Organizations and Society, 7*(2), 167–200. http://dx.doi.org/10.1016/0361-3682(82)90019-8

UNWCED. (1987). *Our common future: A report of the World Commission on Environment and Development.* New York: Oxford University Press.

Vaccari, A. (1997). Constructing the social balance: Consumer Cooperative Italy. In S. Zadek, P. Pruzan, & R. Evans (Eds.), *Building corporate accountability* (pp. 171–88). London: Earthscan.

van der Meer, L. (2007). *Het werk dat telt.* Amstelveen: KPMG.

Weidmann, T., & Lenzen, M. (2006). Triple-bottom-line accounting of social, economic and environmental indicators – A new life-cycle software tool for UK businesses. Presented at the Third Annual International Sustainable Development Conference, Perth, Scotland, November 15–16.

Zadek, S. (1998). Balancing performance, ethics, and accountability. *Journal of Business Ethics, 17*(13), 1421–42. http://dx.doi.org/10.1023/A:1006095614267

PART II

Developing Social Accounting Frameworks

2 Developing Techniques for Stewardship: A Scottish Study

MASSIMO CONTRAFATTO AND JAN BEBBINGTON

Introduction

The normative ideal of stewardship can be observed as motivating organizations operating in a variety of sectors (primarily associations, trusts, non-profit organizations, and social enterprises). These organizations, in the main, are seeking to protect and enhance resources (such as land, forests, fisheries, or all of "god's creation") for common human good and describe their actions as promoting stewardship. The aspirations expressed by stewardship-oriented organizations have resonance with the commitments made by regions, countries, and supra-national bodies to pursue sustainable development (see United Nations World Commission on Environment and Development, 1987; Department for Environment, Food and Rural Affairs, 2005; Scottish Executive, 2005), as well as with more organizationally focused agendas that seek to ensure the accountability of organizations for their social and environmental impacts. In the latter context, this desire sits under the umbrella of corporate social responsibility (see Caroll, 1999, for an introduction to the history of this concept; and Crane & Matten, 2008 for an overview of the literature in the area). Regardless of organizational status (for profit or not for profit), social accounting has sought to systematically analyse "the effects of an organization on its communities of interest or stakeholders" (Mook et al., 2007, p. 2). This activity, however, has rarely (in the social accounting literature) been framed as an attempt to understand if stewardship has been achieved. Rather, the notion of accountability is offered as the normative motivation for social accounting (see Gray, 1992; Gray et al., 1996). The focus on stewardship in this chapter has been dictated by the case organization that forms the empirical context of our project. In particular, between October 2007 and March 2009 we worked in partnership with the Falkland Centre for Stewardship (itself part of Falkland Heritage Trust) as it sought to understand the implications of embedding stewardship of natural, social, cultural, historical, and financial assets within its operations. At the same time, the case organization sought to develop an appreciation of how accounting and reporting technologies could assist with that task.

As a result, this chapter seeks to achieve three tasks, all of which are aimed at deepening our understanding of stewardship, accountability, and the role of accounting tools in supporting these two concepts. First, the chapter explores how the case organization conceptualizes the notion of stewardship. Second, the possible connections between stewardship and accountability are explored. Finally, the extent to which social accounting tools and techniques could support an evaluation of stewardship is suggested. The evidence base that is brought to this task was developed from a longitudinal action research engagement between the organization and the authors of this chapter. Evidence is drawn from information that the organization has put in the public domain, from interviews with individuals who work within the organization (as staff, trustees, and beneficiaries), as well as observations from workshops conducted with organizational participants. In addition, reflective diaries written by researchers inform the observations made.

The remainder of the chapter is organized in the following way. In the second section we describe the case study organization and place it within the context of social economy organizations. In the third section, the notion of stewardship will be discussed and the connections between stewardship and accountability (as conceptualized in the social accounting literature) will be explored. The penultimate section will explore how social accounting could assist in supporting the pursuit of stewardship. Finally, some concluding remarks are made.

The Case Organization

It is not straightforward to identify the case organization for this work. This arises from the history of the estate of Falkland as well as its current institutional arrangements. Falkland is a village in the Kingdom of Fife (which is itself on the east coast of Scotland, bounded by the Firth of Forth and the Firth of Tay – "firth" being the Scots term for a river estuary). Falkland has had a long association with the Stuart monarchs of Scotland and was the location of their hunting palace. The Palace of Falkland (built around 1540) still exists and was transferred to the National Trust of Scotland in 1952. The case organization is found on the estate that was once the king's property, although ownership of the land has changed several times since those early days. The more modern origins of the estate date from 1820, when the estate was bought by Professor Bruce, who built many of the buildings and landscape features (for example, ponds and paths) that are now present. In 1887, the estate was purchased by the Third Marquis of Bute and after his death the estate passed to Lord Crichton Stuart whose descendant, Ninian Stuart, is our key contact in the case organization. The estate is no longer privately held by Ninian but rests in a set of trusts, the main one of which is the Falkland Estate Trust (a private trust). In addition to this trust there are two other relevant organizations: Falkland Rural Enterprises Limited (a for-profit organization that manages the commercial activities of the Estate) and Falkland Heritage Trust (FHT). It is this latter body that formally was the case organization with whom we interacted for this work. Specifically, FHT is a charitable trust (founded in 1994) with the specific purposes of: (1) protecting the historical features of the House of Falkland and its designed landscape; (2) promoting access to the estate; (3) promoting the philosophy and practice of stewardship, locally and beyond, through – among others – educational programs, workshops and learning events (these descriptions are drawn from FHT documents that were in the public domain at the time the study was conducted). Of the various activities undertaken by this body some deserve a little more elaboration.

The House of Falkland was built between 1839 and 1844 with interiors that date from the 1880s. The house is an "A"-listed building; that is, it conforms to legal description of being a building of "national or international importance, either architectural or historic, or a fine little-altered example of some particular period, style or building type" (as per the Town and Country Planning Listed Buildings and Conservation Areas, Scotland Act 1997). This designation exists because of the interiors of the house (which are in the arts and crafts style). Currently the house is leased and operates as a school. In terms of what we will be considering later in this chapter, the house is important as it is an element of the cultural assets for which stewardship must be exercised. Since 2000, FHT has also carried out a major restoration of the landscape on the estate including reclaiming lost paths, rebuilding new bridges, replanting woodlands, and enhancing biodiversity.

In 2004 an operational unit called Falkland Centre for Stewardship (FCS – see http://www.centreforstewardship.org.uk/index.htm) was constituted within FHT. Since then, it has concerned itself with promoting the principles and practices of stewardship through different programs and activities. In particular, it describes itself as existing "to promote the practice of stewardship locally and the philosophy of stewardship in 21st century Scotland and beyond." FCS has undertaken a number of initiatives that are designed to help people and institutions develop the capacity to act as stewards; the Big Tent Festival (see http://www.bigtentfestival.co.uk/) is an exemplar of the types of activities being undertaken. This festival is the largest annual eco-festival in Scotland and 2010 was its fifth year.

Technically, the case organization we worked with was the FHT. Although there are clear legal boundaries between the various elements of the larger organization (the estate), all organizations can be seen as being part of a group of entities that provide stewardship of what we conceptualized as the "Falkland system." We use the term system explicitly to indicate that this is a group of entities that are linked through relationships of interdependence (Masini, 1970). Although any system is composed of distinct-distinguishable elements, the whole represents a unitary reality that is more than merely the combination of these single elements. In this vein, it is possible to envisage the "Falkland Estate" as a system that results from the formal and informal relationships that link the entities within it.

These entities, however, are distinct from the village of Falkland itself, which is made up of various privately owned houses and businesses. The linkages between the estate and the village, however, are numerous and reflexive in nature. Indeed, one FHT trustee (himself a historian) suggested that over the centuries, the estate has been the "centre of gravity" of Falkland, of its people and their lives and that "the estate is the whole. It is the centrepiece of Falkland ... When I speak about the Estate I mean the lands, the houses and historic buildings, the present and past community of Falkland people." Moreover, included within the "Falkland system" are traditional forms of knowledge that allow the landscape of the place to be maintained as well as the history of where the place has come from and the work that was done by previous generations to create what is seen today.

As is evident from the above description, the entity over which or for which a stewardship function is being exercised is fraught with definitional issues from the outset. This poses some problems if one requires a clear entity in order to produce an account (with the entity notion being central to any conception of accounting). A more fluid conception of the entity, however, sits well with the ideas about stewardship that we will examine in the next section. Indeed, on a poster reflecting on the importance of stones, it is suggested that the estate is (metaphorically) the "guardian" and the "steward" of the Falkland universe of symbols and meaning, which have been preserved, nurtured, and protected until the current time. The poster suggests that the history of the estate is, above all, the histories of the women and men who over the centuries have devoted their energy and even their lives to the place of Falkland (regardless of what particular entity these individuals were working and living within). Some of these individuals have their names inscribed in stones on the estate. For the case organization, stone has enormous significance and is considered sacred because stones "provide the structure of our landscape, homes and route way, underpinning the fabric of our communities" (Falkland Heritage Trust, n.d.). This aspect is reinforced by Ninian (the Steward of Falkland) who states that "stone is present today as the main building material, and stone for me represents the enduring structures which stewards maintain over generations" (Falkland Centre for Stewardship, 2004).

To close, the definition of the entity that we were working with was complex from the outset of this study. If one takes a very narrow view, our case organization is FCS and its operations. If the view is broadened, then FHT is most probably the formal case entity. What was evident throughout this work, however, was that the numerous elements that come together at the place of Falkland make a narrow definition of the entity unwise. This is due to the interlocking nature of the various trusts that legally "own" the land where our case organizations operate, as well as the ethos of the leaders of these organizations that all elements are interconnected and interdependent. Moreover, a very strong interconnection is lived through the family line of our key contact. It is clear from the way he talks about FCS and the estate that he personally connects the past to the present as well as having a strong focus on how the current can shape the future. For our contact (even if he does not use these terms explicitly), the need for sustainable development as a response to global and local social, environmental, and economic collapse is evident, and FHT, FCS, and the activities of the broader estate are all part of that mission.

It is also relevant to ask whether the case organization is part of the social economy – and, if it is, what sort of social economy organization it is. Noting that the term "social economy" is itself contested, Falkland appears to fit within the broad parameters of the concept in terms of being privately owned (albeit through trusts) and having both an economic as well as a social mission. There is a variable degree of emphasis on the social and economic mission of the various elements of the Falkland "system," but what is clear is that FHT and FCS have social outcomes at the heart of their activities and are especially motivated by the need to act as stewards for the natural, social, economic, and cultural aspects of the place of Falkland. At the same time, the extent, history, and private trust nature of FHT is in contrast to many social economy entities. There is no formal way to bridge these differences, except to say that the ethos of the FCS (which informs the wider Falkland system) is similar to those that inform many social enterprises. Likewise, some of the specific activities enabled by the FCS are similar to those undertaken within the social economy (education, building community capital, creating public events for change/celebration, and providing a context within which public goods might be created and enjoyed). In the next section the concept of stewardship will be discussed in more detail with particular reference to its meaning and significance in the context of Falkland.

Stewardship

In order to better understand the notion of stewardship, a four-stage investigation was undertaken. First, we examined a sample of organizations that one could infer (from their names) had been founded on the need to ensure stewardship. We then considered the explanations they provided as to how they knew if they were conducting themselves according to the principles of stewardship. Second, we conducted a literature review of academic articles in the fields of economics, business ethics, and management/accounting to uncover if there was any consistency in their use of the term stewardship. Third, through examination of literature from the case organization, interviews, and a workshop we sought to understand how FHT/FCS conceptualized stewardship. The final task reported in this section is a comparison of the concept of stewardship with that of accountability. This comparison was undertaken because it was apparent that there are some conceptual connections between these terms. Moreover, given that social accounting tools and techniques are predicated on accountability, their relevance to the case organization could only be established if the relationship between accountability and stewardship was first understood.

Stewardship-Based Organizations

A web-based search of organizations claiming that their activities are informed by stewardship was carried out in order to develop a tentative taxonomy for the stewardship-based organizations that we examined. In addition, the tools that appeared to be used by these organizations were investigated. Both tasks were focused on providing a "standard" against which the case organization's understanding of stewardship could be compared. Seven organizations were examined in depth (though it is important to note that the search did not yield a large number of organizations) and from these a three-part taxonomy could be proposed.

Stewardship-based organizations tended to fall into three basic types: (1) those focused on activities in a specified physical location (such as the Peninsular Open Space Trust – see http://www.openspacetrust. org/index.html; the Alberta Stewardship Network – see http://www. ab.stewardshipcanada.ca; and the Pacific Forest and Watershed Lands Stewardship Council – see http://www.stewardshipcouncil.org/about_ us/index.htm); (2) those with a focus on stewardship of a particular resource (such as the Forest Stewardship Council – see http://www.fsc. org; and the Marine Stewardship Council – see http://www.msc.org/); and (3) those which are inspired by the Christian religion (such as the Christian Stewardship Council – see http://www.stewardshipcouncil. net/). These various organizations have similarities and differences from each other. In particular, the place-based organizations have a strong ecological focus with a related interest in people's engagement with and enjoyment of those spaces. Likewise, the resource-based organizations focus on ecologically sustainable behaviours and the need to steward resources. The least similar organizations to those we surveyed are those that are motivated by the Christian tradition, at least in part because their focus is wider than either a place or resource. For these organizations the focus is on conduct that supports the stewardship of God's creation, drawing from the fact that stewardship is frequently mentioned in the Bible. Stewardship within this tradition is very widely conceived of and while it includes environmental stewardship it also extends further than that.

In this respect, FCS shares much in common with the place- and re-source-based stewardship-informed organizations in that it focuses on a particular resource; in our case the resource is geographically contained to Falkland. Moreover, a focus on the stewardship of resources for human well-being is shared with these other organizations. Where FCS differs from all these organizations, however, is in its focus on the stewardship of its built/cultural heritage and the traditions that have supported the development of the Falkland Estate. In this respect, FCS's focus is wider than those of the place- and product-based organizations but not as wide as the Christian ideal of being a steward for all of creation.

As a result of this investigation we determined that some of the tools that are used by these other organizations might usefully inform our work. For instance, among others, the definition and presentation of a code of conduct as to what activities underlie good stewardship was seen as a way to clarify the principles that should guide conduct. Moreover, standards that allow for an evaluation of whether other organizations are operating in accordance with stewardship standards is evident in the work of both the Marine and Forestry Stewardship Councils. The ability to transfer these approaches to the work of FHT, however, was limited. This will be discussed later in the chapter.

Stewardship in the Academic Literature

An analysis of the academic literature on this subject was also under-taken with the purpose of identifying key aspects that could assist in conceptualizing stewardship. While there was not a great deal of literature in this area, what does exist provides a possible nesting of the various conceptions of stewardship – from relatively narrow specifications to very broad conceptions of the term.

The conventional accounting literature provides the narrowest conception of stewardship. For example, Gjesdal (1981) explores steward-ship by drawing on a narrow agency framework where it is assumed that managers act as stewards on behalf of owners' interests, with financial accounts being produced as a result of this relationship. In addition, this perspective assumes that the manager is motivated to behave in a way that maximizes his/her utility. In this framework the principal is represented by the shareholders/stockholders group, with the source of the duties/responsibilities for the relationship being identified as legal requirements established by contract or by extant law.

The time frame over which stewardship is to be achieved is relatively short and the resources that are entrusted are mainly financial and economic. While the term stewardship is used by Gjesdal (1981), we would argue that his definition is not cognate with that of the organizations examined previously, nor is it with FCS's conceptualization of the term.

To the extent that the management literature mentions stewardship, it is seen as an alternative model of governance and managerial motivation (see, for example, Davis et al., 1997). In Davis et al.'s paper (1997), stewardship is based on a broader principal-agent framework where the manager (agent) acts as a steward for those whose interests and motives are convergent with the objectives of several parties involved in organizational activities. In this approach, the spectrum of subjects involved in the relationship with the steward is not limited to shareholders. As a result, it is assumed that the steward will adopt pro-organization behaviour and seek to reconcile the divergent interests of different groups in order to maximize the organization's interests. It is further presumed that in doing so the manager/steward will maximize his/her utility, because there is the assumption of alignment between the steward's interests and those of the organization (Davis et al., 1997). This conception of stewardship chimes with that of the mainstream: the idea of a corporate social responsibility wherein a social contract exists that creates broader obligations than those enshrined in law and where it is possible to create a commonality of interests between an organization and its stakeholders.

Finally, the broadest conception of stewardship is that based on a Christian theological perspective. Enderle (1997) explores this theme in the literature and refers to a document produced by the European Ecumenical Assembly, *Peace with Justice for the Whole Creation* (1989), where it is stated that "God the Creator upholds and loves all his creatures. Therefore they all have a fundamental right to life. God the Creator has given humanity a special place within the Creation … *We are to be stewards within God's world*" (p. 177, emphasis in original). From this perspective, therefore, stewardship does not imply ownership because

> God the Creator remains the sole owner, in the full sense of the term, of the entire creation [and as a result] *stewardship* involves respect and care for all human and non-human beings and rules out their total instrumentalization. (Enderle, 1997, p. 177–178, emphasis in original)

As it evident, the theological perspective broadens the spectrum of resources to be stewarded as well the time frame of reference. In addition, the duties for stewardship in this conception arise from moral and spiritual requirements.

These various theoretical conceptions map onto the organizations reviewed earlier in the chapter. Most obviously, the Christian-based stewardship organizations draw directly from the perspective exemplified by Enderle (1997). None of the organizations examined have as narrow a conception as that promulgated by Gjesdal (1981). Rather, the situation we studied is more akin to that described by Davis et al. (1997) as well as being similar to the stewardship perspective described by Caers et al. (2006). This similarity is also stronger due to the small size of the FCS and the fact that its principal is actively involved in the organization. In addition to those organizations considered above, there are many organizations that seek to inculcate the skills and ethos of stewardship in some form of educational program (see, for example, http://umanitoba .ca/faculties/coned/access-afp/afp/programs/diploma/aesd/752.html – an example that may be familiar to Canadian readers). While these are clear links between these activities and the practice of stewardship, these sorts of educational programs were not included with the organizations reviewed above; although they are concerned with understanding and teaching about stewardship, they do not constitute organizations that are directly seeking to steward a particular set of resources.

Stewardship at Falkland

Ninian Stuart (the steward of the estate during the study) often starts his story of who he is and the context in which FCS was developed with an explanation of the derivation of the word steward (the spelling of this concept and his name are linked, with Stewart [with a t] being the Scottish derivation of steward). In particular, the term stewardship is used to indicate the responsibility that is held by someone with regard to the property of others (and hence has some resonance with the Christian-based notion of stewardship). This includes the responsibility to "look after" (*Collins Cobuild Advanced Learner's English Dictionary*, 2003) the resources and assets which have been entrusted to the steward. The word stewardship itself is derived from the Anglo-Saxon word Stiweard or Stigweard. Etymologically, Stigweard has the meaning of "house guardian," derived from stig (hall, pen) and weard (guard, keeper – see the *Dictionary of English Etymology Concise Oxford Edition* [Hoat, 1993]). The steward had a vital role in the Middle Ages because he (invariably) was an officer who managed the interest of an estate on behalf of his employer. This latter conception is in keeping with the history of Falkland as well as the role that Ninian has, and it is often drawn on by Ninian when he recounts the journey that has brought him to desire a move from a privately held and enjoyed estate to one that has broader social objectives.

In its contemporary manifestation, the concept of stewardship has motivated many of the activities that have been undertaken by Falkland entities over the recent past. Stewardship is regarded by the FCS as a comprehensive set of principles and values designed to both guide its operations and to shape its relationships with stakeholders. In the specific historical and social context of Falkland, stewardship is envisaged as

> the act and art of holding, nurturing and vitalizing assets for others – including the next generation. The asset in question may be an organization, a tradition, a building, a landscape, or the highest level of the planet's natural resources and ecosystem. (Drawn from discussions with staff of FCS and material on FCS)

The articulation of stewardship as the art and act of "holding, nurturing and vitalizing" (ibid.) also has particular meaning. In this context the use of the word "art" is important as it derives from the Latin *ars*, a term meaning "the mastery of doing something," which itself requires a certain amount of talent. Indeed, art is something more than a technique (from Greek *tekhne*, meaning "manual skills, ability in making something"). As a result, stewardship is more than a set of rules and methods that can be passed on. Given this conception it is difficult to see how a complete description of what it means to be a steward could be encapsulated in a code of conduct or in any other set of standards (as per those used by other organizations using stewardship as a guiding principle). Indeed, stewardship was described at various times over the case study period as involving a nurturing attitude that is supported by actions.

In terms of actions, a steward was conceptualized (by FCS staff and publications) as being the holder of "something precious," and someone who cares about and protects its growth and development. In Falkland those important and precious things to be nurtured are the property's natural, ecological, social, and cultural assets (such as "historical buildings, landscape and traditions"). Indeed, FCS describes actions as including re-skilling our communities ... [in order to allow the understanding of] the impact of today's decisions on climate change for future generations. We are adapting old ideas of stewardship to the needs of our modern, fast changing world with an organic farm that is starting to produce affordable food for our local town, by upgrading miles of paths to strengthen our connections with neighboring communities, planting thousands of trees and considering plans for allotments and wood fuel production. (See http://www.centreforstewardship.org.uk/index.htm)

Within this quote, as well as in our interviews and observations of FCS practices, there is explicit reference to future generations. This is an important observation to be kept in mind when we consider the connections between stewardship and some relevant concepts (for example, social accountability) that are commonly used in the social accounting literature.

One distinctive aspect of the conceptualization of stewardship provided by FCS is the linking of the past to the current – and from there the current to the future. Indeed, the FCS once stated that "good stewards draw from the past, mind the future and always look beyond themselves" (FCS's previous website). In this manner stewardship was envisaged as the "red thread" that connects the past, with its memories and traditions, to the future, passing through the present. To some extent, from this perspective, the temporal barriers which separate past, present, and future appear to be more blurred. Indeed, this aspect was described in more detail during an interview where a member of the FCS stated that

stewardship involves actions drawing from the past, seeing the moment and handing on to the next generation ... metaphorically is like a spiral ... it is a process where a person, the steward, draws and takes from the past and passes this past to someone else who becomes himself/herself a steward. This second steward, which receives the "baton," has the responsibility to pass it to another person, who will pass to another and so on.

It may be that the specific characteristics of the Falkland Estate (having been passed along a family line) encourage this focus on the nature of time and the passing on of a legacy. Moreover, while the particular organizational form of the Falkland Estate has varied over time, for the most part the core of the land and the activities that take place on it have endured. This is a relatively unusual position compared to the other organizations that were reviewed in this chapter (and corporations more generally), which tend to have shorter lives. It is plausible to hypothesize (but impossible to prove) that the longevity of the estate has led to the development of the stewardship mission and that, given the relative youth of many organizations (combined with a lack of familial continuity of "ownership"), this perspective will be relatively rare for organizations that have hitherto featured in the social accounting literature.

An additional distinctive conceptualization of stewardship also emerges in the use of the analogy that stewards use their heads, hands, and hearts to inform their actions. In particular, the work of FCS has been described as using

> hands to continue some of the threatened skills and traditions of the past, our heads to work out the most effective way to revive the estate with limited resources and our hearts and instincts to anticipate and envisage the next 100 years. (FCS's previous website)

This use of the trilogy links directly to the work of Patrick Geddes (see http://www.patrickgeddestrust.co.uk and Stephen [2004] for a brief history of Geddes) who lived and worked in regions adjacent to Fife. This "heads, hands and hearts" trilogy arose often in interviews and interactions with FCS staff. For example, one person explained that these three "H's" symbolize the pillars of the good stewardship. The hands symbolize the manual skills to manufacture and the ability to work by following traditional methods. The heads express the need to adopt rules and design systems to manage the resources (natural, ecological, social, and financial) which have been entrusted to the current generation, and which a steward is responsible for. Finally, the hearts give the sense of emotional involvement and commitment on the part of the steward who nurtures and protects assets on behalf of others. If this conception holds, being a good steward requires a spiritual engagement with the estate and its resources, including traditions and cultural heritage. In particular, in an interview with an FCS member, it was explicitly stated that

> it is important to stress that there is a spiritual commitment in being and acting as a steward. In fact, as stewards we feel a duty to act on behalf and for the benefits of others. (FCS interviewee)

Another individual noted that

> what really makes stewardship different from other concepts is this strong
> sense of commitment to doing. Stewardship is about giving, it is a choice
> driven by the heart. To be steward means to act on behalf of others even if
> you are not necessarily required to do that. (FCS interviewee)

In this respect, the manifestation of stewardship evolving in FHT and
FCS is akin to that of the Christian-based organizations and the literature described above, but without an explicit religious basis. Rather, the
basis for stewardship arises from a moral and spiritual (in the broadest
sense) requirement to act well for a place and for those not yet born in
that place. This conception is different from attitudes and motives usually assumed or described in the social accounting and corporate social
responsibility literatures.

In summary, in Falkland the concept of stewardship has inspired the
vision and mission of a set of organizations – and in particular FHT
and FCS. The notion of stewardship has been used to both formulate
the mission of these organizations and, on the basis of this, to achieve
the definition of their strategic objectives. However, in order to make
the concept of stewardship a more established and embedded reality
in the organization, staff and trustees at FHT had recognized a need
to translate stewardship principles and their mission into managerial
systems designed to both guide their daily operations and shape relationships with their stakeholders. Therefore, as part of this process
of operationalizing the principles and values of stewardship, a project
was undertaken in partnership with the staff and trustees of FHT in
order to identify, propose, and develop tools to account for the current social, environmental, and economic status of Falkland, as well as
techniques to pursue a stewardship-infused vision for managing the
resources entrusted to it. Before turning to this stage of the work, however, we will undertake a brief discussion of the possible relationship
between stewardship and accountability.

Stewardship and Accountability

Stewardship has a great deal in common with accountability as both involve a relationship between two (or more) parties (described as principal and agent), where the second acts on the behalf of the other to
do/refrain from doing particular things. A steward manages assets on

behalf of the principal (in FCS's case, current and future people and possibly the history of the place of Falkland) in the same way as accountability relationships are defined (see Gray et al., 1996). The proposition that these two concepts are linked was discussed at a seminar held in December of 2007 involving researchers, trustees of FHT/FCS, and other interested parties. It was agreed there that the problems addressed by stewardship and accountability are largely the same, as are many of the issues that have to be resolved in order for each concept to be operational.

At that same time, however, the two concepts were considered to be distinctive; it was proposed that stewardship is a special case of accountability where the asset to be "looked after," the time scale on which care is being exercised, and the range of stakeholders forming part of the stewardship relationship are all broader than the relationships most often identified within accountability-focused social accounting literature. In particular, at FCS the nature of the assets to be stewarded is different from the norm found in traditional organizations (including, for example, heritage and cultural assets). Second, it was determined that the time frame of the analysis for FCS is generational as well as annual. There was also the sense that the place of Falkland was part of the steward's concern although the location itself was not wholly within any one person's control or ownership. Indeed, one trustee of the FHT noted that

> the framework of social accountability is definitely a good starting point for exploring the problematic issues of the stewardship model. However, there is a need to adapt the model of social accountability by taking into consideration the different features which characterize stewardship. (FHT interviewee)

From a social accounting perspective, these conclusions also raise the possibility that current notions of accountability, because they have tended to be focused on for-profit organizations, may themselves be narrower than they could be. Indeed, Gibbon (2009) raises the possibility that the social accounting literature conception of accountability could be widened considerably if it drew from perspectives on accountability developed in the third sector (see Ebrahim, 2003a, b and Goodin, 2003), in the NGO sector (see O'Dwyer & Unerman, 2007 and 2008), as well as in broader theoretical frames (for example, Lehman, 1999; Roberts, 1991 and 1996). Indeed, Ninian asked,

What does it mean to be a steward? How can I be a good steward? I still think that these questions remain even if we have a lot of experience ... Stewardship is such a big concept. There is no way that a "good keeper" could do and cover everything. To some extent, it is probably a matter of what I do not do rather than what I do.

This sort of reflection is indicative of the argument of Miller (2002) where he suggests that

accountability is saturated with politics and emotions ... to give an account ... is to given an account of oneself ... to display oneself as a social actor with all its associated uncertain, complexity and messiness. (p. 554)

Indeed, the way in which one might provide such an account was investigated during this study and forms the basis of the next section.

Tools for Stewardship

This section seeks to outline the extent to which existing social accounting tools and techniques could usefully be brought to bear on the particular situation of FHT and FCS. We have noted that the moral imperative of stewardship being used to guide the actions of these organizations is based on a conception of accountability that is broader than that most usually considered in the social accounting literature. In particular, there are likely to be additional stakeholders within the accountability relationship, perhaps most notably the place of Falkland itself as well as the past and future generations living there. Moreover, given the focus on heritage assets as well as the need to preserve and strengthen the knowledge required to renew these assets, it is likely that any account of the actions of FHT and FCS will require accounts of the impact of these activities. To complete this part of the project, there was an iterative process of engagement between researchers and Falkland from April to July of 2008, concluding with a seminar to discuss the outcome of this work. This resulted in the following observations as to how social accounting tools and techniques could support the pursuit of stewardship in the case context.

In the first instance (and after a review of various approaches), the process by which an account for stewardship could be developed was thought to best be guided by the process methodology (the Social Audit Methodology) developed by Social Audit Network Limited.

This organization is a not-for-profit company, limited by guarantee and based in the UK, whose mission is "to promote and support social accounting and audit as the preferred means whereby organizations operating in the community, social economy and public sectors report on their social, environmental and economic performance" (see http://www.socialauditnetwork.org.uk/). This methodology could be used either for a single entity within Falkland (such as FHT) or for the "Falkland system" as a whole. Most usually a social audit focuses on a discrete entity, but the possibilities of doing an account for a wider group of entities must exist given the nature of the situation. Moreover, it would be plausible to suggest (but difficult to demonstrate) that a social account of the town itself would be valuable to set alongside any account of the Falkland Estate-based account.

This methodology proceeds in four stages (the following material is drawn from Social Audit Network Ltd.'s website at http://www.social-auditnetwork.org.uk/). First, a planning phase is undertaken where the organization clarifies its vision and mission, identifies its strategic objectives, and describes the activities that will allow it to meet the objectives. Further, at this stage a stakeholder map is produced that states who the organization affects or who has an interest in it. These stakeholders will be both internal and external to the organization, potentially including those with no formal links to it. The second phase of the work involves the actual accounting, where (after having established the scope of the social accounting process) a specific social bookkeeping system can be developed and tools identified in order to collect relevant qualitative and quantitative information for measuring organizational performance, and to compare these measurements with the values and objectives of the organization. (Potential tools for Falkland itself will be discussed later in this section.) Next, there is a reporting and auditing stage where the qualitative and quantitative, financial and non-financial information collected during the previous stages are synthesized into the social account. Finally, these accounts are audited by a panel of social auditors who evaluate whether the information reported has been properly obtained and if it constitutes a "fair and honest" reflection of what has happened in the organization. The social report is then made available and accessible to various stakeholders who may be interested in the initiatives undertaken by the organization and the results obtained from them. The way in which one might develop social accounts is reasonably well understood in the literature, with Dey et al. (1995), Gray et al. (1997), and Gibbon (2009) providing insights into this process.

Beyond a focus on methodology, it was also apparent that a number of specific accounting techniques could be suggested that would map well to the "core business" of FHT as well as linking to their stewardship mission. In particular, three accounting tools of potential value were identified (after a wider search for possible techniques): (1) accounts of biodiversity; (2) accounting for heritage assets; and (3) accounting for systems of knowledge. What is worth noting here is that each of these techniques is relatively underdeveloped in the social accounting literature, yet the areas they cover are intimately connected to the mission of FCS as well as the various activities of the Falkland system. Each of these will now be considered in turn.

Accounts of Biodiversity

Based on the methodology developed by Jones & Matthews (2000) and Jones (2003), it is possible to develop a biodiversity account that would allow the recording, managing, and reporting of (at least) some of the natural systems that can be found at Falkland. These include habitats (land- or water-based) and their flora and fauna. The purpose of this methodology (according to Jones & Matthews, 2000) is to develop an inventory of natural components that represent a significant part of an organization's capital. Such an approach would chime well with the activities of FHT and especially its woodlands. These woodlands are managed "to ensure the health of the trees, to produce usable timber for industry and an income for the Estate, and to *enhance the environment*" (Falkland Estate Trust, n.d.; emphasis added). Further, the symbolic importance of wood to the FHT is evident in literature about Falkland. For example, wood has always had a prominent role for the residents of Falkland because it represents one of the three elements (together with stone and water) that "literally and metaphorically" characterize the estate and make it unique. Indeed, "wood is ever present in Falkland: in our ancient oak forests, in our Victorian landscaping and our 20th century commercial activities" (Falkland Stewardship Forum Report, 2004). Moreover, some data already exists that could support the creation of such an account as biodiversity has been monitored on the estate for a number of years.

Accounting for Heritage Assets

The concept of heritage assets has been used to describe assets that are significant due to their cultural and historical characteristics, including works of art, historical buildings, ancient artefacts, documentary collections, geophysical assets, and environmental assets (see Hooper et al., 2005 and Barton, 2005). The role that these assets play in local, national, and international contexts in terms of preserving, protecting, and enhancing history, culture, and the natural environment is widely recognized (Barton, 2005). In the context of Falkland, two different groups of heritage assets were identified: (1) artistic heritage assets (for example, the House of Falkland with its works of art/antiques); and (2) natural and environmental assets (including the landscape surrounding Falkland, which itself was created during the Victorian era). These assets play an important role in the context of this study because they are (in the case of the house) unique to Falkland and also because they provide income to the various entities.

Accounting for heritage assets involves several steps. First, an inventory of assets would have to be created, distinguishing between buildings, paintings, works of art, monuments, and furniture (along with records of any disposals and acquisitions, if relevant). In addition, the preservation and management policy for the assets should be described so that the likely future state of these assets can be assessed and any risks identified. Information of this sort already exists for much of the heritage assets within Falkland.

Accounting for Systems of Knowledge

In the management and business literature, systems of knowledge (comprising an interrelated set of resources including information, know-how, abilities, and skills) represent a key resource for the development and success of any organization (see Nonaka & Takeuchi, 1995 and Davenport & Prusak, 1998). Such a realization suggests that there is a need to adopt appropriate and effective organizational procedures and mechanisms to protect, preserve, and enhance knowledge. During the analysis we identified that in the Falkland system, and specifically in FHT, systems of knowledge exists including: (1) know-how about the principles and practices of stewardship in managing resources; (2) skills and expertise in undertaking activities such as craft practices, sustainable agriculture, or woodland management; and (3) the knowledge which is derived from maintaining good relations with communities and stakeholders. As with the previous examples of accounting tools, a systematic identification of knowledge, the way it is retained, shared, and developed, as well as the risk that it could be lost would all be required as part of an account of stewardship. For example, knowing who knows what about various practices is important, as is the knowledge of who could mentor others to develop these skills. In addition, running workshops to create new skills is part of the activities of FCS, as are seminar series aimed at developing knowledge and capacity about how to create a more sustainable world.

In summary, in this stage of the project we identified specific accounting tools that could be used to support (and provide an account of) the stewardship mission of FHT/FCS. These included a methodology for developing an overall view of the impact of FHT as well as specific techniques that focused on significant components within FHT. Due to resource constraints these particular accounts have not yet been developed by the case organization, but this section does illustrate that it is possible (at least to some extent) to capture the outcomes of acting as a steward in this particular context.

Concluding Remarks

In this chapter we have provided a narrative about a seventeen-month journey (itself part of a longer engagement) that we undertook in partnership with individuals who work within what we have called the "Falkland system." FHT and FCS (themselves social economy organizations) had adopted stewardship as their motivating rationale and were keen to explore what (if anything) social accounting practices could contribute to their activities. A series of conclusions can be drawn from the work undertaken here.

While stewardship could at first glance be seen to be synonymous with accountability, it does not appear to be so in this instance, thereby raising issues for our existing conceptualization of accountability. In particular, we found that stewardship (as conceived of by the case organization) has two distinctive aspects: (1) the time frame of analysis, the scope of stakeholders, and the object of the account is broader than that in much of the accountability literature; and (2) the ethos that was brought to the activity by case participants differs from mainstream corporate social responsibility rationales. Each of these elements will now be considered in more detail.

First, the time frame over which stewardship activities have been pursued by the FHT is much longer that is traditionally expected or articulated within the social accounting literature. This would appear to have arisen in part due to the unique characteristics of the case organization as well as the nature of the assets to be stewarded. In both instances a generational time frame would appear to be the appropriate frame of reference because assets such as built heritage, woodlands, and landscapes change and evolve over these sorts of time periods. This is not to say that reporting should not be considerably more frequent than that in a generational account but that the standards for evaluating progress should include consideration of this longer time frame. In addition, given the length of time that the estate has existed, it is natural for its steward to think for the long term. To phrase this as accountability would seem to be too narrow (depending on what form of accountability is being discussed – see Gibbon, 2009) and as such the use of the word stewardship as the principle guiding these actions is a more fitting description. Moreover, the explicit recognition of stakeholders who are yet to be born as well as the conception of a place itself as being a stakeholder speaks to a wider notion of stakeholders than is usually seen in the literature. As the scope of that for which a steward is held accountable expands, it is also natural that the range of stakeholders to whom responsibility is owed expands. It could also be argued that stewardship links more readily to sustainable development than does corporate social responsibility. Indeed, Bebbington et al. (2007) suggest that accounting for sustainable development would require an ecosystem-based account in order to reconcile organizational and natural systems. It may well be that in Falkland this intersection of interests has naturally arisen.

Second, the ethos expressed by participants in the case study organization was also important. While there remains for the Falkland system (as for any organization) a need to remain financially viable, the constraints that are placed around its potential activities are driven by a stewardship vision and ethos. Ninian plays a pivotal role in this study as the "keeper" of the ethos of the place, but he is not the sole definer of that ethos. In this respect, he plays a complex but important role as both being a guardian of the Falkland vision as well as enabling others' visions for Falkland to develop and become part of the place. It is hard to image this case organization without Ninian, but there must be a time (albeit hopefully far into the future) when a passing of influence and mentoring would have to take place. How this could be done and the way in which the vision and ethos of the place would change as a result is unknown but these are the sorts of challenges that all hereditary and long-lived assets face (whether they be in individual or collective ownership). It is also the case that at the current moment in time the vision for the estate is performative in nature (that is, it is evidenced by actions taken/not taken). This latter point will be returned to below.

The final element of the study explored whether it would be possible to account for stewardship in the case organization. Using conventional social accounting tools and techniques it is clearly possible to provide accounts for some aspects of this organization's activities. The social audit methodology could usefully provide a base from which such an account could be developed and, as described in the main body of this chapter, particular accounting tools could be used to provide an account of particular aspects of these activities. While the organization (for reasons of resource availability) has not currently developed any formal interlinked accounts of the nature suggested here, it is not the case that no accounts exist. Rather, accounts of activities are found by way of information boards on the estate, carved stones, leaflets, public lectures, and the annual Big Tent Festival. It may be that these sorts of accounts are equally (if not more) powerful than a formal paper-based accounting process (although both would have value in their own right) and may be considered as part of the universe of all possible accountings (Gray et al., 1996) through which stories and events are narrated. If more formal accounts (along the lines envisaged here) were developed it would be hard to predict with any degree of certainty what would develop as a result. It is likely, however, that the organization would seek a wide array of stakeholder engagement in any such process in order to understand what impact these accounts would have as well as what actions would be likely to flow from any such accounts (and the interactions surrounding them).

In summary, stewardship can be seen as informing the actions of this social economy participant. The way this concept is developed within the case organization is considerably wider, deeper, and more radical than that most usually observed in the social accounting and corporate social responsibility literatures. Indeed, it could be argued that their conception is closer to the way that sustainable development has been conceptualized at a national scale. Further, many of the aspects considered by the estate (ecological sustainability of activities, social and economic interconnections, and more participative forms of governance) find resonance in the sustainable development literature. In addition, we believe that this case provides a glimpse into a possible articulation of what it means to be responsible for a diverse set of assets. In the case organization, the assets themselves are also unusual in that they comprise a historical built environment, landscapes, and a bio-diverse ecology. There are ways in which an account of these interactions can be constructed – and if these were to be played out in this organization it would be likely to generate further insights. To close, we will leave with a personal reflection (written in a diary of research reflections) about one of the authors' experiences of Falkland – a place to which we grew very attached over the course of this project.

> This is the first time that I am at Falkland in the night. The atmosphere is fabulous. I pass through the main gate and walk along a small road which brings me to a narrow path which is covered over, as if it is protected by the tall and majestic pine and oak trees on either side. The surroundings resound with symbols and meanings embedded in the history of this place. Finally, I reach the top of a small hill, where a house emerges from the quiet of the surrounding nature. This house gives a sense of harmony between human and nature, and for the first time I have the feeling of understanding what stewardship may mean. (Reflections before the Lecture Evening of the 1st November 2007, Diary of Reflections)

REFERENCES

Barton, A. (2005). The conceptual arguments concerning accounting for public heritage assets: A note. *Accounting, Auditing & Accountability Journal, 18*(3), 434–40. http://dx.doi.org/10.1108/09513570510600774

Bebbington, J., O'Dwyer, B., & Unerman, J. (2007). Postscript and conclusions. In J. Unerman, J. Bebbington, & B. O'Dwyer (Eds.), *Sustainability accounting and accountability* (pp. 345–49). London: Routledge. http://dx.doi.org/10.4324/NOE0415384889.ch18

Caers, R., Du Bois, C., Jegers, M., De Gieter, S., Schepers, C., & Pepermans, R. (2006). Principal-agent relationships on the stewardship-agency axis. *Nonprofit Management & Leadership, 17*(1), 25–47. http://dx.doi.org/10.1002/nml.129

Caroll, A.B. (1999). Corporate social responsibility: Evolution of a Definitional Construct. *Business & Society, 38*(3), 268–95. http://dx.doi.org/10.1177/000765039903800303

Collins cobuild advanced learner's English dictionary. (2003). Glasgow: HarperCollins Publishers.

Crane, A., & Matten, D. (2008). *Corporate social responsibility* (Vols. I–II). London: Sage.

Davenport, T.H., & Prusak, L. (1998). *Working knowledge: How organizations manage what they know.* Boston, MA: Harvard Business School Press.

Davis, J.H., Schoorman, F.D., & Donaldson, L. (1997). Toward a stewardship
   theory of management. *Academy of Management Review, 22*(1), 20–47.
Department for Environment, Food and Rural Affairs. (2005). *One future – dif-*
   ferent paths: The UK's shared framework for sustainable development. London:
   Department for Environment, Food and Rural Affairs.
Dey, C., Evans, R., & Gray, R. (1995). Towards social information systems and
   bookkeeping: A note on developing the mechanisms for social accounting
   and audit. *Journal of Applied Accounting Research, 2*(3), 36–69.
Ebrahim, A. (2003a). Accountability in practice: Mechanisms for
   NGOs. *World Development, 31*(5), 813–829. http://dx.doi.org/10.1016/
   S0305-750X(03)00014-7
Ebrahim, A. (2003b). Making sense of accountability: Conceptual perspectives
   for Northern and Southern nonprofits. *Nonprofit Management & Leadership,*
   14(2), 191–212. http://dx.doi.org/10.1002/nml.29
Enderle, G. (1997). In search of a common ethical ground: Corporate environmental responsibility from the perspective of Christian environmental stewardship. *Journal of Business Ethics, 16*(2), 173–81. http://dx.doi.
   org/10.1023/A:1017944430213
Falkland Centre for Stewardship. (2004). Interview with the Steward of Falkland Estate, *Falkland Stewardship Forum Report of first meeting,* Falkland Centre for Stewardship. Falkland.
Falkland Estate Trust. (n.d.). *Falkland Estate.* Official leaflet produced by Falkland Estate Trust. Falkland.
Falkland Heritage Trust. (n.d.). *The importance of stone poster.* Official Poster
   produced by Falkland Heritage Trust. Falkland.
Gibbon, J. (2009). *Enacting social accounting within a community enterprise: Actu-*
   alising hermeneutic conversation. PhD Dissertation. Saint Andrews: University of St. Andrews.
Gjesdal, F. (1981). Accounting for stewardship. *Journal of Accounting Research,*
   19(1), 208–31. http://dx.doi.org/10.2307/2490970
Goodin, R. (2003). Democratic accountability: The distinctiveness of the third
   sector. *European Journal of Sociology, 44*(3), 359–96. http://dx.doi.org/10.1017/
   S0003975603001322
Gray, R. (1992). Accounting and environmentalism: An exploration of the
   challenge of gently accounting for accountability, transparency and sustainability. *Accounting, Organizations and Society, 17*(5), 399–425. http://dx.doi.
   org/10.1016/0361-3682(92)90038-T
Gray, R., Dey, C., Owen, D., Evans, R., & Zadek, S. (1997). Struggling with
   the praxis of social accounting: Stakeholders, accountability, audits and

procedures. *Accounting, Auditing & Accountability Journal, 10*(3), 325–64. http://dx.doi.org/10.1108/09513579710178106

Gray, R., Owen, D., & Adams, C. (1996). *Accounting & accountability: changes and challenge in corporate social and environmental reporting.* London: Prentice-Hall.

Hoat, T.F. (1993). *Dictionary of English etymology concise Oxford edition.* Oxford: Oxford University Press.

Hooper, K., Kearins, K., & Green, R. (2005). Knowing "the price of everything and the value of nothing": Accounting for heritage assets. *Accounting, Auditing & Accountability Journal, 18*(3), 410–33. http://dx.doi.org/10.1108/09513570510600765

Jones, M.J. (2003). Accounting for biodiversity: Operationalising environmental accounting. *Accounting, Auditing & Accountability Journal, 16*(5), 762–89. http://dx.doi.org/10.1108/09513570310505961

Jones, M.J., & Matthews, J. (2000). *Accounting for biodiversity: A natural inventory of the Elan Valley Nature Reserves.* London: ACCA.

Lehman, G. (1999). Disclosing new worlds: A role for social and environmental accounting and auditing. *Critical Perspectives on Accounting, 24*(2), 217–41.

Masini, C. (1970). *Lavoro e Risparmio.* Torino: UTET.

Miller, C. (2002). Towards a self-regulatory form of accountability in the voluntary sector. *Policy and Politics, 30*(4), 551–66. http://dx.doi.org/10.1332/030557302760590378

Mook, L., Quarter, J., & Richmond, B.J. (2007). *What counts: Social accounting for nonprofits and cooperatives* (2nd ed.). London: Sigel Press.

Nonaka, I., & Takeuchi, H. (1995). *The knowledge-creating company: How Japanese companies create the dynamics of innovation.* New York: Oxford University Press.

O'Dwyer, B., & Unerman, J. (2007). From functional to social accountability: Transforming the accountability relationship between funders and non-governmental development organizations. *Accounting, Auditing & Accountability Journal, 20*(3), 446–71. http://dx.doi.org/10.1108/09513570710748580

O'Dwyer, B., & Unerman, J. (2008). The paradox of greater NGO accountability: A case study of Amnesty Ireland. *Accounting, Organizations and Society, 33*(7–8), 801–24. http://dx.doi.org/10.1016/j.aos.2008.02.002

Roberts, J. (1991). The possibilities of accountability. *Accounting, Organizations and Society, 16*(4), 355–68. http://dx.doi.org/10.1016/0361-3682(91)90027-C

Roberts, J. (1996). From discipline to dialogue: individualizing and socializing forms of accountability. In R. Munro & J. Mouritsen (Eds.), *Accountability, power, ethos and the technologies of managing* (pp. 40–61). London: Thomson International Business Press.

Scottish Executive. (2005). *Choosing our future: Scotland's sustainable development strategy*. Edinburgh: Scottish Executive.

Stephen, W. (2004). *Think global, act local: The life and legacy of Patrick Geddes*. Edinburgh: Luath Press Ltd.

United Nations World Commission on Environment and Development. (1987). *Our common future (the Brundtland Report)*. Oxford: Oxford University Press.

3 Fair Trade Intermediaries and Social Accounting: The Case of Assisi Organics

DARRYL REED, ANANYA MUKHERJEE, J.J. MCMURTRY,
AND MANJULA CHERKIL

Recent work has highlighted the importance of social accounting (SA) for social economy (SE) actors in a range of sectors. Another realm of SE activity into which SA could be fruitfully extended is certified fair trade (FT) products. The adoption of SA by individual FT organizations would seem to be a relatively straight forward task, although it would probably have to involve a range of tools targeted at different stakeholder groups. FT, however, is a complex practice that is characterized more by the relationships between organizations than just the activities of single organizations. The more involved these relationships get, especially as value chains become longer, the more complicated it becomes to incorporate SA into FT, especially with relation to actors in the middle of the chains. This chapter examines the case of one such FT intermediary, Assisi Organics, a garment manufacturer in the India state of Tamil Nadu, and highlights the challenges and importance of incorporating the role of such intermediaries in the analysis of the realization of social value added in FT value chains. The chapter begins with an extended introduction to the practice of FT before going on to examine the particular problems of social accounting that arise among intermediaries in FT value chains.

An Introduction to Fair Trade

There are several types of initiatives that are commonly associated with the genesis of FT. It has become common to distinguish between early "charity trade" (which involved ad hoc importing of handicrafts made by vulnerable groups, e.g., refugees, orphans, etc.), "alternative trade" (which was based upon a critique of the dominant trade system and involved establishing alternative markets based upon solidarity which paid fairer prices), and "solidarity trade" (which had much in common with alternative trade but demonstrated a special concern with supporting governments and movements in the South that were promoting alternative forms of development, e.g., Tanzania, Nicaragua) (Low & Davenport, 2005; Hockerts, 2005; LeClair, 2002).

Out of these traditions have arisen the two contemporary branches of FT. In the first of these branches, the practice of FT is defined in terms of commitment to FT principles and participation by small producers in democratically controlled organizations that are joined together in an umbrella body, the World Fair Trade Organization (WFTO). In the other branch, the practice of fair trade has become associated with the certification of (agricultural) products (not producer organizations), which have been produced under fair conditions. While this branch of FT was initiated by a small producer organization and a development NGO, the range of participants has become much more diverse over the years, including larger corporations and agricultural estates. Participation in this branch of FT is defined not by allegiance to FT principles but by conformity to minimal standards established by national labelling initiatives (LIs) and their umbrella organization, the Fair Labelling Organization International (FLO). It is this latter variant of certified FT that is the concern of this chapter (Low & Davenport, 2005).

The Origins of Fair Trade Certification

The origins of certified FT can be traced directly back to a group of Mexican coffee farmers. In 1983 members of seventeen Indigenous peasant communities in Oaxaca, Mexico, came together to form the Union of the Indigenous Communities of the Region of the Isthmus (Unión de Comunidades Indígenas de la Región del Istmo, UCIRI). While the development of this organization was a response to a variety of circumstances (including the role of local middlemen in the exporting of coffee), it is not coincidental that the movement it set in motion developed during a time when a fall in coffee prices threatened to decimate small coffee producers. This drop in coffee prices, however, was not just a normal market fluctuation due to climatic conditions. Rather, it was the result of the deregulation of the international coffee market, part of a larger trend of neo-liberal economic reforms around the globe which emphasized the need for "free trade" and the aligning of local prices to world prices. It was in this context of plunging coffee prices induced by neo-liberal reforms that UCIRI initiated a proposal to develop a certification process for fairly traded coffee. This resulted in the development of Max Havelaar Foundation in the Netherlands in 1998. Over the next decade a variety of other national certifying bodies would emerge in developed countries. In 1977, seventeen of these bodies joined together to form FLO (VanderHoff Boersma, 2009; Fridell, 2007; Waridel 2002; Roozen & VanderHoff Boersma, 2001).

Corporate Participation

Before the advent of certification, fair trade was almost exclusively comprised of small SE actors who maintained close relations in very short value chains. With the introduction of certification, however, three major changes involving the participation of conventional firms have occurred to make the practice much more complex. One of the basic purposes of establishing a certification system was to expand the distribution network for FT coffee to conventional retail outlets, especially large grocery chains (later specialty shops and other retail chains would also be targeted). Initially, retail outlets were not involved as licensees, but over time there has been a significant move in this direction. The second development was the entrance of large agro-food corporations, as well as small- and medium-sized enterprises (SMEs), into the FT market as licensees. This first occurred in a significant way among retail coffee chains and service providers, but has now spread to other products as well. The third major change has been the incorporation of estate production within the FT network. While this move was initially seen as a concession to a shortage of production by small producers in some sectors, the use of estate production has grown rapidly in recent years (Reed, 2009; Fridell, 2007; Murray & Raynolds, 2000).[1]

One way to conceptualize the nature of the changes brought about by the entrance into FT of these three types of large conventional businesses – large retail grocery chains, large agro-food processing companies, and large agricultural estates – is through the notion of value chains (see Table 3.1).[2] With the introduction of FT certification, as indicated in Table 3.1, the original alternative trade value chain involving only SE actors (1) would continue to exist as alternative trade organizations (ATOs) became certified. What changed, however, was the fact that some ATOs embraced the notion of expanding distribution through conventional distribution channels (large supermarkets) and

Table 3.1. Four Variants of the Fair Trade Value Chain

Type of the Value Chain	Level of Corporate Involvement	Nature of Exchange
(1) Wholly social economy	None	Solidarity-based relations
(2) Social economy dominated	Retail	Solidarity-based relations
(3) Corporate dominated	Retail, licensing	Socially regulated market relations
(4) Wholly corporate	Retail, licensing, production	Socially regulated market relations

in the process created a new variant of the FT value chain (2). With the entry of large agro-food corporations into FT, another variant of the FT value chain would emerge (3) as these corporate licensees distributed their products through grocery retailers or (as was the case with coffee retail chains) through their own distribution networks. Finally, the introduction of estate production would lead to another development in the FT value chain (4).

In terms of our concern with SA and SE actors, what should be noted at this stage is that two quite distinct groups can be differentiated among these four variants of the FT value chain. On the one hand, the first two variants continue to be (predominantly) characterized by exchange relations based upon solidarity between SE actors (except for the inclusion of corporate retailers at the end of the second chain). On the other hand, the latter two variants are based upon liberal exchange relations between conventional for-profit firms and small producer organizations (3) or merely liberal exchange relationships between conventional businesses (4) (Reed, 2009).[3]

Competition with Fair Trade

The inclusion of corporate actors into FT has a number of potential implications with respect to the governance of labelling bodies, the prospects for local development, the primacy of small producers, and so on (Mukherjee Reed & Reed, 2009). One of the most significant consequences for our purposes (and one which is closely linked to the others) is that these changes mean that SE actors (both Northern licensees and Southern producers) have to compete against large corporations and estates. In this competition, corporations and estates have distinct advantages, especially with respect to controlling costs and making profits.

In the North, this competition is primarily between SE licensees and large agro-industrial corporations. Here, corporations tend to be much larger and have greater access to resources than most SE licensees. More significantly still, perhaps, is the fact that corporations approach FT differently from SE enterprises. As profit-oriented organizations, corporations enter into FT primarily with an eye to capturing a niche market and/or for other strategic purposes (e.g., image washing, placating potential opposition, or even undermining the initiative by watering down its standards). As such, when they engage in FT, corporations at best conform to minimum standards (e.g., paying the FT minimum price and social premium) rather than to FT values. Any efforts that they undertake to build capacity among small producers – if they source from small producers – are linked to their interests (e.g., in quality control, cost reduction) rather than those of the producers (e.g., to gain information about markets, to move up the value chain into processing, developing related products, etc.). Moreover, they typically only purchase a very small proportion of their total production as certified FT goods (usually well under 5 per cent) (Reed, 2009; Renard & Pérez-Grovas, 2007).

SE licensees, by contrast, are generally motivated by their commitment to FT values. As such, their goal is not to minimize costs and maximize their own value, but to drive as much of the value as they can down to producers at the bottom of the chain. To this end, they seek to provide small producers with as much information and resources (to increase local capacity) as they can, while developing the market in the North (through education and advocacy). This means that SE actors almost inevitably have higher costs structures and work on smaller profit margins. While these practices are appreciated by small producer organizations, they can make SE licensees quite vulnerable (Fridell, 2009).

In the South, the introduction of estate production in FT has meant that small producers too increasingly have to compete against corporations and private owners of large estates. While the introduction of estate production was originally justified on the basis of a lack of sufficient small producers in some agricultural sectors (especially tea, bananas), the use of estate production has been extended to all but four fair trade sectors. This development has been strongly opposed by producer organizations, especially in Latin America (where they are particularly concerned by efforts to extend plantation production to the coffee sector). Small producer organizations not only believe that estate production goes against the original intent of FT, but are very concerned about having to compete with large estates which are likely to have significant cost advantages due to economies of scale (and the fact that they do not invest in the development of the broader local economy). Small producers fear that this may lead to their marginalization in the FT network and even to their elimination in the worst case scenario (VanderHoff Boersma, 2009; Murray & Raynolds, 2000).

Social Accounting in Short Fair Trade Value Chains

The notion of SA originally arose in the 1970s and then, after a period of dormancy, was revived in the 1990s (see chapter 1). The practice of SA seeks to expand the conventional field of financial accounting by "accounting" for the full impact – both financial and social – that firms have on a range of stakeholders (beyond investors). In analysing social impact, SA initially tended to report in non-monetarized forms, using both quantitative methods (e.g., descriptive statistics) or qualitative methods (e.g., simple narratives, ethnographic studies, etc.), or a combination of the two.[4] In addition to this form of social reporting, two other basic SA types of tools have been developed. One tool is an elaborated method to approximate the monetary worth of the social value-added (SVA) that firms produce through providing services and member/employee contributions, for example, social return on investment (SROI), SVA statements. The other seeks to provide measures that integrate both financial and social performance, for example, blended ROI, expanded value-added statements (EVAS) (see Table 3.2). In principle, the SA practices of firms should also involve independent "social auditing." In reality, however, this would not seem to be the norm. To the degree that firms engage in social auditing, it is more likely to be done through their participation in some form of independent reporting initiative (Gray, 2001; Mook et al., 2003; Quarter et al., 2009).

Nicholls (2009) has argued that in recent years SE actors and "social enterprises" more generally have become extremely aware of the strategic importance of engaging in both social and financial reporting. As a result, such institutions have been developing and adopting "new reporting practices that go beyond the requirements of regulation to act as strategic innovations designed to drive improved performance

Table 3.2. Social Accounting Tools

Monetized Statements			Non-Monetized (Social) Statements	
Financial	Social	Integrated	Quantitative	Qualitative
• Income Statement • Balance Sheet • Value-Added Statement	• Social ROI •SVA Statement	• Blended ROI • EVA Statement	• Descriptive Statistics	• Simple Narrative • Ethnographies

impact and better functioning stakeholder accountability" (2009, p. 759). A basic reality that many social enterprises confront is that they have to interact with a variety of stakeholder groups (e.g., donors, members, clients, consumers, government agencies and regulators, etc.). Communicating efficaciously with such varied actors may require a variety of reporting tools. As a result, Nicholls argues, not only have social enterprises been innovative in developing new tools, but they are increasingly employing a mix of options extending across a spectrum of financial and social reporting tools which can be used to address combinations of specific organizational goals and stakeholders. Such a practice, which Nicholls calls "blended social accounting," enables social entrepreneurs "to capture the holistic complexity of organizational outputs and impacts" (2009, p. 764) and, thereby, to develop a more comprehensive strategic approach to reporting.

In principle, a blended approach strategy to SA should appeal to Northern SE firms engaged in FT. (Below, we also examine the potential importance of a blended approach to Southern actors.) Indeed, one of the examples that Nicholls provides of a social enterprise using such a blended strategy is Café Direct, the largest FT coffee company in the UK. Again, the reason such an approach should be attractive is because FT enterprises, such as Café Direct, typically have multiple audiences that they want to connect with (including consumers, NGOs, Southern producer organizations, labelling bodies, development agencies, foundations, etc.). In practice, however, it seems that most FT licensees have not been particularly innovative in this area. While many, if not most, SE actors do engage in some aspects of social reporting, this is typically limited to non-monetized forms. Apart from the prominent case of Traidcraft, the literature reveals few other examples of FT licensees engaging in monetized forms of SA. Similarly, Traidcraft offers one of the few examples of a genuine social accounting program among FT licensees (Dey, 2002, 2007; Dey et al., 1995).

For their part, while they are most commonly presented as the beneficiaries of the social value added of Northern SE licensees, Southern producer organizations are creators of social value added in their own right. Members of producer organizations donate large amounts of time to their organizations as well as to the programs that promote the development of the larger community (Waridel, 2002; Roozen & VanderHoff Boersma, 2001). They are also frequently able to procure time from volunteers and to access resources from international and local NGOs. The value added provided by producer organizations increases the individual and collective capacity of their members and also provides social and physical infrastructures and other benefits for their larger communities.

Just as for Northern SE licensees, there would seem to be potentially significant benefits for Southern producer organizations in being able to quantify the social value added that they generate and to express this in some form of blended approach to SA. Such an approach could help them to provide local and regional government, international foreign aid agencies, and other donors, as well as FT labelling bodies and FT consumers, a more accurate account of their contributions to development (and to distinguish themselves from their rivals, such as large estates participating in FT or other rival labelling bodies).

In the South, however, a couple of different factors seem to have inhibited such a development becoming widespread among small producers. The first of these is a lack of resources and knowledge around SA. By definition, most small producer organizations are composed of marginalized people, who have very limited resources. Such groups, especially primary co-operatives, are unlikely to have any familiarity with the notion of social accounting (though some of the managers of second-level co-operatives might have some awareness). Second, the dynamics around reporting in producer organizations have largely been driven from the outside (from funding agencies, development NGOs, certifying bodies, Northern buyers, etc.). These, largely Northern organizations, as institutions, are to some extent less interested in how Southern small producers are themselves generating value and communicating this to their stakeholders than they are with how small producers are recipients of their beneficence. It is these Northern organizations, which have the resources to engage in social reporting, that drive the reporting agenda. As a result, most of the social reporting that occurs derives from a "development project" perspective and is based on impact assessment frameworks established by development agencies rather than social accounting tools.[5] This is not to say that producer groups themselves are not involved (there has, indeed, been an increasing tendency to incorporate participatory components to such frameworks) and that they are not of use to small producers, but to recognize that it is the agenda of Northern organizations driving the reporting.

Social Accounting in Fair Trade Intermediaries (in Longer Fair Trade Value Chains)

The literature on FT focuses primarily on small producers and Northern licensees (and retailers). The reason for this is that originally intermediaries did not play a significant role in FT. This was by design. Small producers wanted to eliminate intermediaries in order to have more direct relationships with consumers and to capture more of the value in the chain. Two changes in FT, however, would significantly increase the role of intermediaries, especially non-SE intermediaries. The first of these was the entrance of large agro-industrial corporations into FT. Brought into the market by a combination of factors other than a commitment to FT values (e.g., opportunities for exploiting niche markets, consumer pressure, concerns about public relations, etc.), these corporations were more inclined to incorporate their existing value chains into the FT system rather than alter them in any substantive way. These chains were composed almost exclusively of conventional companies that would continue to serve different intermediary roles (as buyers, processers, importers, etc.) within FT value chains (Bezençon, 2007). The second change that induced a greater role for intermediaries involved the introduction of new products, which required more complex and more stages of processing, such as cocoa and cotton.

It is this second phenomenon that is of interest to us, for while most of the intermediaries involved in processing are conventional firms, there is potentially a significant role for SE actors (especially in less capital intensive forms of processing) to add social value. Such actors may have FT or any of a variety of other social purposes as their primary mission. Whatever their primary social purpose, however, they will probably be at a loss to fulfil their mission if they are forced to compete entirely on the basis of cost competition. Thus, they need to find ways to market themselves (most of which should also assist their SE partners in the chain). SA potentially provides an important basis for doing this. In what follows, we will examine a particular case, that of Assisi Organics, to illustrate both the potential and importance of social value creation by SE intermediaries in FT value chains and how this might be more effectively documented for different target audiences.

The Case of Assisi Organics

Assisi Organics[6] was initiated in 1994 by a group of Sisters of the Immaculate Heart of Mary, Cherthala (Kerala). As Franciscans, the sisters have a special mission to work with the poor and disadvantaged. Historically, a major thrust of their endeavours has been to work with victims of leprosy. As leprosy has been largely eradicated in recent years, the nuns have shifted their attention to working with other marginalized groups, especially the poor and the disabled. Among their various activities, the nuns operate a range of schools from the primary level up to community colleges as well as technical schools. They also have schools for disabled and disadvantaged youth, operate orphanages, and run several hospitals and old age homes.

One of the schools that the nuns operate is a boarding facility for hearing and speech impaired girls. The girls enter at the age of six and study until the 10th standard. A basic problem that these young women were facing was not finding work once they had finished school. They did not have obvious career paths and most of them were not in a position to marry. They generally had to return to their families where they were largely confined to the house and not able to integrate into society very easily. An attempted suicide by one of the girls brought home to the sisters just how serious the situation was.

This event instilled in one of the nuns, Sr. Michael Francis, a deep desire to establish some sort of program to help these young women. As the sisters had a convent close to Tirupur, one of the major garment districts in India, she decided to start a garment business that could serve as a training and an employment program that would teach the women tailoring skills and provide them with work. This was a controversial decision as many members of the congregation did not see setting up a business as part of their mission. Still, despite some opposition, Sr. Michael Francis continued with her plan.

In 1994 a younger colleague of Sr. Michael Francis, Sister Vineetha Francis, came to Tirupur with ten graduates of the school to set up a firm. Although they did not have any real knowledge of the garment industry, their goal was to establish a facility in which the young women could learn tailoring skills and gain employment. While the original plan was to work only with hearing and speech impaired young women, it soon became apparent that they would need to expand their vision. There was a large pool of poor women in the area who needed employment, so the decision was made to expand the original mandate to include poor and other marginalized women in the scheme.

It took two years before Sister Vineetha and her colleagues established Assisi Organics as a business. In the first few years, it was a very small operation. Over time, however, it grew significantly and today employs approximately 120 young women as well as a more skilled, local labour force of about sixty, which includes men and women.

Mission

The mission of Assisi Organics is essentially twofold. The original purpose of the company, as noted above, was to provide training and employment for young girls who were hearing and speech impaired. This mission was soon extended to include economically disadvantaged women. In this regard, Assisi Organics can be understood as a social purpose business, that is, a business that was set up with a specific social goal in mind: training workers and generating employment.

When the sisters established Assisi Organics the original understanding was that the young women could come and work for a period of four to five years. During this time they would not only learn skills and have an income, but Assisi would provide them with a yearly bonus (to be paid upon leaving). The latter was intended to help them "get settled," that is, arrange for marriage. It was generally assumed that most women would probably not continue on in the formal workforce after marriage (though they were not prohibited from doing so). While this was the trend in the early years, today more of the women are interested in continuing to work after marriage. This has led Assisi to rethink its policies, both in terms of training and retention of workers. At this stage, however, no solid proposals have been developed.

At Assisi a second purpose – in addition to employment and training – has emerged as a result of its financial success. Because Assisi has become a profitable venture, the nuns have been able to finance a number of other social programs in which they are involved. Among these are a cancer hospital, an old age home, and several schools. In this sense, Assisi functions as a particular type of social enterprise – a business that provides a surplus which is used for the primary mission of the owners (in this case, a range of charitable activities).

Ownership and Legal Structure

Assisi Organics is incorporated under the Indian Companies Act (1956) as a partnership. There are six partners, all of whom are sisters of the order of the Immaculate Heart of Mary, Cherthala. The reason that the business was established as a partnership rather than a not-for-profit business relates back to the reservations from some members of the congregation as to whether the order should be involved in setting up a business. Given the disagreements over this matter, setting up Assisi as a partnership was the most expeditious option. Assisi Organics is owned entirely by the sisters, with Sister Vineetha serving as the managing partner.

More recently, the sisters have been thinking of incorporating the company as a not-for-profit business. This would provide them with some tax benefits. They have not yet taken this step, however. Another possible benefit of such a move could be greater transparency in that the business would have to provide more information about the use of their surplus. While the nuns use the surplus for social purposes, there has not been any regular reporting of exactly where the profits go (but see below).

Business Strategy

As its name implies, Assisi Organics competes exclusively in the organic cotton market. All of the garments it produces are certified organic. Aware of the tremendous negative impact that Bt and traditional cotton farming has had on cotton farmers, the sisters see their commitment to 100 per cent organic production as an issue of social justice and not just a business strategy. Indeed, there are hidden costs within the business strategy: many of the knitwear goods that Assisi provides are typically offered as cotton-synthetic blends. The decision to offer only 100 per cent organic cotton products thereby significantly limits the markets in which it can compete. Similarly, Assisi's move into the FT market is based not merely on expediency and the desire to exploit a niche market; it also reflects the company's strong commitment to social justice. In short, while Assisi demonstrates that competing in ethical markets, such as the organic and FT cotton market, can be profitable,

Table 3.3. Total Sales Turnover (Rs millions)

Year	Export		Domestic	Total
	Organic	Fair Trade Organic		
2005–6	54.7		1.1	55.8
2006–7	37.8	27	2.7	67.5
2007–8	48.3	39.9	8.0	96.2
2008–9	80.3	47.5	61.5	189.3

its decision to compete in these markets reflects its commitment to so-cial justice more than a strategic direction.

There is still room, however, for strategic considerations in ethical markets. Assisi's twofold mission clearly provides it with a unique sell-ing point among Indian garment manufacturers. Similarly, its Catho-lic identity provides it with another unique selling point that should facilitate sales in such areas as sales of uniforms and spirit wear (e.g., branded T-shirts, sweatshirts) in Catholic educational institutions. This is an aspect that Assisi has yet to actively exploit, but is open to examin-ing. Currently, it provides uniforms for only one school in the UK. The recent opening up of the U.S. market (with its large number of Catholic schools and universities) would seem to provide even more potential.

Assisi's strategy has enabled it to consistently increase its sales from its inception (see Table 3.3). As noted above, Assisi originally started in organic garments and these still provide the largest component of its total sales. It was in 2005–6 that Assisi started to produce for the FT organic market. Here, too, there has been consistent growth in its sales over the past three years. While Assisi does produce a small amount of garments for domestic consumption, its primary focus has been on the export market. A recent development has seen Assisi provide yarn and cloth to domestic producers. This was responsible for a large bump in sales during the past year.

Organizational Structure

While Assisi organics is owned by a group of nuns, it is run by a pro-fessional management team. Although Sister Vineetha is recognized as the managing partner, she is more inclined to work on the sewing lines with the women than to oversee business operations. This task of oversight primarily falls to the general manager, who has been with the firm from the start. Like most start-ups, Assisi has had to begin small and develop over time. In terms of its organizational structure, this has meant that early on the general manager had to assume a variety of different tasks. Gradually, Assisi has been able to establish separate departments for merchandising, human resources, production, and so on.

In order to attract managerial talent, Assisi is forced to pay competitive salaries. What really seems to draw managers to Assisi, however, are the less tangible benefits. Primary among these are job satisfaction and a more relaxed work environment, which includes less pressure and shorter working hours because of its work culture that tries to limit overtime.

The development of professional management is an ongoing task. This is especially the case in human resources. Historically, the nuns have tended to solve issues on a personal basis, taking into account their knowledge of the individual workers and their circumstances. This extends to such issues as allowing time off and paying bonuses towards a marriage dowry. The issue of marriage payments is a particularly delicate and tricky issue. Officially, the payment of dowry is illegal in India, but in practice it is very widespread. For large sections of the population, arranging a marriage without a dowry is not a realistic possibility. For their part, the sisters at Assisi have addressed this issue with an informal system of providing each single woman with a bonus of approximately 10,000Rs for every year worked. While the human resources department appreciates the compassion behind this approach (which is at the basis of the organization), it has been trying to develop a more systematic policy for dealing with such circumstances. It is concerned that this practice might be associated with opportunistic schemes employed by other firms,[7] and is focused on finding more efficacious ways of addressing the deeper cultural values and inequitable social relations that such practices tend to reinforce.

Capacity

As a cutting, making, and trimming (CMT) unit, Assisi undertakes several key activities in a much longer value chain (see Figure 3.1). First, Assisi purchases ginned cotton and sends it to be spun, knitted/ woven, and dyed/printed. It then produces the garments and exports them. Most of Assisi's subcontractors are in the Tirupur region of Tamil

Figure 3.1. Assisi Value Chain

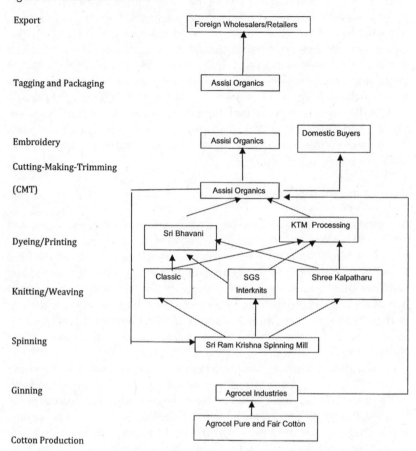

Nadu, while its cotton is primarily procured from Agrocel Industries, which is headquartered in Gujarat.

While Assisi is not a large operation, it can undertake a complete range of CMT activities. It has a full array of standard machinery, which enables it to produce a fairly wide variety of goods. With the recent addition of new Singer sewing machines in 2012, Assisi's capacity has reached 9,000 pieces per day (with a workforce close to 330). Assisi's current product range includes T-shirts, polo shirts, sweatshirts and hoodies, men's dress shirts, women's blouses, various sports jerseys, and pants. Assisi does not have its own design section, but rather works with designs provided by its buyers. While Assisi's product range is not as extensive as some of its large competitors, the management of Assisi is confident that it can produce all standard forms of apparel that buyers might want. As noted above, one limitation that Assisi faces as an exclusively organic producer is that it cannot offer the same range of fabric (i.e., synthetic fabrics) that its larger competitors offer.

Wages and Working Conditions

As noted above, there are two basic categories of workers at Assisi. On the one hand, Assisi's core mandate has been to train and provide employment for differently abled and economically marginalized women. These women typically enter as unskilled workers, although some have had training in tailoring. They are generally between eighteen and twenty-four years old and they stay in the hostel located on the factory grounds. On the other hand, Assisi hires skilled workers from the local area. These include both men and women, and they tend to be older and are usually married.

Wage rates in Tirupur are governed by an agreement between the Tirupur Exporters Association and six of the seven major unions in India (Kizhisseri & John, 2006). These wage rates vary according to skill level, with cutters and tailors being the more skilled occupations. While there are wage rates set for the skilled positions, most of these employees work on a piece-rate basis. This is their preferred option as it provides them more flexibility and a higher income. These skilled positions are in relatively high demand. Assisi has to follow the pattern of paying skilled workers on a piece-rate basis in order to secure their services.

Unskilled workers typically work on an hourly wage rate as set by the Tirupur wage agreement. Assisi tends to pay a slightly higher wage rate and pays double time for overtime work (as is required by the agreement). The work week is forty-eight hours long (six days a week). On average the lowest paid workers earn approximately 2500 Rs per month, not including overtime. Overtime typically does not exceed four hours per week (Kizhisseri & John, 2006).

The regulation of working conditions in Tirupur is based upon Government of India standards. At Assisi all of the basic health and safety standards appear to be met. The workplace is clean, with adequate toilet facilities. There does not appear to be any forced overtime. Moreover, most of the workers were effusive in stating their satisfaction with the working conditions.[8]

There is a workers' association in place. This association, however, does not really function as a union. Primarily, it makes suggestions to the nuns about relatively minor issues. It is not clear how many of the skilled workers actually belong to a union. Unions in India are associated with political parties and workers at a given plant are free to join whichever union they want. This fact, along with the reticence of workers to disclose their affiliation, makes it difficult to be certain how many workers belong to unions.

Retention

When the sisters established Assisi Organics the original plan was that young, disabled women could come and work for a period of four to five years. During this time they would not only learn skills and have an income, but Assisi would provide them with a yearly bonus (to be paid upon leaving). The latter was intended to help them "to get settled," that is, arrange for marriage. It was generally assumed that most women would probably not continue on in the formal workforce after marriage. This is still the dominant trend among the younger differently abled and economically marginalized women, despite the fact that all of the women speak very highly of their employers and are appreciative of the opportunity that they have been offered. Among the skilled workers, the pattern is different. These workers, too, are generally content with their situation, but have remained (or plan to remain) on the job longer than five years.

Training and Advancement

While the majority of the younger women still leave after about five years with Assisi, more of them are expressing an interest in staying in the workforce after marriage, either in the garment industry or in some other sector. A small, but growing number of them are staying on at Assisi, while a few have taken positions in other factories in Tirupur when they return to the workforce after their marriage (some of whom reportedly want to return to Assisi).

At Assisi, the unskilled women workers receive on-the-job training and may advance from being helpers to becoming tailors or supervisors (of packing, inspection, etc.). Some of them would prefer to have more formal courses as well as on-the-job training. A number of the young women are also very keen to get more training in other areas, especially in computers. Assisi is currently looking into setting up a small computer training facility for them.

Accounting for the Contributions of FT Intermediaries

As noted above, Assisi operates as an intermediary in a complex value chain. In this chain, Assisi creates not only economic but also significant social value. It does so in a number of roles and a variety of ways that affect and/or appeal to a number of (potential) stakeholders. Assisi, however, has been slow to develop any forms of social reporting, much less a conscious blended approach combining a range of forms tailored for different stakeholder groups. In what follows, we provide an overview of the different ways in which Assisi generates value added and how it might report on these to relevant stakeholder groups.

Assisi as a Conventional Intermediary

Like any other firm in the middle of a chain, Assisi adds economic value in the conventional ways. These include paying wages and taxes, accumulating capital, and making profits. These value added forms can be expressed in standard accounting approaches or what Mook et al. (2003) refer to as "restricted value-added statements." They can also be expressed more graphically (though not as precisely perhaps) in the breakdown of the cost structure of an individual product, such as a T-shirt (see Table 3.4).

In Table 3.4, the fabric costs represent the purchase of external goods and services. The manufacturing costs represent the value-added flowing to employees, while the margins reflect the value added going to investors (partners). Included in the fixed costs are taxes (the value added that flows to government) and the costs of capital (amortization).

Assisi as a Social Purpose Firm

Assisi is not just a conventional intermediary, however. It has a social purpose. This affects both the economic and the social value added that

Table 3.4. Cost Structure of a Fair Trade, Organic T-shirt
(Men's large, dark colour, 280 grams, 200 grams per square metre)

Process	Rs/kg	Rs/unit
Yarn	215	60.2
Knitting	10	2.8
Dyeing	100	28
Compacting	6.5	1.82
Subtotal	331.5	92.82
Losses (7%)	23.21	6.5
Fabric Cost	354.71	99.32
CMT		12
Trims		8
Printing		6
Subtotal		124.32
Rejection (2%)		2.49
Manufacturing Cost		126.81
Margin (15%)		19.02
Subtotal		145.83
Fixed Costs/extras		25
Total Costs*		170.83

*Exclusive of final transportation and shipping costs

it generates. In terms of the former, Assisi's commitment to marginal-ized women means, as noted above, that it not only meets basic minimum wage rates (including overtime rates) but also exceeds these rates.

In terms of social value added, Assisi makes contributions in a couple of key areas. First, there is the training, education, and counselling that the women receive from the nuns. While such services would not show up on a standard value sheet, costs could be calculated for these services and they could be incorporated into social value added statements. Another major source of value added comes in the form of savings that arise when differently abled women are brought into the paid labour force. Economic independence means that these women are not an economic burden on state coffers (or their families), but rather contribute to state revenue as taxpayers.

The major stakeholder groups with whom Assisi potentially needs to communicate regarding these issues include (1) charities and foundations (that might be interested is supporting Assisi through grants); (2) labour activists and unions that have expressed skepticism about the labour conditions under which FT and organic cotton is transformed into garments; (3) SE importers and distributors (and their investors), along with public purchasing policy managers who want to promote and patronize Assisi as a more ethical form of production (especially with regard to labour rights and environmental practices); (4) ethical consumers (who might have concerns about labour rights, marginalized groups, etc.); and (5) "disability" activists and organizations (who might want to promote and support Assisi but only if labour and other standards are acceptable). Assisi will probably want to communicate with these different groups in various, overlapping ways. Labour activists, for example, will probably be very keen to see financial statements (with value added by labour) as well as descriptive statistics on labour conditions. Charities and foundations, as well as disability activists and organizations, could want to see descriptive statistics and might want more information about the number of women affected. As well, they could want to see some statement of the social value being added by Assisi itself (as a further assurance of the commitment of Assisi to the differently abled vis-à-vis its role as an income generator). For their part, while consumers might be more interested in hearing stories about how individual women's lives have been transformed by the experience of working at Assisi, they could be reassured by descriptive statistics.

Assisi as a Social Enterprise

While Assisi is formally a for-profit partnership, in practice it is run as a particular type of social enterprise in which the (after-tax) profits of the company are used to fund social causes. The social causes that Assisi funds are closely related to the mission of the sisters' order and the institutions that they run. These include teaching, health and social welfare programs, and community development projects (see Table 3.5). While the profits that Assisi makes would show up (in a monetized form) as value added on a restricted value added statement (as profits), the actual social nature of the value added does not. One way to break down the nature of these social impacts is between the benefits directly provided in the form of services to clients (e.g., students, patients) and

Table 3.5. Assisi's Support to Charitable Organizations (Rs)

	Year		
Organization	2006	2007	2008
Old Age Home	100,000	100,000	100,000
Orphanage	300,000	450,000	400,000
Nursery Schools for Poor	200,000	175,000	230,000
Financial Help For Education for Poor	300,000	600,000	250,000
Cancer Hospital	1,250,000	3,700,000	12,550,000
Other Hospitals	425,000	600,000	735,000
Leprosy-Rehabilitation	250,000	425,000	475,000
Community Development	375,000	350,000	400,500
Women's Marriage	611,500	892,000	440,000
TOTAL	3,811,500	7,292,000	15,580,500

the knock-on effects. The former value can be captured quite easily in a social valued added sheet by signifying the profits generated by Assisi as a contribution to the community. The knock-on impacts from the provision of services to clients are quite varied, potentially involving cost savings for the broader community (e.g., in the form of a reduction of social problems), income impacts (e.g., in enabling people to be more productive), and a variety of quality-of-life improvements. Many of these knock-on effects of the provision of social services are more resistant to quantification than the services themselves.

Again, Assisi could potentially benefit from better communicating the value added it provides as a social economy enterprise to different stakeholders in different ways. Perhaps the most prominent group of stakeholders that Assisi needs to communicate with are charity and development organizations concerned with the provision of services to marginalized groups (especially Catholic organizations). Such organizations will probably want to see descriptive statistics (to understand the extent of the impact of Assisi contributions) as well as ethnographies (to understand more clearly the manner in which Assisi impacts clients and other stakeholders). An EVA analysis could be important, however, to demonstrate the efficacy of supporting a social enterprise as a means to contributing to social welfare provision. A second key groups of stakeholders to which Assisi could report are social enterprise foundations. Such organizations might be willing to provide funds for the development of Assisi on the basis of a combination of its social value added as an employment generator for marginalized women and its contributions to the provision of social welfare programs as a social enterprise. Such organizations will probably want to see monetized accounts of the impact of Assisi, such as in the form of SROI SVA reports. (Both of these major groups of stakeholders will also be interested in the generation of simple narratives, which they can use in their own fundraising and publicity campaigns.)

Assisi as an Organic and Fair Trade Intermediary

Finally, Assisi is an intermediary in the organic and FT value chains. As such, Assisi workers do not benefit directly from the enterprise's participation in the chain (as small producers and agricultural workers do in the FT value chain through the payment of minimum prices and a social premium). Workers, however, do share in the benefits that accrue to Assisi as a company through its participation in FT. The primary way Assisi can benefit is through its ability to exploit a niche market, in this case an ethical market, which it is able to do in large part because of its values, which make it a highly valued intermediary.

It is because of its values that Assisi, as an FT intermediary, can actively participate in the realization of social value added in the FT and organic cotton chains. Intermediaries in FT and organic chains can contribute in either of two basic ways towards the realization of social value. On the one hand, they can act in a manner analogous to enzymes in a chemical reaction. That is to say, they are necessary agents in the process of the realization and distribution of social value, but they themselves do not add to the creation of social value themselves and are unchanged by the process. This is arguably the case with many conventional intermediaries involved in the FT and organic cotton value chains. It is for them a purely financial proposition, a niche market which they are happy to exploit if it is profitable. On the other hand, intermediaries can play a much more active role in the realization of social value. One of the key roles intermediaries such as Assisi can play is in the marketing of FT and organic goods, especially in assuaging concerns that consumers and buyers have about the integrity of the chain.

A particularly worrisome aspect of the FT cotton chain has been the labour standards under which FT cotton may be transformed into garments.[9] FT labelling bodies are themselves aware of this problem and their inability to adequately ensure appropriate working conditions in the textile- and garment-making processes. For this reason these labelling bodies only allow merchandisers to claim that the garments they sell contain FT cotton rather than claim that they are selling 100 per cent FT garments. What Assisi provides to SE importers and distributors (and consumers) concerned about these issues is greater assurance that values consistent with FT principles have been respected all through the chain, all the way from the planting of the cotton up to the export of finished garments. While Assisi itself does not pay its own workers any FT premium, it allows for the realization of the payment of such premiums (and the transmission of other forms of social value added in the chain) through ensuring the integrity of the chain. In addition, firms like Assisi actively engage with buyers to encourage them to convert (more of) their product lines to FT and organic cotton.

While it is often difficult for intermediaries like Assisi to tease out the exact quantity of the social value added that they provide, it is clear that they can make significant contributions to FT and organic chains (even if these cannot be effectively disaggregated).

In order to capitalize on its contributions as an SE intermediary – including developing its potential to establish its own FT and organic brand – Assisi needs to communicate with a range of stakeholders. These include FT licensees (especially SE licensees) and their investors, buyers (especially affinity buyers in Catholic universities and schools, alternative fashion houses), and consumers and donors (especially those interested in promoting more sustainable production). Again, these different groups may need to be communicated with in different ways and through different means. Importers and their investors will likely be keener to see not only conventional financial performance indicators for value added but also monetarized indicators of social value added. For their part, affinity buyers and consumers may be more interested in descriptive statistics about the impact of FT and organic production as well as in narratives that highlight particular cases. Assisi (and other licensees) will also be very interested in providing FLO and the LIs with indicators of their performance (especially around labour standards and social value added in this area) in an effort to support the development of more stringent labour standards that will help them compete more effectively on a cost basis with conventional intermediaries.

Finally, to the degree that Assisi's business is dependent upon its ability to source FT and organic cotton, it needs to clearly communicate to producer organizations those values and concerns they share and to emphasize Assisi's long-term commitment to working with them. This might be done through descriptive statistics (of the impact of their social welfare programs and their employment of marginalized women) as well as through engaging narratives.

Conclusion

Since fair trade started as a social economy initiative to help marginalized producers, it has developed in a way that threatens the continued participation of its founding organizations, small producers and ATOs. Inherent compromises in the regulation of FT to promote growth in sales – including the shift from FT principles to minimum standards – have led to a situation in which SE actors have to compete with certified FT corporate retailers, agro-industrial firms, and large agricultural estates. The lack of commitment of the latter to FT principles (along with their size) means that SE actors are typically operating at a significant cost disadvantage. In order to compete, they have to market their commitment to FT principles and their generation of social value added. While many Northern SE licensees loudly proclaim their allegiance to FT principles, few have gone very far in systematically documenting the social value added that they supply through the use of SA and other reporting methods. Similarly, small producer organizations in the South have also not yet been able to develop their own blended SA approaches to reporting. Instead, they have had to (at best) rely on social impact assessments carried out by Northern NGOs and development agencies to document their practices.

As FT continues to evolve (and corporate actors deepen their involvement), the need of SE enterprises for more sophisticated SA approaches to documenting their value added will only increase. This has become particularly apparent with the development of longer FT value chains involving commodities such as cocoa and cotton. In these chains, it is becoming essential for SE producers and licensees to find SE intermediaries (who can actively contribute to the realization of social value added) in order to guarantee the integrity of the value chains. Without such intermediaries, the competitive advantages of SE enterprises at the bottom and the top of the chain (that is, through adherence to FT principles and social value added) are undermined. While such FT intermediaries may not have FT as their primary mandate, they can be effective contributors to FT value chains while pursuing their own social purposes. In order to do this, however, they will need to develop blended SA approaches that allow them to communicate effectively with various stakeholder groups. In this chapter, we have investigated a particular example of an FT intermediary that does not have FT as its primary mission but that contributes to the realization of value added in FT value chains while pursuing its own social purposes. We have also indicated how Assisi might more effectively accomplish these tasks through adopting a variety of SA tools that target its different stakeholders.

NOTES

1 In many countries such as Canada, small- and medium-sized enterprises actually constitute the largest number of licensees (Reed et al., 2010). They do not have the same influence, however, as large corporations.

2 FT practice is more complex than this model suggests, especially with the more aggressive role that large grocery retailers have adopted in controlling value chains and the addition of new products with longer value chains (e.g., cotton). These complexities do not alter the basic point about the existence of different types of exchange (and production) relationships within FT, which result in products of different ethical value.

3 As chains get more complex (as in the case of cotton), a wider range of practices, including mixed forms of value chains, can emerge (Tallontire, 2009). While the basic interests and strategies of the actors involved remain the same in these mixed chains, the more complex set of circumstances can lead to different forms of compromise.

4 It should be noted here that the use of these non-monetized forms of reporting by firms are sometimes referred to as ethical or social audits, even though they do not conform to the standard requirement that audits be undertaken by third parties. See, for example, Richmond et al. (2003).

5 For an example of such reports see IIED (2000). Academics, as well, often draw upon the models of development agencies to development frameworks for evaluations. See, for example, Paul (2005) and Utting (2009).

6 This case is based upon two site visits to Assisi Organics (as well as visits to other firms, NGOs, and meetings with labour leaders in the Tirupur region). In addition to interviewing the leadings executives of Assisi, twenty-nine semi-structured interviews (involving questionnaires) were conducted with

Assisi employees. Fifteen of these interviews were with disabled or economically disadvantaged unskilled young women. All interviews were conducted confidentially in the interviewees' native languages (Tamil or Malayalam).

7 Many companies in the Tirupur region have taken advantage of the vulnerability of economically deprived young women through what is known as the Shumangali scheme. Under this arrangement, young women contract to work with a company (typically for three years) and at the end of the contract they get an additional lump sum payment which they can use for a dowry. It is reported that many firms abuse this practice, often taking the money out of the women's wages rather than giving them a bonus or refusing to pay the bonus when they want to leave. In addition, under this system young women are often treated as bonded labour, frequently being forced to live in hostels, required to work long overtime hours and not having freedom to leave the premises (A. Aloyious, personal communication, February, 8, 2009).

8 This situation contrasts significantly with the general situation of the Tirupur region (A. Chandra, personal communication, February 9, 2009).

9 While there has been an increasing tendency for large supermarket chains, especially in the UK, to develop their own FT brands, Tesco which has its own line of clothing made from FT cotton has come under particular criticism. See, for example, Verdier-Stott (2009).

REFERENCES

Bezençon, V. (2007). *Penetration of fair trade in mainstream distribution: Key management factors and impact. Cahier de Research en Marketing and Management.* Neuchâtel, Switzerland: Université de Neuchâtel.

Dey, C.R. (2002). Methodological issues: The use of critical ethnography as an active research methodology. *Accounting, Auditing & Accountability Journal, 15*(1), 106–21. http://dx.doi.org/10.1108/09513570210418923

Dey, C.R. (2007). Social accounting at Traidcraft plc: A struggle for the meaning of fair trade. *Accounting, Auditing & Accountability Journal, 20*(3), 423–45. http://dx.doi.org/10.1108/09513570710748571

Dey, C.R., Evans, R., & Gray, R.H. (1995). Towards social information systems and bookkeeping: A note on developing the mechanisms for social accounting and audit. *Journal of Applied Accounting Research, 2*(3), 33–67.

Fridell, G. (2007). *Fair trade: The prospects and pitfalls of market-driven social justice.* Toronto: University of Toronto Press.

Fridell, G. (2009). The co-operative and the corporation: Competing visions of the future of fair trade. *Journal of Business Ethics, 86*(S1 Supplement 1), 81–95. http://dx.doi.org/10.1007/s10551-008-9759-3

Gray, R.H. (2001). Thirty years of social accounting, reporting and auditing: What (if anything) have we learnt? *Business Ethics: A European View, 10*(1), 9–15. http://dx.doi.org/10.1111/1467-8608.00207

Hockerts, K. (2005). The fair trade story. OIKOS sustainability case collection. St. Gallen, Switzerland: OIKOS Foundation for Economy and Ecology. Retrieved April 18, 2009, from: www.oikos-foundation.unisg.ch/homepage/case.htm

IIED. (2000). Fair trade: Overview, impact, challenges. Study to Inform DFID's Support to Fair Trade. Oxford Policy Management & Sustainable Markets Group, IIED, London, June.

Kizhisseri, L., & John, P. (2006). *Knitted together: Multistakeholder perspectives on economic, social and environmental issues in the Tirupur garment cluster.* New Delhi: Partners in Change.

LeClair, M.S. (2002). Fighting the tide: Alternative trade organizations in the era of global free trade. *World Development, 30*(6), 949–58. http://dx.doi.org/10.1016/S0305-750X(02)00017-7

Low, W., & Davenport, E. (2005). Postcards from the edge: Maintaining the "alternative" character of fair trade. *Sustainable Development, 13*(3), 143–53. http://dx.doi.org/10.1002/sd.275

Mook, L., Richmond, B.J., & Quarter, J. (2003). Integrated social accounting for nonprofits: A case from Canada. *Voluntas: International Journal of Voluntary and Nonprofit Organizations, 14*(3), 283–97. http://dx.doi.org/10.1023/A:1025614619742

Mukherjee Reed, A., & Reed, D. (2009). Fair trade and development: What are the implications of mainstreaming. *Universitas Forum, 1*(2), 1–8.

Murray, D.L., & Raynolds, L.T. (2000). Alternative trade in bananas: Obstacles and opportunities for progressive social change in the global economy. *Agriculture and Human Values, 17*(1), 65–74. http://dx.doi.org/10.1023/A:1007628709393

Nicholls, A. (2009). "We do good things, don't we?": "Blended value accounting" in social entrepreneurship. *Accounting, Organizations and Society, 34*(6–7), 755–69. http://dx.doi.org/10.1016/j.aos.2009.04.008

Paul, E. (2005). Evaluating fair trade as a development project: Methodological considerations. *Development in Practice, 15*(2), 134–50. http://dx.doi.org/10.1080/09614520500040437

Quarter, J., Mook, L., & Armstrong, A. (2009). *Understanding the social economy: A Canadian perspective.* Toronto: University of Toronto Press.

Reed, D. (2009). What do corporations have to do with fair trade: Positive and normative analysis from a value chain perspective. *Journal of Business Ethics, 86*(S1 Supplement 1), 3–26. http://dx.doi.org/10.1007/s10551-008-9757-5

Reed, D., Thomson, B., Hussey, I., & LeMay, J.F. (2010). Developing a normatively-grounded research agenda for fair trade: Examining the case of Canada. *Journal of Business Ethics, 92*(S2 supplement 2), 151–79. http://dx.doi.org/10.1007/s10551-010-0575-1

Renard, M.-C., & Pérez-Grovas, V. (2007). Fair trade coffee in Mexico: At the center of the debates. In L.T. Raynolds, D. Murray, & J. Wilkinson (Eds.), *Fair trade: The challenges of transforming globalization* (pp. 138–56). New York: Routledge.

Richmond, B.J., Mook, L., & Quarter, J. (2003). Social accounting for non-profits: Two models. *Nonprofit Management & Leadership, 13*(4), 308–24. http://dx.doi.org/10.1002/nml.2

Roozen, N., & VanderHoff Boersma, F. (2001). *L'aventure du commerce équitable: Une alternative à la mondialization par les fondateurs de Max Havelaar.* Paris: Jean-claude Lattés.

Tallontire, A. (2009). Top heavy? Governance issues and policy decisions for the fair trade movement. *Journal of International Development, 21*(7), 1004–14. http://dx.doi.org/10.1002/jid.1636

Utting, K. (2009). Assessing the impact of fair trade coffee: Towards an integrative framework. *Journal of Business Ethics, 86*(S1 Supplement 1), 127–49. http://dx.doi.org/10.1007/s10551-008-9761-9

Vanderhoff Boersma, F. (2009). The urgency and necessity of a different type of market: The perspective of producers organized within the fair trade market. *Journal of Business Ethics, 86*(S1 Supplement 1), 51–61. http://dx.doi.org/10.1007/s10551-008-9766-4

Verdier-Stott, J. (2009). Labels, lies and the law: Opportunities and challenges in mainstreaming fair trade. *Law, Social Justice and Global Development Journal (1).* http://wwwz.warwick.ac.uk/fac/soc/law/elj/lgd/2009_1/verdier-stott

Waridel, L. (2002). *Coffee with pleasure: Just java and world trade.* Montreal: Black Rose.

4 Stakeholder Engagement in the Design of Social Accounting and Reporting Tools

LESLIE BROWN AND ELIZABETH HICKS

In the year 2001, a new retail grocery co-operative opened for business in Atlantic Canada: Consumers' Community Co-operative (CCC). Members from twenty-eight previously independent, locally autonomous co-operatives came together as CCC to rebuild consumer co-operation as an exciting and attractive option in communities where the local co-operative had been struggling (Brown, 2005). By 2005, with the co-operative facing difficulties, the CCC board of directors and the general manager decided that in order to succeed they needed to renew CCC's identity as a co-operative grocery store. Believing that CCC's success rested not only on the conventional factors of quality, service, and price, but also on the co-operative's ability to embed the "co-operative difference" in its business practices, CCC decided to design and implement a co-operative social accounting tool, and to produce a social report based on what they found (Webb, 2007). They believed that this process would help revitalize member engagement, attract new members, reposition CCC in its communities, and provide data to inform strategic planning – especially if the process was opened up to stakeholder involvement. In so doing CCC hoped to ensure its viability and stave off closure. Unfortunately, as will be explained later in this chapter, this was not to be and in 2008 CCC was dissolved. However, their initiatives in the area of tool design and social accounting were not completely in vain, as they have led to further social accounting initiatives by the retail food co-operative sector in the Atlantic Canadian region.

For a period of two years (2006 to 2008) the authors collaborated with CCC in the early stages of designing a social accounting tool and in conducting partnered research on the process.[1] We use the term social accounting generically to refer to the range of efforts to systematically track and report on social and environmental performance, resulting in reports that are variously labelled as, for example, accountability reports, sustainability reports, social audit reports, triple bottom line reports, social performance reports, and corporate social responsibility reports. In this chapter we report on our experience as a contribution to the literature on social accounting and stakeholder engagement.

In the next section of this chapter we discuss the burgeoning interest in corporate social accounting and the proliferation of accounting tools. We argue that social accounting is particularly apt in co-operatives, where a social mission is not an add-on but is a core tenet of the organization. Noting that guides to "best practices" for social accounting now advocate stakeholder engagement in the various stages of the social accounting process, we consider what that might mean for best practices in co-operatives. We suggest that, despite the many challenges they face, co-operatives have a lot to gain by engaging stakeholders in the social accounting process, both because engagement complements co-operative principles and because it contributes to the quality and relevance of the tool and its implementation. Stakeholder engagement can be an affirming process, building cohesion, co-operative identity, commitment, and capacity for innovation across stakeholder groups.

The third section of the chapter draws on our own experiences and reviews our work with CCC. Focusing on stakeholder engagement, we look at the process of determining which stakeholders to engage, how they were involved, and the challenges faced in the process. In reviewing lessons learned, we conclude that it is important to be very clear about the purpose of stakeholder engagement, to develop strategies for handling situations where stakeholders disagree, to use multiple methods of stakeholder engagement (including both "representative" and "inclusive" forms), and to distinguish between stakeholder management and more profound stakeholder engagement (Svendsen, 1998; Belal, 2002). Stakeholder engagement can manifest as one-way top-down communication but also in many more co-operative and co-creative forms (Rixon, 2008; Svendsen & Laberge, 2006; Stakeholder Research Associates Canada Inc., 2005b). We put forward the case for the value of intense and broad-ranging co-creative approaches to stakeholder involvement, rooted in respectful, inclusive, and dynamic relationships.

At the end of the chapter we give a brief overview of an initiative in social accounting and reporting among co-operatives in the Atlantic region. We then offer concluding comments and observations, stressing the need for further research on social accounting and stakeholder engagement in co-operatives.

Social Accounting, Stakeholder Engagement, and Co-operatives

Accounting for Non-financial Performance

Despite claims by analysts such as Friedman (1970) that the only social responsibility of business is to increase profits, significant attention is now being paid to the social and environmental impacts of businesses. Variously seen as a response to external demands for transparency and accountability (Deloitte, 2004; CGAAC, 2005; KPMG, 2008), as recognition of a moral duty to assess and report on social and environmental impacts (Gray et al., 1995; Unerman & Bennett, 2004; Wheeler, Colbert, & Freeman, 2003), as desirable for instrumental reasons summed up as the "business case" (Oracle, 2005; Bent, 2008; Ligteringen & Zadek, 2005), or as some combination of all of these, corporate social responsibility (CSR) is now part of the discourse around the role of business in society. For co-operatives this discourse is welcome indeed, since they typically do not see profit as their raison d'être.[2] Codified in the "Statement of Co-operative Identity," co-operative values, principles, and organizational form reflect a complex purpose, both economic and social, which distinguishes them from investor-owned, for-profit businesses (International Co-operative Alliance, 2006).[3]

However, many leaders and members of co-operatives are concerned that co-operatives can drift away from the International Co-operative Alliance (ICA) co-operative principles, often without being aware of their failings in areas of, for example, democracy, education, or concern for the community (Kurimoto, 1996). There is often a sense that co-operatives are naturally different and deserve loyalty, respect, and business success on that basis. Social accounting offers co-operatives a way to express their complex identities and reduce the risk of displacement of the very practices and priorities that set them apart. "Without the inclusion of both non-financial and financial reporting, members will not have a full understanding of the extent to which the co-operative is fulfilling its purpose" (Robb, Rixon, Maddocks, & Hicks, 2011). Social accounting can help assess whether a co-operative has lived up to its claims, can demonstrate successes and shortfalls in operationalizing co-operative principles, and can provide stakeholders with information previously unavailable to them.[4] The fit between social accounting and an organization's core goals and structures is arguably closer for co-operatives than for investor-owned corporations.[5]

Some of the literature on CSR makes substantial claims for the positive business impacts of social reporting. For example, Oracle (2005) argues that social accounting can contribute to cost savings, increased profits, increased shareholder value, more investors, and attracting employees, while simultaneously enhancing relationships with customers, the community, and other stakeholders and positively impacting the organization's reputation. Social accounting is also said to contribute to proactive management and innovation (Bent, 2008) and to help drive performance by providing legitimacy, normative clarity, functionality, a basis for learning and engagement, clear communications, and materiality (relevance) (Ligteringen & Zadek, 2005). As with corporations, advocates of social accounting by co-operatives often make a "business case," claiming that social accounting can contribute to organizational efficiency and performance in much the same ways as outlined above: more members, enhanced attractiveness to employees, better relations with communities and other stakeholders, risk management, greater efficiencies, more informed decisions, and so on (see Euro Coop, 1999, for a list of benefits). These claims do not go unchallenged. In the longer run people may simply become cynical as social accounting is used more as an effort to manage perceptions rather than an instrument for real change (Spence, 2009). Cooper and Owen (2007) argue, for example, that producing reports does not necessarily enhance accountability.

Many businesses, including co-operatives, do some form of social accounting and their reports are widely available on the Internet (for example, see http://www.sustainability.com; Brown, 2009), though they use different approaches and practices (Cooper & Owen, 2007). Accounting firms often provide social accounting services, but accountants are concerned that while businesses are normally required to report on their financial position in accordance with well-established standards,[6] the development of social and environmental accounting and reporting (also known as non-financial accounting and reporting) is still in its infancy. In response to the deficiencies of conventional accounting and reporting standards (Hicks et al., 2007; Bebbington & Gray, 2001), there has been an explosion of interest in tools for social and environmental accounting, auditing, and reporting, as well as in "assurance standards" (e.g., AccountAbility, 2008; IFAC, 2011).

Among the best-known guidelines and other tools to assist organizations are the "Global Eight" (McIntosh et al., 2003): the UN Global Compact; the ILO Conventions; the OECD Guidelines for Multinational Enterprises; the ISO 14000 series; the GRI; the Global Sullivan Principles; Social Accountability 8000 (SA 8000); and AccountAbility 1000. The ISO 26000 Social Responsibility standard is a recent addition to this repertory of tools (International Organization for Standardization, 2010). There is little uniformity among the tools in terms of their objectives, quality, comprehensiveness, content, applicability (be it universal, sector specific, international, or geographic), or in the approach to their development (Gilbert & Rasche, 2008; CGAAC, 2005; Friedman & Miles, 2006). This hampers comparability across organizations and makes it difficult to know which tool to use when getting started in social accounting. There is strong support for creating a global standardized reporting framework (Institute of Chartered Accountants of England and Wales, 2009; Deloitte, 2006; Ligteringen & Zadek, 2005).[7]

Though standardization has obvious advantages, some say the field can benefit from experimentation, flexibility, and customization of existing tools, at least for the time being. Many organizations are at the early stages of identifying their information needs and developing the necessary accounting and reporting systems for gathering information about and reporting on their performance (CGAAC, 2005). They may need to customize an existing tool or develop a new one in order to measure what is important to an organization's stakeholders. Issues can vary depending on "a company's size, location, or industry and information needs, and interests will vary depending on stakeholder group" (CGAAC, 2005, p. 83). Few of the most widely used tools work well in small organizations, and they are limited in their applicability to non-profits. In recognition of the latter problem, GRI has produced sector-specific supplements including guidelines for not-for-profit organizations and other NGOs, though not for co-operatives.

For co-operatives, these matters are of considerable importance. While existing tools have some relevance and are used by some of the larger co-operatives (Brown, 2009), they fail to capture the essence of the "co-operative difference" as described above. The International Co-operative Alliance recommends that "a common and consistent methodology be developed at a global level to measure co-operative difference and CSR performance" (Cronan, 2007). A few co-operative-specific tools are currently available or in development: Co-operatives UK (2006), Co-operative Environmental and Social Performance Indicators;

New Economics Foundation (2009), Tools For You; Euro Coop's (1999) co-operative principles approach to social reporting; Christianson's (2007) Co-operative Sustainability Scorecard; and the Co-op Index for worker co-operatives (Novkovic et al., 2009). As yet none of these tools is as comprehensive as the ones listed by McIntosh et al. (2003), and none has gained wide currency.

Stakeholder Engagement as a Core Element of Social Accounting

According to Stakeholder Research Associates Canada Inc. (2005a, p. 13), stakeholder engagement is "an umbrella term that covers the full range of an organization's efforts to understand and involve stakeholders in its activities and decisions." Stakeholder engagement is widely defended as a core component of social accounting (AccountAbility, 2011; GRI, 2006; Stakeholder Research Associates Canada Inc., 2005a; Quarter et al., 2009; International Organization for Standardization, 2010). The Global Reporting Initiative (GRI) asserts that "failure to identify and engage with stakeholders is likely to result in reports that are not suitable, and therefore not fully credible, to all stakeholders" (2006). It is thought to offer many other benefits as well, for example: operational and strategic improvement, increased knowledge, stronger relationships characterized by accountability and trust (AccountAbility, 2011), and greater operational understanding of the meaning and value of sustainability (Stakeholder Research Associates Canada Inc., 2005b).

These potential benefits are as valuable for co-operatives as for any other organization. However, when we consider engagement from the perspective of the co-operative principles we begin to see the unique potential for co-operatives (Brown, 2009). Democracy, education, training and information, co-operation among co-operatives, and concern for community are four of the seven principles of the co-operative form of organization (ICA, 2006). Stakeholder engagement can contribute to education as well as training and information in relation to the various stakeholders involved (internal and external). Treating other co-operatives as stakeholders can bring their perspectives to bear and foster co-operation among co-operatives. Planning for and soliciting stakeholder engagement from the community helps a co-operative to consider what "concern for community" can mean in its own context, and holds a co-operative accountable for its external impacts. Social accounting that engages stakeholders in the process can profoundly deepen a co-operative's democratic qualities as well, beyond the obvious effect of increased access to information. Responsibly done, engaging stakeholders in the process of social accounting enhances responsiveness, transparency, and accountability – all of which are fundamental to democracy.

Let us consider the case of consumer co-operatives, which typically understand democracy as incorporating the following characteristics: boards of directors are elected by the member-owners (one member one vote); any member-owner can run for office; voting takes place at least once per year at the time of the annual general meeting, and as necessary when key decisions are needed (e.g., regarding mergers). Accountability reports measure democratic performance, usually including attendance at annual and special meetings, percentages of members who vote in board elections, the number of candidates, and the number of available positions. Reports often indicate targets for the future and plans for reaching those targets, and may also report on members' perceptions of the adequacy of information sharing as well as their knowledge of their democratic rights and responsibilities.

Less often, co-operatives offer (and report performance on) more participatory forms of democracy, for example: serving on standing or ad hoc committees; taking part in systematic consultations such as focus groups or surveys; attending town hall meetings; and engaging in member-led initiatives of various kinds.[8] Such deepened understandings of democracy promote multiple channels for democratic involvement and participation, including the inclusive, transparent, multi-way dialogue not provided in typical annual general meetings. Social accounting processes commonly engage stakeholders through surveys, focus groups, and dialogue with persons thought to represent a variety of stakeholder perspectives.

Mook et al. (2007, p. xxx) define social accounting as "a systematic analysis of the effects of an organization on its communities of interest or stakeholders, *with stakeholder input as part of the data that are analyzed for the accounting statement*" (emphasis added). Engagement can take other forms as well, ranging from consultation through to empowering stakeholders to make decisions (AccountAbility, 2011), from manipulation through to stakeholder control (Friedman & Miles, 2006), from influence through to co-creation of strategies and policies (Svendsen & Laberge, 2006). Co-operatives interested in deepening democracy will undertake activities that involve broadening access to decision-making power, increasing stakeholder control, and the co-creation of strategies and policies. In a co-creative approach, "a network or web of organizations and individuals comes together voluntarily to address a shared issue, problem, or opportunity," unlike the traditional approach in which "an organization is at the centre or hub of a number of bilateral relationships" (Svendsen & Laberge, 2006, p. 2).

Stakeholders can be invited to participate in determining the purpose and scope of stakeholder engagement in social accounting and reporting, planning the engagement processes, identifying performance areas to be assessed, influencing the measures used, validating the information to be presented in reports, influencing decisions about targets, and suggesting strategies for improving performance (Brown & Hicks, 2007). Stakeholder engagement in the process of developing and refining the social accounting tool offers the additional advantages of drawing on stakeholders' knowledge to help with problem solving, increasing stakeholder knowledge about the organization, and encouraging them to "buy-in" to the social accounting process.

Thus far we have ignored the fact that the profusion of different and overlapping definitions of the term stakeholder is thought by some to endanger the concept, causing it to become "'vague,' 'slippery,' and shallow" (Friedman & Miles, 2006, p. 28). Some of the various definitions that have been proposed include "everyone, everything, everywhere" (Sternberg, 1997, p. 4), "those who are affected by [the organization]," and "those groups necessary for an organization's survival" (Sternberg, 1997, p. 3). The classic definition of stakeholder is that of Freeman (1984): "any group or individual who can affect or is affected by the achievement of the organization's objectives" (p. 46).

From a practical point of view, broad definitions of stakeholder make it difficult to identify all stakeholders and their needs (Rixon, 2008) and may lead to engagement burnout (Government of Canada, 2006). Subdividing stakeholders into primary and secondary categories (Clarkson, 1995) can help narrow the scope, and AccountAbility (2011) offers useful criteria for doing so. Shareholders, customers, suppliers, employees, and local communities are commonly included as key stakeholders of a corporation (Friedman & Miles, 2006). For a co-operative, by contrast, primary stakeholders might include member-owners, employees, elected officials, and management. Depending on circumstances, customers, financial institutions, the community, suppliers, government/regulators, other co-operatives, and competitors may also be identified as stakeholders of a co-operative. (See for example Co-operative Group, 2011; Desjardins, 2010; Vancity, 2010; MEC, 2010.)

Though stakeholder engagement is an important component of social accounting, it is not easily implemented (AccountAbility, 2011, pp. 34–5). Getting the "right" stakeholders to participate is vital, and not easily done (Unerman & Bennett, 2004; Friedman & Miles, 2006; Owen et al., 2001). For example, failing to include employees, or ignoring a concerned local environmental group, may negatively affect the whole engagement process (Stakeholder Research Associates Canada Inc., 2005b). Methodologies that ensure the inclusivity of engagement processes and that fairly represent the stakeholder group need to be agreed upon. Agreeing on forms and degrees of engagement, and in what domains of organizational performance these will take place, can be tricky too – for example, this can include identifying the appropriate balance of involvement and influence across different stakeholder groups. Being inclusive and balancing conflicting interests and tensions is always a challenge, especially when stakeholders come from multiple groups and cultures, or when there are imbalances of power and influence (Friedman & Miles, 2006). Further, not everyone will have the time, skills, and other resources to be as involved as they might want to be. Even in the best of circumstances it is unlikely that all stakeholders' expectations can be met, so it is important to have open discussions with stakeholders about these matters. Finally, engagement must be genuine. Stakeholders need to know that the process is not mainly an exercise in "stakeholder management" (Svendsen & Laberge, 2005). If the process is perceived to be transparent, and if stakeholders are involved in setting up the process and evaluating it at its end, some of these problems can be mitigated (Owen et al., 2001). For organizations doing social accounting, engaging stakeholders can be expensive; it requires time, money, and other resources as well (Government of Canada, 2006; Friedman & Miles, 2006). This may be particularly problematic for small and medium-sized organizations, such as many co-operatives and NGOs.

A growing number of frameworks offer guidance in stakeholder engagement strategies, with the AA1000 Stakeholder Engagement Standard Exposure Draft (AccountAbility, 2011) being one of the best known.

Stakeholder Engagement – The Case of Consumers' Community Co-operative (CCC)

In this section we focus on stakeholder engagement in the initial design of a social accounting tool for CCC. Our work with CCC was informed by the following lessons learned from a review of the reports produced by four Canadian co-operatives[9] (Brown, 2009):

1. Existing standards and guides are useful, but there is an appetite for tailoring social accounting tools to individual organizations;
2. Despite considerable overlap across some of these approaches, we are unlikely to see a single tool that all co-operatives use, at least in the near future;
3. Stakeholder approaches are valued but need to be further explored, especially in relation to: determining reasons for stakeholder engagement in the initial creation of the tool, defining primary stakeholders, developing strategies for inclusive engagement, and deciding how to proceed when stakeholders disagree;
4. Stakeholder engagement takes time, money, and skill. These must be factored into decisions on engagement strategies;
5. Anecdotal evidence suggests that significant organizational learning takes place during the process of developing the tool;
6. Stakeholder groups may be unequal in their power, experience, knowledge, and degree of organization, raising questions about how to ensure inclusivity;
7. All the co-operatives that we studied modified their approaches and measures over time, in part as a response to stakeholder suggestions.

Engaging CCC Stakeholders

As indicated above, for a period of two years we collaborated with CCC in the early stages of designing a social accounting tool. Initially, CCC's focus was not on accountability, but rather on social accounting as a tool to help guide their actions and decisions in ways that reflected their co-operative identity and contributed to the renewal of their co-operative. Table 4.1 presents the stages we followed in our work together.

The CCC board of directors authorized the creation of a Research Advisory Committee (RAC), representative of key internal stakeholders, to direct the work (see Table 4.1, stage a). The committee included two board members, the CCC general manager, and an ex officio member – Co-op Atlantic's corporate secretary – as well as the two academics.[10] CCC local store councils were invited to take part, but none of them could dedicate the time (including travel time) to serve on the RAC. With the stores in crisis, council representatives (all of whom were volunteers) were occupied with daily matters. Within a year of CCC's creation, several storefronts had closed, and further attrition continued throughout the project. The academics kept in touch with

Table 4.1. The Stages of Stakeholder Engagement in the Design of a Social Accounting Tool for Consumers' Community Co-operative

Stakeholder Engagement		
Stages in Building a Social Accounting Tool	Who	Nature of Engagement and Validation Process
a. Constituting the Research Advisory Committee (RAC)	RAC composed of: two board members, CCC general manager, and two academics. Ex officio: corporate secretary for Co-op Atlantic. Though invited, no one from a local store council was able to accept the invitation to participate.	Oversight and planning by RAC – framing of the approach (agreeing on mandate and terms of reference, planning the engagement process and collaborative research components); planning for ongoing stakeholder engagement. Regular reports to the full board. Researchers reviewed the literature and presented overview of existing tools.
b. Identifying stakeholders to participate in initial phases of the tool design	Members, local store councils, CCC board, CCC general manager, store managers, and other employees, Co-op Atlantic management, and the Co-op Atlantic board.	RAC developed plans for stakeholder engagement through consultation, negotiation, involvement, and collaboration. CCC board to review and circulate drafts to stimulate discussion and input. Researchers to prepare materials for presentation and discussion at AGM.
c. Selecting the main themes / performance areas to be assessed	Members, local store councils, CCC board, CCC general manager, store managers, Co-op Atlantic management, and the Co-op Atlantic board.	Used recent survey of CCC member-owners + interviews with key informants (CCC, Co-op Atlantic, local store managers) + observations and conversations at meetings of local councils, regional zone meetings, AGMs. Validation of main themes through conversations at meetings; responses to presentations at CCC's AGMs (including responses on evaluation forms); dialogue in an AGM workshop; responses to presentations at board meetings; responses to circulated papers / reports. Other employees were not surveyed in the time available, though they took part in CCC's AGM.

(continued)

Table 4.1. (*continued*)

	Stakeholder Engagement	
Stages in Building a Social Accounting Tool	Who	Nature of Engagement and Validation Process
d. Selection of the specific performance categories (within each theme) to be assessed	Plans not finalized in the time available.	Readied draft documents and made plans for this phase but project ended with CCC's dissolution.
e. Choice of indicators (measures) of performance for each sub-theme / sub-category	Plans not finalized in the time available.	We had prepared illustrative examples for preliminary discussion but project ended with CCC's dissolution.
f. Stakeholder review of draft tool before implementation (and re-drafting if needed)	Plans not finalized in the time available.	Unable to develop full draft of a tool, nor to engage stakeholders in its review, implementation, assessment, and revision.

local councils, as described below, but the lack of a council member on the RAC remained a gap in the study.

While the RAC developed its terms of reference and approach to the process of developing the tool, the CCC board continued work on its strategic plan – a plan that expressly required management to work with the board and the membership to develop the "co-operative difference" with reference to the ICA co-operative values and principles. The board believed that assessing CCC's performance in relation to these principles and values would contribute to its efforts to revitalize member engagement in the co-op, attract new members, and reposition CCC in its communities. Available data showed that many members were disaffected and unsure of what the co-operative stood for (Brown, 2005). The board's directors supported stakeholder engagement in the design, implementation, and review of the tool because they believed that such a bottom-up process would bring stakeholders' knowledge and experience to bear, would result in measures that would be meaningful to key stakeholders, and would also be an educative and positive process for them. In its effort to reconnect with members and customers, this project signified CCC's commitment to accountability and responsiveness.

The RAC developed the broad outlines of an engagement strategy, but the plan was not fully articulated because so much was in flux with CCC. According to the plan, stakeholder engagement would be tailored to the needs of each phase of tool development. Initially (Table 4.1, stage b) the focus was on stakeholders who would be most affected by the potential collapse of the co-operative, and most likely to be able to take action based on the results of the accounting process: member-owners, local store councils, CCC board members, the general manager, store managers, and other employees. Co-op Atlantic management and the Co-op Atlantic board members were also added, both because of their significant impact on CCC and because a CCC collapse would have had significant implications for the Co-op Atlantic system. At this early stage, local producers, non-member shoppers,[11] and the financial institutions concerned about CCC's solvency were not included.

In regards to the selection of themes and performance areas to be assessed, the RAC identified the stakeholders listed in Table 4.1, stage b. How to engage them was a matter of considerable concern and debate. The RAC discussed various methodologies, drawing on a variety of social science approaches that were both quantitative and qualitative. While consultation was valuable, the RAC wanted to incorporate opportunities for dialogue as well. Compromises were necessary, however, as the RAC's budget was minimal and time was of the essence. Thus, at stage c, the RAC decided not to collect new feedback from stakeholders but rather to draw upon findings from previous collaborative research with CCC that had explored stakeholder views on "the co-operative difference."[12] (See Table 4.1.) As indicated in Table 4.1, we planned a broad circulation of drafts to stimulate discussion and input, followed by a board review and presentation to an Annual General Meeting, in order to incorporate more active influence and control. We planned to validate any conclusions in a variety of venues, from AGMs to local store meetings (Table 4.1, stage c).

The methodologies used in the original research project permitted both triangulation and saturation; the former to increase confidence in the data by referencing similar findings from different methods of data collection, and the latter by continuing data collection until the researcher began to hear the same things from participants (Silverman,

2004; Sandelowski, 1995). The quantitative and qualitative data collection techniques included a membership survey and interviews with representatives of several additional stakeholder groups (CCC board and management, CCC local council members, Co-op Atlantic management, and Co-op Atlantic board members who served as Co-op Atlantic representatives on the CCC board).[13] The interviewees were chosen on the basis of their knowledge of CCC, and specifically included those who were in a position to have a significant, direct effect on CCC.[14] The survey and the interviews explored the meaning of the co-operative difference for key CCC groups, and investigated the elements of co-operative identity at a personal and organizational level. Two stores in two different communities became the focus of more intensive study, including observations at local council meetings and conversations with employees, disaffected members, and shoppers in the stores.

The findings from this previous research provided the basis for a list of core elements of the "co-operative difference" and for the development of a social accounting tool reflective of these key performance areas. Our confidence in the validity of the findings from the survey and interviews was increased by the fact that these findings had been presented, with the opportunity for feedback and informal discussion, at two CCC AGMs (2004 and 2005). In 2005 the delegates participated in a workshop on the meaning of co-operative difference as seen by their various groups. Delegates to the AGMs included board members and local council members from every store in the co-operative. CCC management and Co-op Atlantic managers also attended, but were not delegates. Some of the local council representatives were staff from the stores. Other venues for the validation of our findings included board meetings, RAC meetings, and responses to circulated drafts of papers prior to presentation or publication (Table 4.1, stage c).

By fall of 2007 we had reviewed and conducted the evaluation, further analysed the previous findings, and drafted the list of themes / categories of performance to be assessed. As reported at the 2004 AGM, the key *categories of performance* as identified by members (i.e., what CCC should do) were: (1) success as a grocery business – achieved through strategies suited to a co-operative; (2) success at being rooted in the community – supporting the local economy and being responsive to community needs; (3) success at making membership meaningful – valuing members in demonstrable ways; (4) success as an alternative to other grocery stores – clear and positive identity among members, employees, and in the marketplace. The 2007 analysis of the interview data uncovered

three overarching *themes* indicating a way of doing things, not just what should be done: (1) creating positive relationships; (2) distributing influence and control over the co-operative across the various stakeholders ("having a say"); and (3) offering mechanisms through which stakeholders can proactively engage in controlling their own lives (individuals and communities taking part in creating their own future).

At the intersection of "what to do" and "how to do it," the co-operative difference becomes grounded as an element of a social accounting dialogue and practice. During the study, we prepared a grid with columns identifying the key performance categories gleaned from the CCC research, and rows reflecting the themes that emerged from informants' comments on how to "do" the co-operative difference (Brown & Hicks, 2007). This grid was intended to be the focus of a discussion with stakeholders as part of the engagement strategy (including validation processes) during the remaining stages of the study. Planning for the engagement of employees and non-member shoppers was initiated at this time.

The RAC recognized that attention to the question "how extensive will the engagement be?" must address notions of input, influence, and control, especially if there was disagreement among the stakeholders. While we did not explicitly discuss that crucial issue, the RAC was conscious of the need to develop engagement methods that would go beyond consultation to interweave negotiation, involvement, and collaboration.

Meanwhile, Co-op Atlantic was also making changes. A new "Co-operative Difference Manager" was tasked with working with Co-op Atlantic's member co-operatives, exploring ways to implement the "Four Pillars of the Co-operative Difference": grow Atlantic; member focus; community involvement; co-operative business model (PEI ADAPT Council 2007). As of August 2007 the mandate of the RAC had changed and the project description, as presented in the revised memorandum of understanding for the RAC, became:

> Using the tools and processes of social and ethical accounting, auditing and reporting, work with the Cooperative Differences Manager to imbed the co-operative difference into the culture, strategic planning, and the accountability/reporting system of Co-op Atlantic. Track this intervention.

Several meetings explored whether / how the social accounting tool could integrate the "four pillars" approach. However, as the situation

of CCC continued to deteriorate, concerns about the finances of the co-operative, and Co-op Atlantic's exposure, increased. It was difficult for RAC members to get together, and the process bogged down.

Sadly, these events overtook our research. Late in 2007 Co-op Atlantic and the CCC board decided to dissolve the CCC, a decision that took effect by January of 2008. The remaining seventeen storefronts became corporate stores of Co-op Atlantic and our project was terminated. However, a measure of the success of our work with CCC was that Co-op Atlantic wanted to explore possible directions for a new project. The outcome of several months of discussion with three Co-op Atlantic managers was the Co-operative Sustainability and Planning Scorecard Project, which we will discuss in further detail below.

Experiences with Stakeholder Engagement in CCC: Challenges and Lessons Learned

Table 4.2 presents the main stakeholder engagement challenges experienced during our work with CCC. It also indicates how we addressed these challenges and the lessons we learned along the way. This part of the account is based primarily on the perceptions of the authors of this chapter. We would have preferred to involve the members of the RAC and other stakeholders, but that was not possible under the circumstances.

The challenges identified in Table 4.2 are grouped into four categories: context, previous experience with social accounting, communication, and momentum. Without discussing every point listed in Table 4.2, we can highlight some of the key items. First, there is the matter of context. It is not possible to overstress the significance of the fact that CCC was in crisis. Resource constraints and morale problems associated with the loss of storefronts hampered our work all the way through. Despite these constraints, the board of directors remained committed to the process, the advisory committee members proved extraordinarily dedicated, and we learned that the advisory committee offered a resilient mechanism for engagement and project management. The role of independent academics was important, setting the process apart from the internal hierarchies of CCC and Co-op Atlantic, and the research grant supported the focus on stakeholder engagement processes.

None of the CCC members of the RAC had any experience with social accounting and reporting (or the associated stakeholder engagement),

though the two board members did have considerable acquaintance with the subject. Time constraints prevented us from spending as much time in the learning phase as we had hoped. Instead, we all made the most of any opportunities that arose during the study, realizing the importance of stressing respectful relations and mutual learning along the way.

Communication is fundamental to the process. In addition to the mutual learning that occurs as stakeholders bring their experiences and knowledge to the table, participants also learn by developing a shared understanding of the process they are engaged in – and a "language in common." Face-to-face communication is vital in this, as well as in building trust, especially at first. Part of effective communication is making sure that stakeholder groups are (and feel) adequately represented and engaged. In the CCC project, plans for stakeholder engagement – especially regarding inclusiveness, levels, and forms of engagement – were more implicit than explicit and certainly not transparent to all stakeholders. A lesson for the future is the value of a more clearly developed stakeholder engagement strategy that can be reviewed and modified by stakeholders. The strategy should include: the organization's definition of a stakeholder; the purpose for stakeholder engagement; an explicit rationale for engaging some stakeholders and not others; the ways in which stakeholders are to be engaged (processes and timing); the ways their opinions will be incorporated in designing the tool; strategies for handling disagreements within and across stakeholder groups; and the process for finalizing the tool. We did not reach the point where we had to deal with tensions between stakeholders.

In completing stages c through f (Table 4.1), however, divisions would certainly have emerged regarding which performance categories to emphasize and which indicators of performance to use. Full discussion and agreement on decision rules would have been needed at that time.[15] Our experience reinforces the recognition of stakeholder engagement as a process that is heavily dependent on relationships and open communication. It is vital that the process identify a basis for a shared vision and goals, even though there may be disagreements and divisions. Stakeholder engagement is time-consuming, and that constraint alone is likely to mean that corners will be cut. However, it is vital that those leading the process be mindful of the reasons they are engaging stakeholders and the likely consequences of cutting too many corners. The stakeholders themselves need to know why their participation is valuable. It is important that stakeholders' level of involvement and control

Table 4.2. Experiences with Stakeholder (SH) Engagement during the CCC Project

Challenges	How Challenges Were Addressed (With Varying Degrees of Success)	Lessons Learned
1. Context – CCC was in crisis		
- Acute resource constraints (time, money, personnel) - Uncertainties and pace of change - Stores closing, personnel changes, reactive mode - Finding time for RAC to meet due to other priorities - Opportunities for genuine SH dialogue difficult to find - Relations between Co-op Atlantic and CCC were complicated, with unclear lines of authority - Distance between stores and across four provinces was considerable	- Transparent about resources needed in dire circumstances - Research grant helped by providing additional money and personnel as well as external legitimacy for the idea of social accounting and reporting for co-ops - Cultivated flexibility and good humour - Exercised patience with delays and found creative ways of communicating - Made use of existing opportunities (e.g., piggybacked on others' meetings) - Supported open and respectful dialogue around authority relations (in safe venues)	- SH engagement can be valuable even in dire circumstances - Value of independent third-party researchers in managing challenge of hierarchy - Develop plans for addressing the constraints and opportunities provided by the context - A respected advisory committee, guided by mutually agreed-upon processes, goals, and objectives, is invaluable - Engage the appropriate SHs at the right times and places during the process, being respectful of their constraints
2. Previous experience with social accounting and reporting – new for most stakeholders		
- Takes time and experience to become comfortable with social accounting and reporting and the stages of the work - Takes time and experience to devise and implement methodologies for inclusive and transparent stakeholder engagement - Difficult for people to understand the potentials for flexibility in the tool design - People may not understand the tool as a work in progress that can be modified and changed as it is used, unlike a financial audit	- Answered questions as they arose - Two members of the RAC were knowledgeable about social accounting and reporting - Took every opportunity to answer questions, anticipate need for extra information - Provided RAC with URLs for social reports by other co-operatives	- Allow time for mutual learning and value that as part of the process - Make sure there are different channels through which people can raise questions and concerns; facilitate open discussion of these matters - Draw in examples, and possibly invite speakers, from other co-operatives that are doing social accounting and reporting - Respect and discuss concerns that social accounting changes the expectations and evaluation criteria for managers of co-operatives

(continued)

Table 4.2. (*continued*)

Challenges	How Challenges Were Addressed (With Varying Degrees of Success)	Lessons Learned
3. Communication – numbers of people and groups, and great distances		
- High-speed Internet not available to all SHs - Search for a "language in common" takes time - Limited opportunities for face-to-face meetings, even for RAC - Making sure stakeholder groups are, and feel, adequately represented and engaged - The General Manager was not able to be very involved - Did not address matters of degree of influence and control for the different stakeholder groups	- Communications with the RAC relied on electronic communication, with face-to-face meetings when possible - Effective communication with other SHs was more difficult. Used email, telephone, face-to-face as much as possible; others' meetings provided sites for formal and informal communication (e.g., board, council, zone, AGMs) - Conducted some interviews with disaffected members located by word of mouth - Had plans for reaching under-represented SHs, but did not have opportunity to incorporate non-managerial employees and non-member shoppers in the process	- Take time to build respectful relationships, build common language, share knowledge, share power, and work through conflicts - Devise proactive and transparent communication strategies, including face-to-face communication - Develop and agree on clear objectives, processes, and a collaborative work plan - Incorporate an explicit (transparent) SH engagement strategy in the plan; review and modify it regularly - Allow time for check-ins with SHs about the process and for validation and evaluation along the way
4. Momentum – keeping the project moving at the pace desired by CCC and Co-op Atlantic		
- The CCC and Co-op Atlantic members of the RAC were volunteers; this was an "extra" job - The academics were not full-time contract researchers - The pace of progress depended on factors beyond the control of the RAC	- As much as possible the RAC and the academics collaborated on setting schedules and did their best to stay on track	- This problem is not likely to go away - Communicate openly about progress, or lack thereof - Regular review of the schedule and agreement on any changes

be clearly specified. Unless stakeholders' expectations for impact line up with their actual experiences, disaffection may result. We came to appreciate that a co-creative approach can help ensure that such concerns are addressed (Svendsen & Laberge, 2005).

Any engagement strategy must be the subject of review and dialogue among the key stakeholders, who in turn will influence its further development – time for reflection and evaluation should be built into the process. Fortunately, the process of designing a social accounting tool and of doing social accounting is iterative in nature, offering opportunities to rectify early mistakes and to adapt to changes in circumstances.

In summary, despite not completing the actual tool, the project achieved some notable successes. For one, stakeholder engagement helped to generate a vision of co-operative identity that many key stakeholders could embrace, and which could have become the focus for constructive dialogue had the process continued. Also, from the perspective of capacity building, many co-operative members and leaders were exposed to the idea of social accounting during the study, and to discussion about which categories of performance should be measured. By and large people were enthusiastic. They felt that social accounting fit well with the co-operatives' commitments to democracy and transparency, and allowed them to assess themselves on criteria valued by their stakeholders. CCC board members and key people in Co-op Atlantic management were convinced that social accounts could provide valuable information for strategic planning. The idea was taking hold that co-operatives could not unthinkingly apply the dominant business models and strategies, and that social accounting and reporting could help in identifying alternative paths. Stakeholders embraced the idea that stakeholder engagement was essential in the development of such an accounting tool.

Next Steps: Co-operative Sustainability and Planning Scorecard Project

The work with CCC led to the Co-operative Sustainability and Planning Scorecard Project, in collaboration with Co-op Atlantic and seven autonomous co-operatives (four francophone and three anglophone). At the time of writing, this work is ongoing (see http://www.cooperativedifference.coop/page/40-Atlantic-A1-Sustainability). When the CCC project was terminated in 2008, three Co-op Atlantic managers and the

Figure 4.1. Transition from CCC Social Accounting Tool Project to Co-op Atlantic Scorecard Project

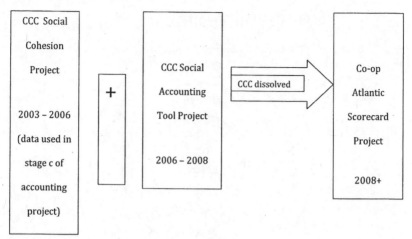

researchers met over several months to consider possible directions for a new project (see Figure 4.1).

As before, a first step was the formation of an RAC. This time, the members of the RAC were Co-op Atlantic managers from the marketing and communications department and from public affairs, as well as the corporate secretary and three academic researchers, including the two authors.[16] The RAC members were already familiar with the idea of social accounting and have been committed, innovative, supportive, and comfortable with discussion and debate.

The Co-op Atlantic members of the RAC assumed a leadership role in the initial development of the tool[17] and identified key stakeholders in local co-operatives (see Figure 4.2). In the tool design phase, completed in May 2012, the focus has been on engaging leaders (board members and management) most deeply, with members and staff having some opportunities for input along the way. They and the other stakeholders will become more involved as the tool is implemented.

Co-op Atlantic launched the project at the May 2009 Co-op Atlantic Annual General Meeting, at which time the delegates heard about the scorecard project and interested co-operatives were invited to participate. The RAC followed up with those who expressed their interest by making a presentation to that co-operative's board of directors

Figure 4.2. Diagram Presented at Co-op Atlantic's May 2009 Annual General Meeting

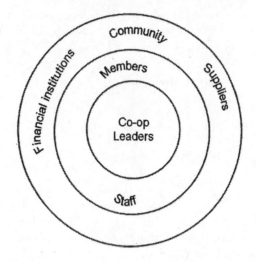

Co-operative stakeholders

and issuing an official invitation to become a pilot project co-operative, describing the goals, the process, and the time commitment involved. Each pilot project co-operative formed a Pilot Project Committee (PPC), deciding whom to recruit after discussing the suggestions from the RAC. The three- to five-member committees included board members and management, and in some cases other stakeholders as well. The RAC conducted workshops and met regularly with the PPCs at each stage of the tool-development process. The PPCs reported to their boards and some reported to their co-operatives' AGMs. Together with the PPCs, the RAC prepared reports and staffed information tables at the Co-op Atlantic AGMs in 2010 and 2011.

The RAC developed a stakeholder engagement plan to guide the revision of the initial tool and to finalize its first iteration. We also agreed on guidelines for situations where pilot project co-operatives disagree on various elements of the tool. Finally, we used stakeholder input to improve the tool and will continue to do so, making it adaptable to the contexts of individual co-operatives.

The work has been, and continues to be, informed by the lessons learned while working with CCC. Through this process, we have learned the importance of, for example: developing a stakeholder engagement strategy appropriate to each stage of the work; emphasizing regular and open communication (face-to-face where possible); carefully considering the composition of the RAC and the PPCs; and outlining a clear project description and Memorandum of Understanding – including goals, objectives, a work plan, a schedule, and an identification of everyone's areas of responsibility. We are continuing to monitor the stakeholder engagement process – paying particular attention to the quality of the experiences for the stakeholders, their perceived responsiveness, and the outcomes of the process.

Concluding Comments and Observations

In this chapter we presented the case for social accounting in co-operatives, emphasizing that since co-operatives have a social mission at their core, social accounting has both instrumental and expressive value. Social accounts provide information that is valuable in strategic planning and offer mechanisms through which to express their identity as co-operatives. Further, given the co-operative principles of "education, training and information," "democratic member control," and "concern for community," the stakeholder engagement processes advocated in the literature are particularly apt. As social accounting is developed in theory and in practice, it is steadily being infused with principles of accountability, transparency, and democracy (O'Dwyer, 2005) – all three of which are at the core of co-operative theory.

The partner co-operatives in the projects reported here all value broad stakeholder engagement. Our experience, focused on the development of a social accounting tool for co-operatives, indicates that stakeholder engagement contributes to mutual learning and relationship building. Stakeholders contribute to the quality and relevance of the tool itself, and engagement increases buy-in to the tool. In both CCC and the co-operative scorecard research, the partner co-operatives were positively disposed towards participation in developing the instrument. Their work improved the tool and lent it credibility. Thus far in the scorecard project, feedback from the workshops and the meeting logs has indicated that the PPC members also value learning about their co-operative and about the other pilot co-operatives. These co-operatives engage stakeholders not because they are worried that they are potential antagonists who will make increasingly challenging demands, but because they believe that stakeholders will want to strengthen the co-operative and will contribute a valuable perspective.

This is not to minimize the challenges of this process, including the potentials for disagreement and even conflict within and across stakeholder groups. However, in the process of designing a co-operative social accounting tool, it is possible to accommodate many different priorities. Down the road, when using the tool, assessing performance, and making recommendations for action, disagreements and conflict may more readily emerge. It is vital that there be opportunities for genuine dialogue during which all can feel safe expressing their opinions. For managers and other employees this is of particular concern. Inclusivity becomes more and more of an issue at the implementation stages, too.

In our work thus far we have found that, where opportunity permits, a collaborative process of stakeholder engagement is desirable. Certainly, engaging those who will use the tool in its design – and supplying them with clear criteria for how decisions will be made – is very important. The constitution of a hands-on advisory committee that brings in, and is accessible to, stakeholders is a vital part of the process. The idea is to nurture and expand relationships with stakeholders who are participating in the process of assessing and improving the co-operative's performance across social, economic, and environmental dimensions. Trust and respect are the foundations of this process. Framing the collaborative work in terms of co-creative approaches (Svendsen & Laberge, 2007) orients those involved towards outreach, mutual learning, the common good, and innovation. Acknowledging and dealing with power relations by explicitly considering the idea of a "ladder of participation" (Friedman & Miles, 2006) and the nature of relationships at each of the rungs could help to avoid mistakes or the unintentional betrayal of stakeholder expectations.

All organizations that prioritize stakeholder engagement will face the unavoidable fact that such a commitment comes with costs – in time, money, and personnel. To ensure inclusivity, engagement strategies must be innovative and targeted to the situations of the respective stakeholder groups. It is also important that the process be evaluated at various stages. Other challenges will arise as the project goes on, only some of which can be planned for in advance. A stakeholder engagement plan is helpful, though it is important to be flexible, to take advantage of opportunities that may arise, and to respond to the engagement ideas that stakeholders put forward during the process.

When done well, stakeholder engagement has the potential to be much more than a means of managing risk. It can contribute to an organization's sustainable performance and to the integration of social, environmental, and economic issues into core strategies and business models. Wheeler, Colbert, & Freeman (2003, p. 11) have found that stakeholder engagement can contribute to the creation of a "sustainable organization" culture whereby it seems natural to focus on creating value in economic, social, and ecological terms. Further research is needed on the impacts of social accounting and engagement processes, especially in relation to co-operatives.

Stakeholder engagement is not easy, whether for the facilitators or for those who are being engaged. It is definitely not formulaic. However, evidence is mounting that it is well worth the effort.

NOTES

1 The funding provided by the Southern Ontario Social Economy Node was invaluable in supporting this work.

2 Co-operative membership is open and voluntary, and the members are owners who democratically control their co-operative, which provides them with the goods and/or services that they want within a business framework that they support. Members benefit primarily in proportion to their economic transactions with the co-operative. Profits are the means through which the co-operative can continue to serve its members, not a goal in and of itself.

3 The co-operative principles are: voluntary and open membership, democratic control, member economic participation, autonomy and independence, education, training and information, co-operation among co-operatives, and concern for the community (ICA, 2006).

4 In their 1997 Social Report, VanCity Savings Credit Union heard from its members that they were "disappointed and disillusioned with its traditional banking style" (1998, p. 5) and from other credit unions that it was "becoming increasingly indistinguishable from a bank, and losing touch with its co-operative roots" (1998, p. 24). In response, VanCity made significant commitments regarding its incorporation of the co-operative principles and this has informed its progress ever since.

5 Of course, some co-operatives operate more like conventional businesses (e.g., in relation to concern for community and the management of information), in which case social accounting and reporting is at least as useful

for co-operatives as it is for conventional businesses – and may even stimulate dialogue around the "co-operative difference."

6 In 2011, Canada adopted International Financial Reporting Standards.

7 See Lazarte (2011) for a discussion of the bridges being built across some of these tools and standards.

8 There is an extensive literature on the value of supplementing (or supplanting) traditional representative forms of democracy with participatory forms. For a recent review of participatory democratic theory see Hilmer (2010), and for a discussion of the importance of participatory democracy in co-operatives see Spear (2004).

9 The four were: Alterna Credit Union, VanCity Savings Credit Union, Sustainability Solutions Group, and Desjardins.

10 Co-op Atlantic is a second-tier co-operative owned by 128 retail and producer co-operative members. The co-ops that came together as CCC were all members of Co-op Atlantic. The fate of CCC would heavily impact Co-op Atlantic, which was devoting significant resources to help save CCC.

11 Using other sources, the CCC board had gathered information from shoppers that it was already responding to.

12 Said previous research, supported by SSHRC (2003–6), was led by B. Fairbairn and entitled "Co-operative Membership and Globalization: Social cohesion through market relations." The work with CCC focused on co-operative identity and social cohesion. In 2006, CCC became a partner in the social accounting project and E. Hicks joined the team. This was funded by a SSHRC CURA on the Social Economy and was directed by J. Quarter and L. Mook of OISE.

13 A membership survey went to a random sample of the membership of CCC in May 2004. The response rate was 25.3% (N=223). For the full report, see Brown (2005).

14 Informant interviews totaled twenty-eight: seven board members, including two from the Co-op Atlantic Board; six local council members; the CCC General Manager; five store managers; and nine Co-op Atlantic managers who were involved in the decision to create CCC and who still had significant impacts on its management.

15 Strategies for handling disagreement or conflict must be geared to the situation and can include airing all views to see if discussion helps reduce disagreements, identifying and emphasizing points of agreement that do exist, and facilitating dialogue at key decision points. Where disagreements persist, majority rule, sequencing (when there are more priorities than the co-operative can handle in one time period), accommodating

minority opinions, and a variety of other methods are available (some of which are discussed by Svendsen & Laberge, 2007).

16 In the spring of 2009 a third academic, André Leclerc of l'Université de Moncton, joined the team.

17 Following a presentation by the authors on existing social accounting tools and indicators, Co-op Atlantic decided that the tools did not adequately capture the co-operative difference. Soon after that, Christianson's (2007) new Co-operative Audit Scorecard came to the attention of Co-op Atlantic management. Pulling together what we had learned from the CCC experience and from examples of other tools, and agreeing that the scorecard had to be rooted in the ICA co-operative principles and values, a first draft was prepared.

REFERENCES

AccountAbility. (2008). AA1000 Assurance Standard 2008. Retrieved June 5, 2011, from: http://www.accountability.org/standards/aa1000as/index.html

AccountAbility. (2011). AA1000 Stakeholder Engagement Standard 2011 Final Exposure Draft. Retrieved May 4, 2011, from: http://www.accountability.org/images/content/3/6/362/AA1000SES%202010%20PRINT

Bebbington, J., & Gray, R.H. (2001). An account of sustainability: Failure, success and a reconceptualisation. *Critical Perspectives on Accounting, 12*(5), 557–88. http://dx.doi.org/10.1006/cpac.2000.0450

Belal, A.R. (2002). Stakeholder accountability or stakeholder management: A review of UK firms' social and ethical accounting auditing and reporting (SEAAR) practices. *Corporate Social Responsibility and Environmental Management, 9*(1), 8–25. http://dx.doi.org/10.1002/csr.5

Bent, D. (2008) Competitiveness and sustainability: Building the best future for your business. Institute of Chartered Accountants of England and Wales. Retrieved March 13, 2010, from: http://www.icaew.com/index.cfm/route/160966/icaew_ga/Technical_Business_Topics/Topics/Corporate_governanceCompetitiveness_and_Sustainability/Competitiveness_and_Sustainability_Building_the_best_future_for_your_business/pdf

Brown, L. (2005). *Membership survey. Report to the CCC board of directors.* Moncton, New Brunswick.

Brown, L. (2009). *Accountability practice as a strategy for engaging stakeholders: The co-operative difference and organizational renewal.* Working Paper. Retrieved July 10, 2009, from: http://www.istr.org/conferences/barcelona/WPVolume

Brown, L., & Hicks, E. (2007). *Accounting for the social: Incorporating indicators of co-operative difference into strategic planning*. Presented at the 1st International CIRIEC Conference on the Social Economy, Victoria, BC.

Certified General Accountants Association of Canada (CGAAC). (2005). *Measuring up: A study on sustainability reporting in Canada. Certified General Accountants of Canada*. Retrieved March 9, 2010, from: http://www.cga-canada.org/en-ca/ResearchReports/ca_rep_2005-06_sustainability_1.pdf

Christianson, R. (2007). *Sustainability Scorecard (original draft)*. Retrieved March 10, 2009, from: http://cooperativegrocer.coop/files/SustainableScorecard.xls

Clarkson, M. (1995). A stakeholder framework for analysing and evaluating corporate social performance. *Academy of Management Review, 20*(1), 92–117.

Co-operatives UK. (2006). *Demonstrating co-operative difference: The key social and co-operative performance indicators*. Retrieved July 10, 2007, from: http://offline.cooperatives-uk.coop/Home/miniwebs/miniwebsA-z/cespis

Co-operative Group. (2011). Sustainability report of the Co-operative Group. Retrieved September 6, 2011, from: http://www.co-operative.coop/corporate/sustainability/

Cooper, S.M., & Owen, D.L. (2007). Corporate social reporting and stakeholder accountability: The missing link. *Accounting, Organizations and Society, 32*(7–8), 649–67. http://dx.doi.org/10.1016/j.aos.2007.02.001

Cronan, G. (2007). *2007 Global 300 Launch*. Presentation to the International Co-operative Alliance General Assembly Singapore. Retrieved March 10, 2011, from: www.ica.coop/calendar/ga2007/ga2007-cronan-slides.pdf

Deloitte. (2004). *In the dark: What boards and executives don't know about the health of their businesses*. A Survey by Deloitte in Cooperation with the Economist Intelligence Unit, Retrieved March 13, 2010, from: http://www.deloitte.com/assets/Dcom-NewZealand/Local%20Assets/Documents/In%20the%20dark(4).pdf

Deloitte. (2006). *Added value, long term. Non-financial sustainability key performance indicators on their way into financial reports of German companies*. A survey from Axel Hesse SD-M supported by Deloitte and the German Federal Ministry of the Environment. Retrieved March 13, 2010, from: http://www.sd-m.de/files/Hesse_SD-M_Deloitte_AddedValueLongTerm.pdf

Desjardins. (2010). 2009 Social Responsibility and Cooperative Report. Retrieved September 6, 2011, from: http://www.desjardins.com/en/a_propos/publications/bilans_sociaux/rapport-sociale-2010.pdf

Euro Coop. (1999). *Measuring the co-operative difference*. Retrieved March 15, 2010, from: http://www.eurocoop.org/publications/en/memos/bilansocial.asp

Freeman, R.E. (1984). *Strategic management: A stakeholder approach*. Boston: Pitman.

Friedman, A.L., & Miles, S. (2006). *Stakeholders theory and practice*. [Electronic book] London, UK: Oxford University Press.

Friedman, M. (1970). The social responsibility of business is to increase its profits [Electronic version]. *The New York Times Magazine* 13 September: 33.

Gilbert, D.U., & Rasche, A. (2008). A discourse ethical perspective on social accounting – the case of the "Global Eight." In A.G. Scherer & M. Patzer (Eds.), *Betriebswirtschaftslehre und Unternehmensethik* (pp. 291–313). Wiesbaden: Gabler. http://dx.doi.org/10.1007/978-3-8350-5565-0_16

Government of Canada. (2006). *Corporate social responsibility: An implementation guide for Canadian business*. Retrieved March 9, 2011, from: http://www.ic.gc.ca/eic/site/csr-rse.nsf/eng/rs00126.html

Gray, R., Kouhy, R., & Lavers, S. (1995). Corporate social and environmental reporting: A review of the literature and a longitudinal study of UK disclosure. *Accounting, Auditing & Accountability Journal, 8*(2), 47–77.

GRI Sustainability Reporting Guidelines version 3.0. (2006). Retrieved March 13, 2010, from: http://www.globalreporting.org/NR/rdonlyres/B52921DA-D802-406B-B067-4EA11CFED835/3882/G3_GuidelinesENU.pdf

Hicks, E., Maddocks, J., Webb, T., & Robb, A. (2007). Co-operative accountability and identity: An examination of reporting practices of Nova Scotia co-operatives. *Journal of Co-operative Studies, 40*(2), 4–16.

Hilmer, J. (2010). The state of participatory democratic theory. *New Political Science, 32*(1), 43–63. http://dx.doi.org/10.1080/07393140903492118

Institute of Chartered Accountants of England and Wales. (2009). The prince's accounting for sustainability project, the Climate Disclosure Standards Board. *Representation to the Conference of Parties on Climate Change (COP15) Copenhagen*. Retrieved March 10, 2010, from: http://www.cica.ca/climat-echange/item34206.pdf

International Co-operative Alliance. (2006). *Statement on the co-operative identity*. Retrieved September 9, 2007, from: http://www.coop.org/coop/principles.html

International Federation of Accountants (IFAC). (2011). ISAE 3000 (Revised), Assurance engagements other than audits or reviews of historical financial information – proposed international standard on assurance engagements (ISAE). Retrieved September 9, 2011, from: http://ifac.org/Guidance/EXD-Details.php?EDID=0161

International Organization for Standardization. (2010). ISO 26000 Social Responsibility – Discovering ISO 26000. Retrieved December 19, 2010, from: http://www.iso.org/iso/discovering_iso_26000.pdf

Kurimoto, A. (1996). Restructuring consumer co-operatives and co-operative principles. *Review of International Co-operation, 89*(2), 69–74.

KPMG. (2008). *KPMG international survey of corporate responsibility reporting 2008*. Retrieved March 15, 2008, from: http://www.kpmg.com/Global/en/IssuesAndInsights/ArticlesPublications/Documents/International-corporate-responsibility-survey-2008.pdf

Lazarte, M. (2011). Building bridges: Aligning SR efforts for greater leverage. ISO Focus, March. Retrieved September 5, 2011, from: www.iso.org/iso/iso_focusplus_march_2011_social-responsibility.pdf

Ligteringen, E., & Zadek, S. (2005). *The future of corporate social responsibility codes, standards and frameworks*. Retrieved March 10, 2009, from: http://www.globalreporting.org/NR/rdonlyres/19BBA6F5-9337-42B0-B66D-A3B45F591938/0/LigteringenZadekFutureOfCR.pdf

McIntosh, M., Thomas, R., Leipziger, D., & Coleman, G. (2003). *Living corporate citizenship – strategic routes to socially responsible business*. London : FT Prentice Hall.

Mook, L., Quarter, J., & Richmond, B.J. (2007). *What counts: Social accounting for non-profits and co-operatives* (2nd ed.). London: Sigel Press.

Mountain Equipment Co-op. (2010). Accountability Performance 2009 Interim Report. Retrieved September 6, 2011, from: http://images.mec.ca/media/Images/pdf/accountability/MEC_2009_Accountability_Report_v1_m56577569830970401.pdf

New Economics Foundation. (2009). *Tools for you: Approaches for proving and improving for charities, volunteer organizations and social enterprise*. Retrieved March 15, 2010, from: http://www.neweconomics.org/sites/neweconomics.org/files/Tools_for_You_1.pdf

Novkovic, S., Stocki, R., & Hough, P. (2009). *Participation in co-operative firms: Theory, measures, and impacts*. Working Paper. Retrieved March 3, 2010, from: http://www.msvu.ca/socialeconomyatlantic/English/documentsE.asp

O'Dwyer, B. (2005). Stakeholder democracy: Challenges and contributions from social accounting. *Business Ethics (Oxford, England)*, *14*(1), 28–41. http://dx.doi.org/10.1111/j.1467-8608.2005.00384.x

Oracle and the Economic Intelligence Unit. (2005). *The importance of corporate responsibility*. Retrieved March 11, 2010, from: http://docs.google.com/viewer?a+v&q+cache:oU2cqVu7gC

Owen, D.L., Swift, T., & Hunt, K. (2001). Questioning the role of stakeholder engagement in social and ethical accounting, auditing and reporting. *Accounting Forum*, *25*(3), 264–82. http://dx.doi.org/10.1111/1467-6303.00066

PEI ADAPT Council. (2007). Proud to be different Co-op Atlantic and its community-building role. *PIE Adapt Council Agri-Newsletter*, *6*(9). Retrieved June 26, 2007 from: http://www.peiadapt.com/2007/may1.pdf

Quarter, J., Mook, L., & Armstrong, A. (2009). *Understanding the social economy: A Canadian perspective.* Toronto: University of Toronto Press.

Rixon, D. (2008). *Reporting for public sector agencies: A stakeholder model.* International Workshop on Social Audit, Social Accounting and Accountability. Prague, Czech Republic.

Robb, A., Rixon, D., Maddocks, J., & Hicks, E. (2011). Co-operative non-financial reporting, CEARC iSORP discussion paper no. 6. Retrieved May 4, 2011, from: http://www.smu.ca/academic/sobey/cearc/documents/CEARCiSORPDP6-Non-financialreporting-Feb2011.pdf

Sandelowski, M. (1995, Apr). Sample size in qualitative research. *Research in Nursing & Health, 18*(2), 179–83. http://dx.doi.org/10.1002/nur.4770180211 Medline:7899572

Silverman, R. (2004). *Doing qualitative research.* London: Sage.

Solstice Consulting. (n.d.). *Strengthening the dialogue: Member consultation and communication in co-operatives and credit unions.* Retrieved September 10, 2011, from: http://www.coopscanada.coop/en/orphan/Reports-and-Surveys

Spear, R. (2004). Governance in democratic member-based organizations. *Annals of Public and Cooperative Economics, 75*(1), 33–60. http://dx.doi.org/10.1111/j.1467-8292.2004.00242.x

Spence, C. (2009). Social accounting's emancipatory potential: A Gramscian critique. *Critical Perspectives on Accounting, 20*(2), 205–27. http://dx.doi.org/10.1016/j.cpa.2007.06.003

Stakeholder Research Associates Canada Inc. (2005a). *From words to action. The stakeholder engagement manual.* (Vol. 1). Retrieved March 15, 2010, from: http://www.stakeholderresearch.com/documents/sra-stakeholder-engagement-manual-vol-01.pdf

Stakeholder Research Associates Canada Inc. (2005b). *From words to action. The stakeholder engagement manual.* (Vol. 2). Retrieved March 15, 2010, from: http://www.stakeholderresearch.com/assets/documents/sra-stakeholder-engagement-manual-vol-02.pdf

Sternberg, E. (1997). The defects of stakeholder theory. *Corporate governance: An international review, 5*(1), 3–10. http://dx.doi.org/10.1111/1467-8683.00034

Svendsen, A. (1998). *Why we shouldn't manage stakeholders.* Retrieved May 13, 2009, from: http://www.sfu.ca/cscd-new/cli/resources_shouldnt.htm

Svendsen, A., & Laberge, M. (2005, Fall). Convening stakeholder networks, a new way of thinking, being and engaging. *Journal of Corporate Citizenship,* (Issue 19), 91–104. Retrieved May 13, 2009, from: http://web.ebscohost.com/ehost/pdf?vid=3&hid=9&sid=4c9ef614-324c-4054-bac6-be07282713fe%40sessionmgr4

Svendsen, A., & Laberge, M. (2006). *Beyond consultation: A co-creative approach to stakeholder engagement.* Retrieved March 10, 2010, from: http://www.sfu. ca/cscd/cli/beyondconsultation.pdf

Svendsen, A., & Laberge, M. (2007). *Methods for co-creative engagement: Building healthy communities and sustainable outcomes.* Retrieved February 22, 2009, from: http://www.sfu.ca/cscd/cli/methods.pdf

Unerman, J., & Bennett, M. (2004). Increased stakeholder dialogue and the internet: Towards greater corporate accountability or reinforcing capitalist hegemony? *Accounting, Organizations and Society, 29*(7), 685–707. http://dx.doi. org/10.1016/j.aos.2003.10.009

Vancity. (1998). Social Report. Retrieved January 8, 2007, from: https://www. vancity.com/AboutUs/OurBusiness/OurReports/AccountabilityReport/

Vancity. (2010). Vancity's 2008–2009 Accountability Report, Retrieved September 6, 2011, from: https://www.vancity.com/AboutUs/OurBusiness/ OurReports/AnnualReports/0809AccountabilityReport/

Webb, T. (2007). *Managing the co-operative difference.* Retrieved August 16, 2007, from: www.coopscanada.coop/pdf/meetings/2007institute/Tom%20 Webb%20Jan%2031%20%202007.pdf

Wheeler, D., Colbert, B., & Freeman, R.E. (2003). Focusing on value: Reconciling corporate social responsibility, sustainability and a sustainable approach in a networked world. *Journal of General Management, 28*(3), 1–28.

5 Mixed Methods in Social Accounting: Evaluating the Micro-Loan Program of Alterna Savings Credit Union

EDWARD T. JACKSON AND MICHELE TARSILLA

The purpose of this chapter is to draw lessons from an evaluation of a micro-loan program that combined survey research, logic-model analysis, and stakeholder-engagement methods with other social accounting approaches. Experience from this case study suggests that, while it requires considerable effort and time, such a mixed-methods strategy can enrich the analysis and insights of a performance assessment of a social enterprise. The chapter includes a discussion of the implications of this experience for the broader practice of social accounting.

Methodological Experimentation in Social Accounting

In chapter 1 of this volume, Mook traces the evolution of the field of social accounting. The first wave of the 1970s featured bold experimentation and expectations as the emerging field sought to assert its place alongside traditional accounting methods. In the 1990s, Mook observes, a second wave featured more cautious experimentation and more realistic expectations as the field worked to test its own principles and nascent methods. Tools were created in this period to measure the triple bottom lines and develop social impact statements for companies, and to calculate social return on investment (SROI) and expanded value added statements (EVAS) for non-profits. The third wave began a decade ago and has involved more concerted efforts to shape a *holistic* approach to social accounting "encompassing issues of accountability, performance, and strategic planning" (Mook, chapter 1 of this volume). The Global Reporting Initiative (GRI) and the Balanced Scorecard are well-known examples of integrated, third-wave social accounting models.

The way that social accounting evolves from this point will be important. By measuring and communicating performance, accounting can drive change. This is as true for small non-profits as it is for multinational corporations – and it is especially the case for social economy organizations, which explicitly strive to achieve multiple objectives: social, environmental, and financial. In this sector – which in Canada is populated by tiny, fragile social enterprises as well as large, established co-operatives – social accounting has a special role in informing managers, workers, consumers, suppliers, governments, and community residents of the achievements, failures, and requirements for the improvement of social businesses. And, in light of the turbulent world economy and its local ramifications, it is crucial that social accounting be developed in an adaptive and flexible manner as conditions on the ground change. Indeed, these conditions can sometimes change overnight with startling and devastating consequences to workers and communities, such as when bankruptcies and layoffs ensue. The stakes are very high.

In this regard, it makes good sense to continue to experiment with social accounting methods. Scholars, policy makers, and practitioners all need to test and pilot to discover the most effective and efficient combination of methods; this experimentation will yield crucial and timely insights on the performance of the social economy that will enable these social actors to adjust and strengthen the sector as it proceeds towards an uncertain future. The benefits from social accounting's accompaniment of social economy organizations promise to be real and tangible.

One relevant source of methodological experience and tools for social accounting is that of program evaluation. Three methodological streams in the field of evaluation are worth highlighting. The first is the long-standing use of *mixed methods* in the social sciences (see, for example, Greene, 2007; Hesse-Biber, 2010; Plano Clark & Cresswell, 2007). There is considerable literature on effective ways of blending the use of survey questionnaires, for instance, with focus groups – the quantitative with the qualitative. A second methodological stream is that of *logic model analysis* (e.g., Frechtling, 2007; Morra Imas & Rist, 2009). This technique involves building a model of the inputs, activities, immediate outputs, intermediate outcomes, and long-term impacts that a program claims it is implementing, and testing subsequent performances against this model. Such testing can be undertaken at multiple levels, from the micro (individual, household, enterprise, community) through to the meso (organization) and macro (policy) levels. A third methodological stream involves *stakeholder engagement*, or participatory evaluation, in which the stakeholders in a program play a key role in co-designing, co-implementing, and taking action on the evaluation (e.g., van de Sande & Schwartz, 2011; Jackson, 2005).

This chapter describes – and draws lessons and implications from – a case study that involved the blending of these three methods with other social accounting techniques in order to assess the performance of a larger-scale social economy organization. The case examined here was an evaluation of the micro-loan program of Alterna Savings Credit Union in Toronto, which was undertaken by the Carleton Centre for Community Innovation at Carleton University. The study was carried out from 2008 to 2009, and reported on in 2009 and 2010. In addition to using a survey questionnaire, logic model, and stakeholder engagement, the evaluation also employed the Expanded Value Added Statement (EVAS) (Mook, Quarter, & Richmond, 2007). Prior to this case study, Carleton researchers had already gained experience in blending the EVAS with logic model analysis and participatory strategies in a series of studies of Ontario-based community economic development organizations (Jackson, Harji, & Colwell, 2008; Jackson & Harji, 2009; Tarsilla, 2009).

Micro-Lending: Economic and Policy Context

In today's turbulent world economy, every possible channel to create employment and improve livelihoods must be considered and, ideally, supported. Micro-loan programs typically provide small amounts of credit to enable unemployed individuals, often on social assistance, to establish or expand micro- or small businesses, invest in better housing for their families, or finance their own education and training. Sometimes these programs call for peer groups to monitor the lending process; in other cases, individual loan officers manage a portfolio of borrowers without the peer mechanism. Complementary programs offering business advice as well as financial-literacy and life-skills training are often delivered to borrowers by allied organizations. Across Canada, micro-loan programs have been implemented by credit unions, governments, non-profit loan funds, and non-profit social agencies.

Governments coping with scarce public resources are interested in micro-loan funds for several reasons. Most generally, in an economy where formal employment is shrinking and informal work is expanding, self-employment is an essential option – especially for those workers who have been marginalized in some labour markets, such as immigrants and women. Second, in the present climate especially, the state at all levels seeks to reduce the "social drag" on their budgets of rising rates of unemployment, poverty, and social assistance. And third, governments are interested in tapping new sources of revenue themselves; successful entrepreneurs create revenue flows to the government through direct tax payments and indirectly through the tax payments of their employees and other members of their households.

In Canada, credit unions (or caisses populaires, as they are known in Quebec) have been important managers and supporters of micro-loan programs. Among the country's larger social economy organizations, credit unions are community-based and democratically governed while at the same time being obliged to navigate as viable businesses in the hyper-competitive financial services sector, a sector that has experienced great turmoil since the global debt crisis of 2008–9. In light of these various pressures, most credit unions have framed their support of micro-loan programs as part of their corporate social responsibility (CSR) work. The extent to which the borrowers in a micro-loan program contribute to the bottom line of the credit union business is not an issue that has received much attention from academics or practitioners.

There is, in fact, a worldwide debate on whether and how CSR contributes to business viability (see, for example, Wan-Jan, 2006; Hopkins, 2007). Many boards and executives view CSR more as a luxury than a key company asset or resource. Consequently, they have been inclined to reduce or cut CSR initiatives in the face of serious economic downturns. There are other voices, however, that make the case that strong environmental, social, and governance performance works to reduce investor risk (Hebb, 2008). And Vogel (2005) argues that the business case is strongest for firms that use CSR to differentiate their brands from those of their competitors. He also notes that many companies deploy CSR to attract and retain both customers and employees.

Yet there are other commentators who are critical of CSR and other forms of "philanthrocapitalism." Social transformation should be driven not by market forces and billionaires, writes Edwards (2010), but instead by citizen action supported by governments and progressive foundations. Yet it is here that the social economy can offer a unique convergence of citizen action with social purpose capital. As Quarter, Mook, and Armstrong (2009) explain, social economy organizations generally share four characteristics: social objectives in their mission, social ownership, volunteer/social participation, and civic engagement. For their part, credit unions are democratically controlled financial institutions that express these principles in practical form, and often at a substantially higher scale than most social enterprises in Canada.

The Evaluation of the Micro-Loan Program of Alterna Savings Credit Union

The evaluation of the Micro-Loan Program of Alterna Savings Credit Union was an assessment of a major CSR initiative of a Canadian financial co-operative. The evaluation was carried out during 2008–9, precisely during the period of the worldwide recession that was triggered by the underperformance of mainstream Western financial institutions. The summary of the evaluation presented here is drawn from the full report of this evaluation, entitled "Social Impact Evaluation of the Alterna Savings Community Micro-Loan Program" (Tarsilla, 2010).

Alterna Savings Credit Union

With nearly $2 billion in assets, 120,000 members, and 22 branches in Toronto, Ottawa, and elsewhere in Ontario, Alterna Savings Credit Union is a major social economy business. Awarded the status of an Imagine Caring Company and holding membership in the Canadian Business for Social Responsibility organization, Alterna has earned recognition across Canada as a leader in corporate social responsibility. Alterna's CSR policy calls for initiatives in community economic development (CED), corporate accountability, financial literacy, environmental sustainability, and philanthropy.

The Community Micro-Loan Program

For more than a decade, the credit union's main CED initiative has been the Community Micro-Loan Program, through which Alterna provides small-business loans of up to $15,000 to individuals with strong business plans. Participants generally have a personal annual income of less than $30,000. They are either newcomers to Canada or are on some form of government assistance, or both. In addition, because of their low credit scores or insufficient collateral, Alterna's clients have seen their loan requests rejected by one or more financial institutions before entering the program. The program's financial support is all the more relevant because the community business centres, which help these micro-entrepreneurs to prepare business plans and provide them with advice and training, do not offer financing. However, the added value of the Alterna program is not only the provision of loans to qualifying borrowers. It is also the creation of peer networking and professional coaching opportunities that aim to enhance borrowers' businesses.

The basic output indicators associated with the program were robust. Between 2000 and 2009, Alterna loaned over $1.5 million to some 340 borrowers in the Greater Toronto Area. During the program's first ten years, the average default rate on these micro-loans was 9.4 per cent. However, while the program became closely associated with the Alterna brand, and while some evidence was collected on the program's effectiveness through sporadic interviews with a small number of borrowers, the credit union had never undertaken a systematic evaluation of the program. In the fall of 2008, Alterna commissioned the Carleton Centre for Community Innovation to carry out such a study.

Purposes of the Evaluation

The credit union was interested in using the evaluation to strengthen the program in terms of internal management, external recruitment, and tailoring new financial products to successful borrowers. It also wanted to use the results of the evaluation to mobilize government support in order to expand the program. The overall goal of the evaluation was to assess the financial and social impact of the Community Micro-Loan Program. In terms of objectives, the evaluation aimed to: (1) inform Alterna's new CSR policy, which was being reviewed and revised; (2) provide a better understanding of what was and wasn't working in the program, particularly in terms of anticipating the risks of faulty loans; and (3) contribute to the international debate on the effectiveness of micro-credit as a tool for poverty mitigation, which is a question of considerable interest to governments and civil society alike.

Methodology

Design: The design of the evaluation was non-experimental; that is, it did not involve either a random selection of study participants or the inclusion of a comparison group. In particular, randomization was judged to be unfeasible given the specific nature of the Community Micro-Loan Program. First, the program mainly targeted marginalized groups (and not the general population). Second, the program had been in full implementation status for several years and, as such, did not easily lend itself to comparisons with any counterfactual group. Furthermore, the Alterna evaluation was undertaken on a modest budget; an experimental design was not considered a viable option due to the high costs generally associated with such designs.

Despite these limitations, the Alterna evaluation featured several strengths. First, the study maximized the use of information on past micro-loan borrowers that was already available but had not yet been fully used by Alterna for evaluative purposes; in this sense it was a retrospective evaluation.[1] Second, rather than being purely descriptive, the evaluation assessed the extent to which borrowers' participation in the micro-loan program was associated with expected (and unexpected) outcomes at all levels. The study therefore constituted a relational or predictive evaluation, as well.

Sampling: The survey population was defined as the total number of micro-loan borrowers who had participated in the program between July 1, 2000 and June 30, 2008. This population was stratified by loan size: large ($10,000 to $15,000), medium ($5,000 to $9,999), and small ($0 to $4,999). Focusing on loans provided during the latter five years of the program (2003 to 2008), and for which complete records could be compiled, a stratified sample of fourteen large loans (10 per cent of the sample), ninety-two medium-sized loans (64 per cent), and thirty-six small loans (26 per cent) was drawn. Difficulties in tracking borrowers' mailing co-ordinates and the lack of email addresses, especially for borrowers from earlier years, resulted in the generation of forty-seven survey responses. While not as large a number of respondents as the evaluators had originally hoped for, this total nevertheless represented a 33 per cent response rate.

Data Collection: Employing a mixed-methods approach to data collection, the evaluation relied on the triangulation of findings from data collected from a range of sources, including the following:

1. Key-informant interviews: In order to establish the scope of the study (e.g., key evaluation questions, utilization of the findings), key-informant interviews were conducted with thirteen Alterna staff and Carleton University faculty members with expertise in community economic development (CED) and social return on investment (SROI).
2. Document review: The study also reviewed a wide range of documents – scholarly and professional, online and in hard copy – on micro-finance and CED in Canada and around the world. Upon signing a confidentiality

agreement with Alterna, the lead evaluator also reviewed program files and other hard-copy documents in the credit union's archives, including audits and annual reports over the past decade.

3. Semi-structured questionnaire and focus group: Building on these first two data collection steps, a draft survey instrument – a semi-structured question-naire – with questions on key outcome indicators (employment, credit sta-tus, welfare assistance, etc.) was drafted and then tested with a focus group of six borrowers. The instrument was modified and simplified as a result of the observations of this focus group.

4. Online semi-structured survey: A full-scale, semi-structured survey was then launched, involving mostly closed-ended questions together with opportu-nities for qualitative responses. The survey instrument was posted online for two months, and the sampled borrowers were all encouraged to respond.

5. A second virtual focus group: As the survey's findings were compiled, a second virtual discussion group was convened by the evaluator to validate some of the findings. A Delphi technique was applied online with a conve-nience sample of ten borrowers.

6. Case studies: A total of ten case studies of individual borrowers were also produced, the result of detailed interviews and file analysis. The case studies profiled the experiences of seven borrowers who had paid their loans back on time and whose businesses had performed well over time. The cases also included three borrowers who had either defaulted on their loans or whose businesses had performed poorly following the receipt of their loans. These case studies permitted a deeper understanding of some of the issues emerg-ing from the focus groups and the online survey.

7. EVAS analysis: Using the Expanded Value Added Statement technique, the evaluation also undertook the calculation of the otherwise "hidden" value of non-monetary contributions from the program, particularly with regard to the free services it provided: financial literacy sessions, display-booth space at a downtown Alterna branch, and earned articles in the local media.

Overall, the evaluation sought to assess the program's impact at three levels: the *micro-level*, on the socio-economic status of the micro-loan borrowers and their households; the *meso-level*, on the reputation, brand, and customer loyalty of Alterna as an institution; and the *macro-level*, on the revenues and expenses of the municipal and provincial governments. Table 5.1 presents the logical model of the Community Micro-Loan Program that was developed for the evaluation. This was an important tool in making explicit the program's theory of change. Table 5.2 sets out the relevant impact indicators that the study sought to evaluate at the three levels: micro, meso, and macro.

Table 5.1. Logical Framework for the Alterna Savings Community Micro-Loan Program

Mission Statement: To provide a compelling financial alternative to Canadians through a unique banking philosophy based on co-operative values and focused on professional financial counsel

Program Components	Inputs	Activities	Outputs	Intermediate Outcomes	Final Outcomes	Impact
Small business development loans	Alterna's capital (Credit Union members' shares) 1 full-time Community Micro-Loan Manager 1 full-time CSR Manager	Provision of small loans (maximum $15,000 at prime rate + 6%) upon approval of loan requests submitted by interested applicants	Loans disbursed to qualified applicants in a timely fashion (e.g., within two weeks from the applicants' initial request)	Start-up or expansion of small businesses (including purchase of productive assets, workspace rental, e-commerce development)	Micro-Level (Borrowers) Meso-Level (Corporate) Macro-Level (Policy)	
Free financial literacy programs and professional development opportunities	Volunteer work by both Alterna staff and recognized local business professionals/ instructors	Business financial literacy programs offered to both members and prospective applicants Member display booth and information boards at Alterna branches	Networking Café conducted as planned Presentations made by Alterna CSR officers at local business development centres and training colleges	Members' enhanced understanding and adoption of effective business practices (e.g., business plan development, accounting, marketing) Development of partnerships among borrowers in different fields		

Source: Data taken from Tarsilla (2010)

Table 5.2. Key Community Micro-Loan Program Income and Impact Indicators

Evaluation Layers	Final Outcomes	Impact
Micro-Level (Borrowers)	Increased borrowers' productivity and personal assets	Increased borrowers' payment of federal and provincial income taxes
	Encouraged borrowers' self-sufficiency	Reduced number of borrowers relying on government assistance
	Increased borrowers' annual income	Enhanced well-being of borrowers and their households (including housing, nutrition, health)
Meso-Level (Corporate)	Increased free media coverage of corporate CSR as well as their services/products at large; boosted corporate membership	Increased corporate reputation within the community
	Encouraged development of new products and services specifically catering to the most marginalized and vulnerable population groups (e.g., new Canadians, individuals with no or low credit rating)	Enhanced corporate brand differentiation
	Aided consolidation of Alterna's membership base (e.g., through referral) and enhanced borrowers' opening of additional accounts other than business related (e.g., personal lines of credit, mortgages)	Increased customer loyalty
Macro-Level (Policy)	Contributed to the health and success of the local economy; saved government a large amount of resources otherwise allocated to assistance programs; contributed to federal and provincial revenues due to the borrowers paying higher income taxes over time	Promoted self-employment and entrepreneurship among vulnerable population groups in Toronto
	Fostered the creation of new jobs (e.g., micro-loan borrowers hiring employees to run their business)	Contributed to the reduction in the local unemployment rate

Source: Data taken from Tarsilla (2010)

The main findings of the study were reported to Alterna and the social economy and government sectors in early fall 2009. The full evaluation report was finalized in early 2010 and officially released in spring 2010 by Alterna and Carleton. Alterna (2010) produced and distributed a summary of the findings of the evaluation aimed at lobbying governments for greater support of micro-loan programs. The findings of the study received national media coverage (Grant, 2010).

Micro-Level Findings

The survey found that 81 per cent of borrowers in the Community Micro-Loan Program with incorporated businesses experienced a *change in income*. Of this group, two-thirds saw their income increase: 50 per cent reported income gains of $3,000 or more; and one-third reported that their income had increased by $10,000 or more. Among borrowers whose businesses were not incorporated, income gains of between $1,000 and $5,000 were reported by 45 per cent of these members, while increases of between $10,000 and $15,000 were experienced by one-third. Two-thirds of all respondents indicated that their small business, which had either been launched or expanded by their micro-loan, represented their primary source of income.

The survey also found that 60 per cent of borrowers no longer lived in the same home as they had in the year they received their loan. Of these respondents, 70 per cent indicated that their current home was of better quality than their previous one. While 84 per cent of borrowers were renting before entering the program, only 65 per cent were found to be renting at the time of the study. Before receiving their loans, 8 per cent of borrowers owned their own homes; at the time of the evaluation, 27 per cent, or more than three times as many, were homeowners. In terms of life improvements, 41 per cent of respondents reported that the loan had improved the economic status of their whole family. The most notable impacts reported by this group included financial stability (61 per cent), the purchase of assets (47 per cent), and better nutrition (33 per cent).

Meso-Level Findings

At the meso-level, the evaluation helped to construct a profile of the members being reached by the program. Survey and file data indicated that the Community Micro-Loan Program targets vulnerable or under-served groups in the financial marketplace. Some 62 per cent of bor-rowers were women, a group that has historically faced more difficulty in obtaining finance than men, especially when they have recently ar-rived from other countries. Further, the study found that 75 per cent of borrowers received only one loan from the program. One possible explanation here is that the rapid injection of these funds into the bor-rower's household, combined with the ongoing earning capacity of the business, served to reduce their need for further micro-loans.

The survey highlighted useful information on loan repayment pat-terns, as well. Ninety per cent of borrowers paid their loans back on time. This repayment rate provides evidence that micro-loans consti-tute a solid line of business inside the credit union. For comparative purposes, in 2008, 5 per cent of Alterna's mainstream commercial loan portfolio was in default, while the micro-loan default rate was about 9 per cent.

Perhaps even more importantly for the core business of the credit union, the evaluation found that the micro-loan program acted as a powerful marketing tool, capable of expanding the credit union's mem-bership and helping to retain that membership over time. Indeed, Al-terna has retained two-thirds of its micro-loan borrowers as ongoing customers for other services and products. In fact, more than one-third (35 per cent) of the surveyed respondents stated that Alterna had be-come their primary bank. Furthermore, about two-thirds of borrowers were found to have referred friends and relatives to Alterna. More than one-third (35 per cent) of these respondents had referred an average of three new persons to the credit union, while more than a quarter (26 per cent) had referred an average of four new persons. Indeed, file data showed that micro-entrepreneurs from the Community Micro-Loan Program had brought over $1 million worth of business to Alterna in the form of other financial services and products supplied by the credit union.

The findings suggest that Alterna's Community Micro-Loan Pro-gram has enabled the credit union to build a brand that is perceived positively, particularly among new Canadian communities. The sur-vey showed that, of the 37 per cent of borrowers who had contacted the mainstream banks for a loan, only one-third of this group actually received a loan from these institutions. The success rate for accessing loans from the major banks is about 10 per cent of all borrowers – a rate that underscores the inadequacies of the commercial lending system in Canada. If not for Alterna's program, borrowers would likely have been obliged to turn to other alternatives, such as cheque-cashing operations like Money Mart, which carry much higher interest rates and other onerous terms of repayment.

Macro-Level Findings

With respect to the Micro-Loan Program's effects on job creation, 37 per cent of borrowers surveyed reported that, using the proceeds from their loans, they had hired an average of two employees (full-time or part-time), while 25 per cent had hired an average of four employees. Such employment gains serve to reduce the unemployment rate and the number of citizens benefiting from Employment Insurance, while also generating an increase in income tax and other tax revenue for governments. In fact, the micro-loans catalyzed gains in three different types of tax-revenue streams: federal income tax and provincial income tax paid by employees of the businesses that had been started or expanded with the loans, as well as the income tax paid by the businesses themselves. Furthermore, it is important to note that such outcomes can continue to flow over sustained periods of time – such as, for example, five to ten years, and often much longer.

Moreover, survey data indicated that, while 41 per cent of borrowers had entered the Community Micro-Loan Program on some form of government assistance, only 21 per cent, half of that original cohort, still benefited from government assistance at the time of the evaluation. This is a notable achievement of the program and its borrowers.

Expanded Value Added Analysis

The evaluation also calculated elements of an Expanded Value Added Statement (EVAS), a social-impact method developed at the Ontario Institute for Studies in Education at the University of Toronto (Mook, Quarter, & Richmond, 2007). This EVAS analysis of the Community Micro-Loan Program sought to determine the monetary value of otherwise "hidden" contributions to the program for the fiscal year 2008.

There were three components to this analysis. The first component assigned a value to the nearly twenty free financial literacy sessions, totaling 100 hours of instruction that the program provided to 400 individual credit union members that year. Using tuition fees at local community colleges for similar courses as a standard, it was determined that the average cost of these sessions was $26 per participant, assuming each class was three hours in duration. The total value of this component of the program for 2008, therefore, was estimated to be approximately $205,600.

The second component calculated a value for the free display booth provided to borrowers and their products at an Alterna branch in the centre of downtown Toronto. Guided by commercial fees for similar services (e.g., space and display-booth rental fees) in the downtown core, the EVAS analysis determined that the average cost for such display facilities would be $723 per day. In 2008, the credit union offered this space to a dozen borrowers for three days each. The total value of this service was thus estimated to be $26,028 for the fiscal year 2008.

The third and final component of the EVAS analysis estimated the value of free publicity in magazines and newspapers generated through articles that were earned (not bought) by way of the Community Micro-Loan Program. These articles strengthened Alterna's image and brand within the Greater Toronto Area. The advertising fee rates of a local magazine were found to range between $750 (for non-profits) and $1,795 (for for-profits and government organizations) per ad per issue. The value of the steady stream of articles on the Micro-Loan Program generated in 2008 was thus determined to be about $35,000.[2]

Overall, then, for the three components combined, the EVAS analysis showed that in 2008 the Community Micro-Loan Program created about $266,630 worth of value that would not otherwise be captured in conventional financial statements. This value benefited both the micro-loan borrowers and the credit union as a whole. Note that this calculation was for one fiscal year only; the program created comparable value over multiple years that would similarly have been invisible.

Implications

Core Business Growth

Taken together, the findings of the evaluation of Alterna's Community Micro-Loan Program provide solid evidence that this CSR initiative is a core-growth strategy as much as it is a CED program. In particular, it is worth noting how the program boosted Alterna's core-business growth. First, the high motivation of new-Canadian borrowers to succeed, together with their loyalty to Alterna, appear to be important factors in maintaining a loan default rate at an acceptable level of risk for the credit union. The business line of micro-lending to immigrants therefore would seem to be one of manageable and predictable risk for Alterna, and this could be demonstrated to the credit union's leadership.

Second, micro-loan borrowers themselves generate significant downstream business as they repay their loans and seek larger financing deals and new financial products and services. The credit union benefits by accompanying these member-customers on their financial growth curve. Indeed, 35 per cent of borrowers decided to make Alterna their permanent bank. And finally, two-thirds of the borrowers referred friends and relatives to the credit union, generating new members and even more new business. In this way, the customer satisfaction and reputational gains of the credit union at the household and community levels combined to open new markets to the immigrant community.

Of course, this is not the end of the story. For the new borrowers and for current members whose fortunes are rising, the onus remains on Alterna to respond with additional appropriate, attractive, and timely financial products and services. The credit union must track the progress of these member-customers (and the obstacles they face) in detail, in real time, in order to support their trajectory towards success. Such careful monitoring of its members would enable sustained accompaniment on the part of the credit union.

Policy Development

The evaluation reported here also provides solid evidence in favour of government support for micro-lending to new Canadians. At the micro-level of the study, more than half of all borrowers with incorporated businesses saw their incomes increase, often very substantially. Some 40 per cent reported that the loans had improved the economic status of their families, especially with regard to financial stability. The loans had also helped borrowers to find better housing. Indeed, the percentage of borrowers who were homeowners more than tripled over the course of the program, from 8 per cent to 27 per cent.

These micro-level gains translated into macro-level benefits for governments. Successful borrowers helped to reduce the cost to the state of Employment Insurance by hiring new employees (some 60 per cent of borrowers hired between two and four employees, on average). These employees, in turn, paid taxes, as did the new and enhanced businesses of the borrowers in the program. Furthermore, the Micro-Loan

Program helped to cut the number of borrowers on government assistance *in half*, from 41 per cent to 21 per cent. All of these achievements meant lower government costs and higher tax revenues.

The case is strong, therefore, for government provision of loan guarantees and grants for literacy training, which can enable the credit union and other community-based groups to expand their programs to achieve a meaningful scale. As has been shown, this support can also enable the credit union or other program providers to gain new business while advancing other public-policy objectives: higher employment, lower unemployment costs, lower social assistance costs, and increased home ownership, among others. In turn, these gains contribute to more effective economic and social integration of new Canadians into the larger society.

Social economy financial institutions like credit unions and caisses populaires are ideal partners for governments in undertaking these efforts. These financial co-operatives bring a set of social values to their work along with a commercial capacity and scale that can result in very successful micro-lending and financial-services support for new Canadians as they build their financial success in Canada, step by step. The comparative advantage of these institutions is precisely their civil-society character, combined with their capacity and discipline to manage substantial pools of capital.

For its part, Alterna Savings Credit Union has proven itself as a willing champion of micro-lending and financial-services accompaniments for Canadians on the margins of the economy – and for low-income, new Canadians in particular. The credit union has used the evaluation as a platform to draw attention to its own corporate commitment, policy knowledge, and track record in micro-lending, distinguishing itself from its competitors in the process. Alterna is also engaged in policy advocacy on financial literacy with both the Ontario and federal governments, in association with other social economy and financial-services organizations.

Mixed Methods in Social Accounting

Overall, the case reviewed here suggests that it may be time for the field of social accounting to more intentionally experiment with different combinations of mixed methods for research and evaluation. In particular, while EVAS proved to be an important component of the evaluation of the Alterna Micro-Loan Program, it was the *combination* of this tool and other methods that enabled the study to generate its most granular insights.

There is no doubt that the *EVAS analysis* was an innovative element of the evaluation. The study benefited from the calculation of the monetary value of three components: free literacy training for borrowers, free display space for borrowers' products and services, and free publicity for the program through articles in the print media. This analysis confirmed that the program generates substantial and otherwise hidden value from these three components. And this calculation proved to be useful for decision-makers on the credit union's board of directors as well as those in its management.

At the same time, however, other methods also proved useful. Chief among these was the *semi-structured online survey questionnaire* for borrowers. The questionnaire was long, thorough, and addressed very important performance indicators at the individual, household, and enterprise levels. To be sure, it took considerable time and effort the construct the survey population, particularly in the case of assembling email contacts for sampled borrowers from the earlier years of the program. However, given the range of sophisticated data-management tools available to social economy organizations today, this challenge should be minimized in future studies. The experience of the Alterna evaluation suggests that the design and administration of this kind of survey instrument is ideally carried out by an experienced external researcher. Further, conducting the study over a fairly long period provides sufficient time for the design, testing, and refinement of the tool, for the engagement of respondents, and for the receipt and analysis of completed questionnaires.

The fact that there was no comparison group in the survey is worth noting again. One way of dealing with this limitation is to compare the findings of the Alterna evaluation with those of social impact studies that investigated borrowers enrolled in similar programs in Canada and other similar jurisdictions. Another approach would be to survey a targeted, comparable sample of borrowers in the Alterna program who have not paid back their loans. In this instance, the problem is that relations between these unsuccessful borrowers and the credit union are likely to be strained and distant, and indeed some files may even involve active litigation.

The second technique that also proved to be very important to the study reported here was that of the *logic model*. Making explicit the program's theory of change was useful in more precisely defining and assessing the key outcome indicators of interest in the evaluation. The logic model also distinguished among outcomes at the three levels: macro, meso, and micro. This aided in tracking the various "results chains" of the program and their differential effects on key stakeholder groups – notably borrowers, governments, and the credit union as a whole. Such logic models could play this kind of role in most social accounting exercises and, in so doing, support better-informed decision-making by program managers and policy-makers in planning, implementing, and adjusting social-economy interventions.

Finally, and perhaps most importantly, the Alterna case offers lessons related to *stakeholder participation*. Prior to working together on this evaluation, the Carleton Centre for Community Innovation and Alterna Savings Credit Union had participated in common networks on the social economy in Ottawa and more generally in the province of Ontario. While these earlier experiences involved mostly indirect interaction, they nevertheless provided a platform of mutual respect upon which the project discussed here could be built. For its part, Alterna's senior management agreed to collaborate on the study not only to internally assess the effectiveness of its key CSR activity but also to externally strengthen the credit union's market position, as well as to advocate for more government support of micro-credit programs.

Alterna's participation in this study occurred in phases. During the design of the study and the construction of the borrower database, three key Alterna staff members (including the senior executive responsible for CSR) played an active role alongside the Carleton Centre's researcher and his supervisor. However, when the study was actually being conducted – and notably in the drawing of the sample and the collection and analysis of data – the Carleton team insisted on complete independence, to which the Alterna team fully agreed. Later, upon receiving the evaluation report from Carleton, Alterna's personnel resumed co-leadership of the process, presenting the findings to its annual general meeting, using the study to renew its CSR policy, and disseminating the results of the evaluation to governments and the media.

It must be acknowledged that borrower participation in this study was more limited and narrow in scale than the management's participation. The respondents to the questionnaire participated via that online tool, while a smaller number of borrowers participated in the focus groups. In future studies, borrower engagement could be expanded and their voices amplified in the social accounting process. Nonetheless, the

Alterna case lends concrete support to the view that both strategic and practical stakeholder engagement by key personnel of social economy organizations in social accounting exercises is possible and desirable. Indeed, it is essential. Moreover, the nature of this participation can (and probably should) take different forms and levels of intensity as the social accounting exercise proceeds.

Furthermore, and perhaps most significantly, stakeholder engagement was in practice the facilitator, co-ordinator, and synthesizer of the application of the other methodological tools in the study. In the Alterna case, the co-leaders of the study – Alterna and Carleton – jointly decided how and when to apply the tools. Stakeholder participation was itself the *prime vehicle* for managing and sequencing all the other tools. In this case, stakeholder participation is thus primus inter pares among methods in a mixed-methods study. Indeed, all practitioners of social accounting must be aware of and skilled in techniques for facilitating such stakeholder participation.

Finally, it is important to affirm that the application of this mixed-methods approach was, by most reasonable standards, quite cost-effective. What proved essential was the allowance of sufficient time for the design and implementation of the study. It was also useful that the lead evaluator was experienced and efficient in his conduct of the work. Both of these conditions can be replicated in other social-accounting studies.

Overall, then, the case study reviewed here lends support to the claim that the field of program evaluation is an important source of methodological experience and tools for social accounting. In this case, the use of survey questionnaires among other instruments in a mixed-methods approach (Greene, 2007; Hesse-Biber, 2010; Plano Clark & Cresswell, 2007) and the application of logic model analysis (Frechtling, 2007; Morra Imas & Rist, 2009), together with stakeholder engagement (van de Sande & Schwartz, 2011; Jackson, 2005), all proved to be pertinent to and useful in the social accounting process. There is more to be gained from a more extensive "interaction" between the fields of social accounting and program evaluation.

Conclusion

Over the past thirty years, scholars and practitioners in the field of social accounting have worked hard to distinguish its methods from those of mainstream accounting. New conceptual frameworks and tools have been created to demarcate the mission and methods of the field. The case study reviewed here suggests that benefits can be realized in the field by intentionally and systematically reflecting on and experimenting with the most appropriate combinations of mixed methods, which can yield optimum insights into and understandings of the social performance of enterprises and institutions. The evaluation of the Alterna Community Micro-Loan Program provides one window into the nature and value of a mixed-methods approach to social accounting, and to some of the practical tools that can be combined effectively and efficiently. There are many more such windows to be opened and there is much more to be learned.

ACKNOWLEDGMENTS

The authors are grateful to Susan Henry and Jean Barrett of Alterna Savings Credit Union, and to former Alterna executive Kimberley Ney, for their professionalism, openness, and diligence as collaborators in the design, implementation, and utilization of the evaluation of Alterna's Community Micro-Loan Program. Genevieve Harrison and Sonja Vanek at the Carleton Centre for Community Innovation were valuable allies, as well. We also thank Laurie Mook and an anonymous reviewer for their useful comments on an earlier draft of this chapter. The research on which this chapter is based was supported by a sub-grant from the Southern Ontario Node of the Canadian Social Economy Research Partnerships, which was funded by the Social Sciences and Humanities Research Council.

NOTES

1 For example, the evaluation recaptured information on both the borrowers' incomes and employment status before the start of the program through a review of all the loan-request forms originally submitted by the program's members. These data were all present in Alterna's archives, but they had never been systematically collected or analysed.
2 Interestingly, the presentation of these evaluation findings in public fora between late 2009 and early 2010 gave the Community Micro-Loan Program

additional publicity and therefore contributed to an increase in the value of Alterna's free publicity – and, as a result, to greater brand differentiation within the community.

REFERENCES

Alterna Savings Credit Union. (2010). "Strengthening our community by empowering individuals: Showcasing our success – Alterna's Community Micro-Loan Program." Toronto: Alterna Savings Credit Union.

Edwards, M. (2010). *Small change: Why business won't save the world*. San Francisco: Berrett-Koehler/Domos.

Frechtling, J.A. (2007). *Logic modeling methods in program evaluation*. San Francisco: Jossey-Bass.

Grant, T. (2010). Microcredit programs yield outsized benefits. *Globe and Mail*, April 28.

Greene, J.C. (2007). *Mixed methods in social inquiry*. New York: Wiley.

Hebb, T. (2008). *No small change: Pension funds and corporate engagement*. Ithaca, NY: Cornell University Press.

Hesse-Biber, S.N. (2010). *Mixed methods research: Merging theory with practice*. New York: Guilford.

Hopkins, M. (2007). *Corporate social responsibility and international development: Is business the solution?* London: Earthscan.

Jackson, E.T. (2005). Participatory monitoring and evaluation. In S. Mathison (Ed.), *Encyclopedia of evaluation* (p. 296). Thousand Oaks: Sage.

Jackson, E.T., & Harji, K. (2009) "Measuring the blended value of corporate social responsibility and social enterprise." Presented to the Annual Conference of the Canadian Evaluation Society, Ottawa, 2009.

Jackson, E.T., Harji, K., & Colwell, A. (2008) "Measuring social value in CSR: Lessons from community enterprise in Canada." Presented at the 27th International CIRIEC Congress, Seville, 2008.

Mook, L., Quarter, J., & Richmond, B.J. (2007). *What counts: Social accounting for non-profits and cooperatives* (2nd ed.). London: Sigel Press.

Morra Imas, L.G., & Rist, R.C. (2009). *The road to results: Designing and conducting effective development evaluations*. Washington, DC: World Bank.

Plano Clark, V.L. & Cresswell, J.W. (Eds.). (2007). *The mixed methods reader*. Thousand Oaks: Sage.

Quarter, J., Mook, L., & Armstrong, A. (2009). *Understanding the social economy: A Canadian perspective*. Toronto: University of Toronto Press.

Tarsilla, M. (2009). *Ottawa Community Loan Fund outcome evaluation*. Ottawa: Carleton Centre for Community Innovation, Carleton University.

Tarsilla, M. (2010). *Social impact evaluation of the Alterna Savings Community Micro-Loan Program*. Ottawa: Carleton Centre for Community Innovation, Carleton University.

van de Sande, A., & Schwartz, K. (2011). *Research for social justice: A community based approach*. Halifax: Fernwood.

Vogel, D. (2005). *The market for virtue: The potential and limits of corporate social responsibility*. Washington, DC: Brookings Institution.

Wan-Jan, W.S. (2006). Defining corporate social responsibility. *Journal of Public Affairs, 6*(3–4), 176–84. http://dx.doi.org/10.1002/pa.227

6 The Demonstrating Value Initiative: Social Accounting for Social Enterprises

BRYN SADOWNIK

Those who operate and invest in the social economy seek to demonstrate its value as an innovative means to meet community needs, and to bring about desirable social and environmental change. They want to understand if, and how, their organizations are successful in meeting the objectives for which they were created, and to use that information to improve their performance. But assessing performance and impact for social economy organizations is challenging; one must take into account the limited capacity of social enterprises to conduct assessments, the usefulness of such assessments to social enterprises and their stakeholders, power relationships in evaluation, and methodological challenges in measuring social impact and representing social value creation (Paton, 2003; Shah, 2003; Snibbe, 2006; Kramer, 2005). Nevertheless the advancement and adoption of assessment practices are often seen as critical factors in the development of social enterprise, particularly in legitimizing support (Standing Committee on Human Resources, Social Development and the Status of Persons with Disabilities, 2006; HRSDC, 2006).

A unique community-based project, the Demonstrating Value Initiative, has sought to address this challenge by designing a framework in line with social accounting to help social enterprise operators and investors assess the performance and impact of their enterprise. This includes developing a set of common approaches and processes for assessment that will relate and extend the emerging tools in performance measurement and impact assessment as well as encourage common reporting formats. The initiative ultimately seeks to move the social enterprise sector towards improved practices in performance and impact assessment, leading to improved stakeholder accountability and to better sharing and communication of innovative practices, learning, and social value creation. Originating in 2004 as an informal exploration of assessment methods by a number of Vancouver-based social enterprises and investors, it is now a more formal initiative led by Vancity Community Foundation. The initiative has since received technical and funding support from Coast Capital Savings, Community Economic Development Technical Assistance Program (CEDTAP), Enterprising Non-Profits (enp), Human Resources and Skills Development Canada (HRSDC), Renewal Partners, SAP, and Vancity Credit Union.

Since 2005, the initiative has engaged in various research and development activities, starting with a literature review to understand the state of knowledge around impact assessment methodologies relevant to social enterprises, and followed by informant interviews with social enterprises and investors to understand the needs and challenges surrounding impact assessment. This research established that existing tools/resources were insufficient and that there was a strong demand to develop a framework for impact assessment. Over twenty social operators and investors then engaged in a framework development process that involved multiple design workshops (May 2007; October 2008). (See appendix 1 for a list of participants.) A preliminary "working framework" was then piloted with eight social enterprises and subsequently refined.

The resulting Demonstrating Value Framework guides social enterprises to fully identify their information needs for managing, planning, and demonstrating their value. It then develops a reporting tool ("a performance snapshot") that serves their particular decision-making and communication needs. In addition, the initiative developed an "Investor Lens" to move investors towards harmonizing their reporting demands, as well as a variety of guides, worksheets, and information resources to support the specific information identification, collection, and reporting needs that are unique to social enterprises. While the framework was originally developed for social enterprises, it is also relevant to other organizations within the social economy.

Through the course of this research and framework development, we had the opportunity to explore the practical challenges and practices of performance and impact assessment from both a social enterprise and an investor perspective. In this chapter we share our insights about the interests, needs, and challenges of different parties in the assessment process. We then describe the work of the initiative to address these issues in the development of the Demonstrating Value Framework. We conclude by looking at the particular lessons learned for small- and medium-sized social economy organizations, as well as the next steps for the initiative.

Social Enterprise Needs and Practices

Social enterprise is growing in Canada for a number of reasons that include enhancing the financial stability of non-profit organizations, providing innovative delivery for some community programs, and delivering goods and services that would not otherwise be provided by the marketplace. Individual social entrepreneurs are also developing enterprises independent of non-profit organizations.[1] Social enterprises are unique hybrid entities with financial management and reporting needs that are not adequately addressed by either non-profit or business practices.

Reporting demands associated with funding and financing differ greatly across the sector. In 2005, informant interviews conducted as part of the initiative revealed that reporting requirements range from brief end-of-project summaries to no direct formal reporting to rigorous reporting requirements, including frequent reporting periods, statistical information, audited financial statements, and narrative reporting. Social enterprises expressed considerable frustration with the range and divergent timing of reporting requirements, as well as the lack of dialogue with investors. Another frustration stemmed from the lack of integration between their external and internal reporting (Armstrong, 2006).

As part of our research, we were interested in exploring in more detail the areas in which social enterprises were already active in monitoring and reporting, as well as the areas in which they still needed to develop. At framework design workshops held in 2007 and 2008, we found that the situations and needs of social enterprises were very divergent, particularly as they related to assessment and reporting. For some social enterprises, their main aim in improving reporting was internally focused – either to improve the efficiency of operational reporting systems or for improving communication with a governing body (such as a board of directors or a "parent" nonprofit organization). Others were interested in strengthening external reporting, both to improve their ability to successfully apply for funding/financing and to provide reporting as part of a longer-term funding relationship. Yet another focus was on being able to demonstrate and communicate their value more generally to the community, and on developing a clearer picture of how they contribute to community change.

Investor Needs and Practices

Most investment in social enterprise in Canada occurs by way of grants from charitable foundations and the government, as well as through financing from credit unions and community-based financial institutions. Equity investments are limited. While most sources of private capital are not prepared to engage in below-market loans or investments, some angel investors and venture capital firms who support social enterprise are beginning to emerge in Canada (Hebb et al., 2006).

We explored investors' needs and perceptions around their reporting relationships as part of the informant interviews and workshops noted in the previous section. The interviews revealed that the relationship between most investment organizations and their investees is limited to an assessment process, and that further engagement after the receipt of funding often depended on the motivation of the investee to request closer involvement. Investors felt that it was often challenging to get information from investees, or that the quality of said information was low, especially where there was limited incentive to report. At the workshops, investors expressed an interest in moving towards more standardized reporting, while also recognizing the diversity of the sector and the importance of ensuring that reporting be as simple as possible and provide only information that directly supports decision-making, learning, and the enterprise's success. The investor participants felt that they should take a much stronger role in aggregating information and learning, educating others, and developing the social enterprise sector.

Another theme that emerged at the workshops, and one which was echoed throughout the initiative, was the desire to assess and demonstrate the collective social and/or environmental impact of investments in addition to standard business and organizational performance data. Investors and social enterprises both expressed that they felt pressure and a need for guidance to quantify their social, environmental, and cultural impacts, and to go even further to provide monetized information (such as taxpayer cost savings) about their community impacts. The driving reason for this was to be able to legitimize public support for social enterprise. Based on this need, we looked to the existing research and practice in the social finance community and investigated the value and practicality of capturing these data with our framework-development participants.

The objective of capturing both a financial and a social and/or environmental return ("blended" returns) has been the subject of considerable research and effort on an international scale. This work has been developed in different contexts including the social entrepreneurship movement in the U.S., social enterprise support in the UK, community economic development support in Canada, and in developing the social economy in Quebec and various countries in Europe. We reviewed the projects described in Table 6.1 to help us better understand the issues, approaches, and specific tools that have been developed.

A study of the literature suggests that two different approaches to accountability and reporting are emerging, both of which extend beyond the practical differences in investment programs. The first could be characterized as an *impact-focused* approach to accountability, which is most representative of projects 1, 4, 6, 7, 9, and 12 (Table 6.1). The second could be characterized as *performance-focused*, which is most representative of projects 2, 3, 5, 8, 10, and 11 (Table 6.1). The first approach emphasizes impact measurement and results. Investors want to know that the investments they make are achieving their desired results, and they want evidence of the impact their dollars are having on the world. This view is strongly associated with venture philanthropists, who have done a lot of work to advance impact measurement methods.[2] While many different methods are developing, the one that has received the most attention is the calculation of a Social Return on Investment (SROI), which seeks to develop standardized metrics that represent both social and financial value. Measurement of social returns is based on establishing an impact map to represent how the activities of the enterprise lead to changes in social outcomes, to isolate the impact of the enterprise relative to what would have happened anyway, and to show the influence of other factors on that outcome. Many supporters of social enterprise see that focusing on impact is crucial. For instance, Jeremy Nicholls, in a "think piece" commissioned for the UK government, emphasizes that measures are needed that reflect the result of the social enterprise's work (the outcomes) rather than simply summarizing its activities. He also notes that it is important for enterprises to take into account what would have happened without the influence of their enterprise (Nicholls, 2007).

Table 6.1. International Studies Relating to Investor Reporting

Organization	Project(s)
1. Office of the Third Sector / The Department of Trade and Industry, Small Business Service, United Kingdom	Think piece (2008); Research program around SROI (2008–10)
2. Social Enterprise Partnership, United Kingdom (led by the New Economics Foundation)	Quality and Impact Project (Social Enterprise Partnership, 2003; Social Enterprise Partnership, 2004)
3. Research Initiative on Social Enterprise (RISE) Columbia Business School, USA	Double Bottom Line Project (Clark et al., 2004); A Discussion Among Grantmakers (Goldman Sachs Foundation and the Rockefeller Foundation, 2003)
4. SROI Working Circle[3] led by the Blended Value Project of the Hewlett Foundation (2003–4); Update led by Scholten & Franssen and Social Venture Technology (SVT) Group, USA	A Framework for Approaches to SROI Analysis (Olsen and Nicholls, 2005); Social Return on Investment: A Guide to SROI Analysis (Scholten et al., 2006)
5. Foundation Strategy Group, USA	From Insight to Action: New Directions in Foundation Evaluation (Kramer et al., 2007); Measuring Innovation (Kramer, 2005)
6. Social Venture Technology Group, USA	Various tools including an open-source Impact Database Social Metrics
7. REDF, USA	OASIS, Ongoing Assessment of Social Impacts (Twersky & BTW Consultants, 2002); Social Return on Investment Collection (Emerson, Wachowicz, & Chun, 2000)
8. Réseau d'investissement social du Québec (RISQ) and other investors groups, Canada	Guide for Analysis of Social Economy Enterprises / Guide d'analyse des entreprises d'économie sociale (RISQ, 2005)
9. Benchmarking Philanthropy Task Force, World Economic Forum's Global Leaders for Tomorrow	Philanthropy Measures Up (Global Leaders for Tomorrow, 2003)
10. Keystone Initiative Based at AccountAbility, United Kingdom	The Keystone Method (Keystone, 2008)
11. University-based research in Québec[4]	Evaluation Methods Research Program (CRCÉS) Evaluation-related research projects within ARUC-ES / RQRP-ES
12. Rockefeller Foundation Impact Investment Collaborative, USA	Impact Measurement Approaches (Olsen & Galimidi, 2008)

In contrast, the *performance-focused* approach questions the need, wisdom, and practicality of focusing on impact. For example, Tim Broadhead, President and CEO of the J.W. McConnell Family Foundation, questioned grant makers' insistence on demonstrable results, speaking of the danger of a "so-called 'misplaced concreteness' – assuming that everything can be defined in terms of results, especially quantifiable ones" (Broadhead, 2004). In his opinion there is considerably more value in seeing that an investee has a clearly defined goal and a strategy for realizing it, and in providing some way of monitoring progress to ensure they are moving in the right direction. A study by FSG Social Impact Advisors about evaluation practices at U.S. foundations argues for a similar approach, noting that more foundations are abandoning the constraint of objectively demonstrating the impact of a specific grant in favour of performance-centred approaches that encompass a wide range of activities and provide foundations and their grantees with current information and actionable insights (Kramer et al., 2007).

Impact measurement has also been critiqued in program evaluation circles, based on the unsatisfactory results of requiring that recipients be accountable for achieving impact through tools such as results-based management. Earl, Carden, and Smutylo (2001) argue that linear, "cause-and-effect" thinking contradicts the understanding of development as a complex process. They further note that the drive to claim credit for impact interferes with the creation of knowledge and limits risk-taking, innovation, and the creation of partnerships. There are few good examples of isolating impact. Fry, Haklay, and Esterhuizen (2007) similarly argue that common practice deductive approaches limit learning and understanding about social impact.

Measuring impact is challenging for a number of reasons. One reason is that methods can be difficult to understand and resource-intense to apply. There may also be a lack of methods whatsoever, or there may be many divergent methods to choose from. Certain methods may also be inappropriate to the needs of the user (for instance, they could be intrusive to the people that social enterprises are aiming to help). Given that social enterprises are working to effect change in a wide number of areas (e.g., food security, improving air quality, preventing climate change, and improving health and well-being, to name a few), it can be challenging to keep abreast of and know how to use these methods.

Another reason why measuring impact is challenging is that it is difficult to tease out the social enterprise's specific role in these changes. The social enterprise may influence change in conjunction with other events and the activities of others who are working towards the same objective. Isolating the impact of the social enterprise is difficult without a scientific study that establishes a control group (which is costly, impractical, and even impossible in many cases).

An Investment Criteria Survey for the investor participants in the Demonstrating Value Initiative was conducted to explore the importance of "truly measuring impact" and to see what particular criteria were critical in informing investment decision-making. The survey listed a comprehensive list of sixty-nine criteria under eleven categories.[5] Respondents were asked to review the criteria and rank each criterion's importance in their decision to support a social enterprise. For each criterion they could select "high," "medium," "low," or "N/A." They could also add criteria that were not included. The survey also asked how the respondent's organization determines whether criteria are met and their processes for assessing and following up with groups to determine their alignment with their criteria.

Respondents from ten investor organizations that participated in the October 2008 workshop completed the Investment Criteria Survey online. Investors found that most criteria were considered to be relevant; "N/A" was rarely chosen. The top twelve criteria chosen by investors are listed in Table 6.2. The top criteria in the following table (Table 6.3) relate to the capacity and ability of the social enterprise to deliver on its mission and on its ability to show adequate financial analysis and cash flow. Most investors were in agreement about these top criteria – the standard deviation for these responses was minimal.

The survey included the criteria of wanting an investee to show their impact. Interestingly, while the ability to show and value impact is important, it ranked behind most other criteria that related to an organization's mission, including:

• the capacity of an organization to deliver on its strategy/plan;
• the positioning of an enterprise to address a specific need in the community;
• the clarity and strength of the mission;
• the viability of the strategy/plan to address the mission;
• the alignment of the mission to the investor's strategy; and
• demonstrated skill and expertise to address the mission.

Table 6.2. Top Twelve Criteria, Investment Criteria Survey

Category	Criteria	Rating Average	Standard Deviation
Social Enterprise Management's Track Record	Ability to deliver	3.00	-
Rationale for the Business and Concept Viability	Sustainability of enterprise over time as evidenced by planning and past operations	3.00	-
Social/Environmental Mission – General	Capacity of organization to deliver on its strategy/plan	3.00	-
Financial Status	Adequacy of financial analysis and projections	3.00	-
Social/Environmental Mission – General	Positioning of enterprise to address a community need	2.89	0.33
Financial Status	Reasonable and clear accounting of costs	2.89	0.32
Status	Evidence of clear planning processes (business, strategic, marketing, etc.)	2.88	0.35
Status	Clear articulation of viability and sustainability	2.88	0.35
Rationale for the Business and Concept Viability	Realistic activities and time frames	2.80	0.42
Social/Environmental Mission – General	Clarity and strength of the mission	2.80	0.42
Social/Environmental Mission – General	Viable strategy/plan	2.80	0.42
Financial Status	Adequacy of cash flow	2.80	0.42

Note: The average rating is calculated on the following weighting for the responses: high = 3, medium = 2, low = 1, N/A = 0, divided by the number of responses.

Table 6.3. Top Criteria by Category, Investment Criteria Survey

Category	Criteria	Rating Average	Standard Deviation	Part of Top 12
Social Enterprise Management's Track Record	Ability to deliver	3.00	–	Yes
Rationale for the Business and Concept Viability	Sustainability of enterprise over time as evidenced by planning and its past operations	3.00	–	Yes
Social/Environmental Mission – General	Capacity of organization to deliver on its strategy/plan	3.00	–	Yes
Financial Status	Adequacy of financial analysis and projections	3.00	–	Yes
Status	Evidence of clear planning processes (business, strategic, marketing, etc.)	2.88	0.35	Yes
	Clear articulation of viability and sustainability	2.88	0.35	Yes
Governance	Clear and direct leadership from the organization for the enterprise	2.70	0.44	No
Human Resources	Suitable employment conditions	2.63	0.52	No
Social/Environmental Mission – Employment Enterprises	Strategy appropriate for work, skills, and capacity of the target population	2.60	0.70	No
	Positive employment outcomes for target population	2.60	0.70	No
Operations	Have mentorship and technical assistance where needed	2.60	0.52	No
Quality of Assets	Sufficiency of capital assets	2.57	0.53	No

(continued)

Table 6.3. (*continued*)

Category	Criteria	Rating Average	Standard Deviation	Part of Top 12
Links to the Community	Strength of community or sector support	2.40	0.84	No

Note: The average rating is calculated on the following weighting for the responses: high = 3, medium = 2, low = 1, N/A = 0, divided by the number of responses.

Development of the Demonstrating Value Framework

Method Overview

As noted in the introduction, the Demonstrating Value Initiative originated in 2004 as an informal exploration of assessment methods by a number of Vancouver-based social enterprises and investors. This led to a small research project by the Potluck Café and Catering Society (and funded by Vancity) that researched methodologies, conducted informant interviews about the practices and needs of social enterprises and investors, and outlined a possible plan to develop a national framework that could address these needs. This exploratory work was overseen by a steering committee comprised of social enterprise operators, investors, and others involved in social enterprise development. This project was then developed in November 2006 and involved the following activities in 2007 and 2008:[6]

1. Recruitment of social enterprises and investors to participate in the development, piloting, and refinement of a framework based on a mix of activities and geographic locations. (Participants are listed in appendix 1.)
2. Development of a "working" framework and supporting tools that built on, adapted, and integrated existing methods and tools, and developed the current practices of project participants. This work was based largely on a Concept Paper and a Framework Development Workshop held in May 2007.
3. Piloting of the working framework and its supporting tools with eight of the twelve social enterprises who participated in its design. (See appendix 1 for a list of the pilots.) In the piloting process, all of the social enterprises identified information needs and reporting processes that they wished to

improve or develop. The enterprises were then provided with support as they refined and/or developed monitoring and reporting systems that would address their top priorities.

4. Exploration of standardized reporting and indicators with social enterprises and investors, which led to the development of an "Investor Lens" to guide reporting.

5. Refinement and release of the framework and tools based on the lessons learned from the pilot implementation. A website was developed in May 2009 that contains the framework and tools (http://www.demonstratingvalue.org). A technical assistance program was developed by Vancity Community Foundation in order to provide facilitation and technical support to organizations wanting to use the framework.

The overall development goal of the framework was to move the social enterprise sector towards improved practices in performance and impact assessment, leading to improved stakeholder accountability and better sharing and communication of innovative practices, learning, and social value creation. The development sought to be practical in nature by developing resources and tools that would be specific to the needs of social enterprise development in the Canadian context.

The research conducted in the early part of the initiative (2005–7) – including informant interviews, workshop discussions with social enterprise operators and investors, and a literature review – strongly pointed to the need for better technical and resource support for social enterprises and their stakeholders that would help them identify, develop, and use information more effectively. Fundamentally, this means supporting both social enterprises and investors in identifying what information is useful to gather, establishing effective systems for gathering said information (through monitoring systems and assessment), and developing better systems for using it (by communicating the information clearly and improving processes for using it in decision-making processes) (see Figure 6.1 below). We learned that many social enterprise participants had developed their monitoring and reporting procedures largely in response to externally driven information demands, and/or particular operational crises that alerted them to the importance of tracking certain types of information. They sought to change this pattern to proactively develop monitoring and reporting systems that would specifically support their short- and long-term decision-making and could communicate their value to specific stakeholders. Inherent in this was the need to be able to build on existing

Figure 6.1. The Focus of Demonstrating Value

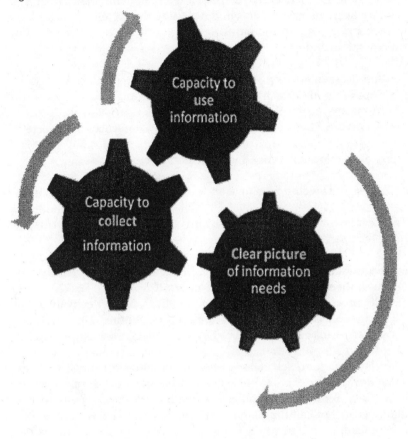

processes and systems and to be able to integrate reporting for different audiences (management, board, funders, partners).

The Demonstrating Value Framework

The Demonstrating Value Framework that arose from this collaborative effort was a collection of tools and concepts aimed at helping social enterprises to ask the right questions about their work and develop systems for tracking and communicating their value. The key focus was to help social enterprises take the time to proactively work out what information is most useful to them in order to better manage, plan, and communicate their work, and in developing the systems that respond to their priorities and the particular stage of their development. The framework includes:

- A process to develop strong monitoring and reporting systems;
- Support to undertake the mapping process and to develop systems through a technical assistance program;
- An Investor Lens to foster shared reporting practices by investors.

These elements are described in more detail below.

A Process to Develop Strong Monitoring and Reporting Systems

The Demonstrating Value Process aims to help a social enterprise do three things:

- Gain a clear picture of its critical information needs and how to meet them in an "Information Blueprint";
- Design a "performance snapshot" report to more effectively use information for management, planning, and fundraising;
- Improve an organization's capacity to collect information.

In order to accomplish these goals, the organization must first take some time to clearly work out what information it needs to collect and how it will use it. The organization can then design its own "performance snapshot" and implement the systems that it needs. This work is designed to involve multiple stakeholders in the social enterprise – all of those parties who will use the information as well as those who will produce it.

The process is based around a key question that is asked of the organization: "What do you want to know and show?" The Demonstrating Value Lenses, a conceptual framework, then helps focus the organization's efforts to develop monitoring and reporting systems based on the additional questions shown in Figure 6.2.

In terms of the first question – *"What information is useful?"* – the framework guides social enterprises to identify information needs in three areas: business performance, mission performance, and organizational sustainability. Business performance refers to the business and financial success of the social enterprise. Mission performance refers

Figure 6.2. Demonstrating Value Lenses

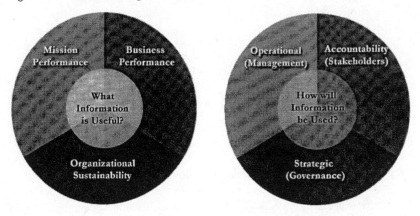

to the ability of the social enterprise to successfully contribute towards the social, cultural, and environmental objectives set out in the organization's mission. Organizational sustainability refers to the ability of an enterprise to attain, develop, maintain, and renew resources in order to meet its purpose.

In terms of the second question – *"How will information be used?"* – the framework helps the social enterprise to represent different information needs and flows so that monitoring and reporting systems can be integrated and respond as efficiently as possible to different needs. These components include: an operational perspective (to support decisions by management and staff); a strategic perspective (to support decisions by a governing body such as a board); and an accountability perspective (to foster support for the enterprise from external and internal stakeholders, including investors).

Specifically, the Demonstrating Value Process sets out the following steps.

Step 1: Information Mapping

In this step, stakeholders map out an *information blueprint* of their organization. This is a picture of what they do and want to do, as well as the information needs associated with managing, planning, and communicating the value of their work. This mapping work includes laying out:

- Who matters (the stakeholders) and what they need to know;
- A vision for better reporting;
- The goals of the organization;
- The activities that the organization is undertaking in order to achieve these goals, as well as the value these activities create for the business and in the community;
- Information that would be essential in knowing whether goals have been reached, whether activities are going well or need to be adjusted, and the value created by the organization. (This information should be prioritized where possible.)

Step 2: Assess Data Collection and Define Improvements

Once an organization has developed an *information blueprint*, it can then determine how it will meet its information needs. This includes defining key indicators and monitoring approaches in more detail, determining what the organization is already monitoring, and assessing what it could improve (or, in the case of a new organization, what systems should be developed). The focus should be on the priorities highlighted earlier and on the information that is going to be represented in the *performance snapshot*. Lastly, monitoring approaches and indicators should be prioritized and an action plan developed with clear timelines and responsibilities. The output of this process is called a *systems assessment and action plan*.

Step 3: Design Reporting

The organization designs a *performance snapshot* based on the specific information that it has identified in the *information blueprint*. A *performance snapshot* is a simple, visual way to present the performance and value of an organization to its boards, funders, investors, and staff. It shows the key information that people need in order to make informed decisions about their enterprise and manage its different business, social, environmental, or cultural goals. This integrated, comprehensive picture of how the organization is doing not only supports the enterprise in seeing the trade-offs and synergies of different goals but also helps stakeholders to see the value that the enterprise creates in their community. (An example of a *performance snapshot* is available on the following website: http://www.demonstratingvalue.org.)

Designing a *performance snapshot* is not about developing another report. It is about developing a management and communication tool that the organization can use on an ongoing basis to make better decisions and to engage stakeholders in the issues that matter. The design process takes some upfront work to consider what the *performance snapshot* will look like, what will be included, and how it is going to be used.

Step 4: Implement Monitoring and Reporting

In this step, the organization improves data collection by streamlining and improving existing systems (such as accounting systems, record keeping, surveying, data management, etc.) and developing new ones. These are undertaken according to the key priorities outlined in the organization's *systems assessment and action plan*. At the same time, they will develop a *performance snapshot* and implement it in MS Word, MS Excel, or reporting software such as SAP Crystal Dashboard Design. Once launched, the *performance snapshot* can be integrated into meetings and used to inform and report to the organization's different stakeholders on a regular basis. It can start simply and be developed in depth over time.

Investor Lens – Guidance to Investor Organizations

The investor participants at the October 2008 workshop discussed whether and how they could adjust their reporting demands to be more harmonized with each other. There was a strong willingness among the participants to do this, though this will more difficult for some investors than others. Investors felt that one way to achieve this greater harmony would be through the development of a common performance report, which the social enterprise would develop primarily for its own management, planning, and communication needs.

The participants felt that it was important for the social enterprise's own information to drive the development of good monitoring and reporting systems within the enterprise, and for investor's information needs to be based on this core information collection – this perspective can be seen as a kind of "lens."

The *Investor Lens* performance report template was developed for investor organizations to use in managing their social enterprise investments. The aim was to help investors gain useful information that would not only support their investment decisions but also their overall investment strategies, as well as supporting the social enterprise sector as a whole. The use of the template and the parallel development of monitoring and reporting capacity in social enterprises are both aimed at achieving greater consistency in reporting, improving the quality of information, and improving how information is used.

The template proposes common content areas and reporting formats that social enterprises can use to provide information to investors about their performance. It is not expected for all parts of the template to be relevant to every type of investment. The template distinguishes between results from a business perspective and those from a (social) mission perspective; separates objectives from results; distinguishes strategies from objectives; and suggests a classification scheme.

Lessons Learned and Next Steps

The overall objective of the Demonstrating Value Initiative was to move the social enterprise sector towards improved practices in performance and impact assessment, leading to improved stakeholder accountability and better sharing and communication of innovative practices, learning, and social value creation.

Was the initiative a success? What have we learned from the process? What else remains to be done? To answer these questions, we reflect on the direction taken in this initiative, the lessons learned so far, and the next steps in the process.

Early on in the initiative we made a decision not to focus the project on piloting the Social Return on Investment (SROI) methodology with Canadian social enterprises, even though this approach has garnered a lot of attention within this sector. Instead we chose to look systematically at challenges in the generation and use of information by social enterprises and their stakeholders, and to develop a framework that could address these challenges. The initiative adopted this focus for several reasons:

1. *Data Quality.* We found in our research (particularly informant interviews and participant workshops) that social enterprises and investors face many challenges in developing good monitoring and reporting systems to satisfy their basic information-related needs for operational, planning, and communication purposes. Organizations typically develop systems in a responsive and piecemeal fashion. Data quality improvement should be

the priority before delving into such realms as the monetization of social and environmental impact.

2. *Methodological Limitations and Uncertainty.* Although there is considerable interest and activity aimed at promoting the development of a standardized SROI methodology, key questions remain about the usefulness and integrity of an aggregate SROI indicator. This includes the method's inability to quantify and monetize many important outcomes, lack of clarity around cost perspectives, and a strong reliance on assumptions around discount rate, benefit period, and impact attribution and deadweight.

3. *Information Technology Advancements.* There are many new technological advancements that make it possible for small organizations to combine and publish information in engaging and interactive formats, even with relatively little financial investment and technical skill. For instance, by using reporting software (such as SAP Crystal Dashboard Design) and web publishing applications, diverse information formats such as images, video, figures, and databases can be combined in an interactive way and made available online. We felt it would be valuable to explore how these technologies could be applied to portray a spectrum of information for decision-making and transparency. So, rather than bringing social and environmental impact data into a financial metric, as in SROI, we found it would be more effective instead to succinctly combine financial metrics with other information formats.

Moving forward, there may be considerable potential for organizations in the social economy to use the Demonstrating Value Framework to improve the breadth and depth of their reporting, leading to improved stakeholder accountability as well as better sharing and communication of innovative practices, learning, and social value creation. Nevertheless, we can only do this by building on what we have learned from the initiative so far. We comment below on key challenges in this process and our perspectives on overcoming them.

Key Challenges and Possible Solutions

Ability of an Organization to Take on the Demonstrating Value Process and Work through It

Our experience so far with organizations using the Demonstrating Value Framework has shown that, while there is considerable enthusiasm and interest in mapping information needs, developing a performance snapshot, and improving monitoring systems, it can be difficult to manage this work and stay focused. The key reasons for this are limitations of staff time and resources, and in some cases technical challenges. In small organizations, single individuals are responsible for many duties, and pressing operational issues can easily delay the steps of this process. Also, staff turnover and vacant positions can create considerable delay. During the piloting, various levels of assistance were provided by project staff to facilitate use of the framework.

Some possible long-term solutions to this might be to improve the design of the Demonstrating Value Process by increasing its modularity so that it is less overwhelming; and by identifying manageable goals for the process. For instance, an organization with low technical capacity should seek to develop a performance snapshot as an MS Word document, and consider using reporting software only at a later stage.

In addition, it could also be beneficial to develop a technical assistance program to support social economy organizations that want to use the framework. This technical assistance would include facilitators that could help organizations to map an information blueprint and design a performance snapshot. Specialized technical expertise could also be brokered if required. This program would need to include the training of technical assistance providers as well as funding mechanisms to offset the cost of assistance to organizations.

Methodological Challenges in Measuring Social and Environmental Outcomes

While data in any area can be challenging to collect, mission-related outcome data are particularly difficult because outcomes often happen outside of an organization's direct operational sphere, and may occur within different time frames than the organization's intervention. Processes to access existing data in a government or private agency, or to collect new data, can be costly. In a resource-constrained setting, even learning about what methods and tools exist can be difficult. In the piloting process, we were able to help organizations to research methods and access data, but support is still needed for the long term.

In order to address this issue, more resources need to be developed that can support both the sharing of meaningful outcome data and the sharing of tools that can collect this data. In the Demonstrating Value Initiative we sought to develop a "Monitoring Ideas Library" to guide organizations to relevant data and tools. Given the resource constraints of the project, this library is currently limited to listing data sources and collection methods of interest to the pilot organization's mission areas. However, there is considerable potential to use Web 2.0 tools to further develop this library and to create a forum for organizations to share practices with one another.

Investor Demand for "Impact" from the Social Economy Organization They Fund

While there is considerable variation in what investors demand from organizations in applications and reporting, many ask for measurements of "impact" without being clear about what they are asking for, and they generally offer little guidance or support on how an applicant or investee might provide this information. This continues to be a challenge for many community-based organizations.

Some ideas for long-term solutions to this challenge include better education for investors about the state of impact assessment practices and methodologies, which will help them to ultimately receive better quality information about mission impacts; and the development of tools and support for investors to work out what they "want to know and show" about their investment support, as well as how they can best use the information they receive from those they are invested in. As more social enterprises and other social economy organizations develop performance snapshots and improve data quality, investors can learn more about what these organizations deem to be important and feasible to track about their business performance, social/environmental mission, and organizational sustainability. At the October 2008 workshop, investor participants were open to and interested in the idea of basing their information needs on what their investees themselves deemed important.

Next Steps

Since the completion of the framework development in 2009, Vancity Community Foundation has been working to disseminate the framework and foster its use by social enterprise operators and other organizations that support the sector. In order to move to improved practices, the initiative must build on this foundation and use the relationships and tools that have been developed. What follows is a brief summary of the important work that still needs to be done.

Development of a Support Program

Vancity Community Foundation is developing a program to support the use of the framework. This includes promoting the framework, maintaining and further developing the online learning program, and providing technical assistance. The technical assistance aspect of this program will address the challenges that some social enterprise pilots faced in terms of finding the time, resources, and expertise to identify and implement monitoring and reporting solutions. A key issue faced in developing this program was the question of how to fund it and make it accessible to social enterprises with limited resources (many of which would benefit greatly from receiving technical support).

Development of Tools That Are Specifically Geared to New Social Enterprises

The tool development was informed by social enterprises that were already established prior to this project. We believe that the framework and tools are applicable to the needs of new social enterprises as well. It would be valuable to test this assumption, and to adapt/develop new tools as necessary. A few different areas for this could be: (i) the integration of the conceptual framework into business planning tools; and (ii) the establishment of monitoring/reporting "packages," which new social enterprises could adopt, that would include financial accounting software, mission-related monitoring software (where applicable), and reporting software (like Crystal reports) with pre-established templates that are specific to social enterprise.

Keeping the Tools Up-to-Date and Fostering the Development of New Tools

The scope and technical sophistication of the tools already developed through the initiative reflect what could still be developed with the resources of the project. The initiative should foster the further development and refinement of these tools, ideally using an open-source model. Ideas for this process include the development of performance snapshot templates for social enterprises in specific lines of business and with specific types of missions. This project could begin with the social enterprise models that are more common (e.g., thrift stores, supportive employment) and progress to the less common models. Further development of indicators in the Monitoring Ideas Library is also important. This could include the identification of core indicators that are determined to be most important by the organization's stakeholders (i.e., social enterprises, investors, government). It could also include developing the database as a web-based application (it is currently run in Microsoft Access) and setting up the means for social enterprises and investors to contribute directly via a collaborative wiki. At minimum, the website needs to be maintained, and the resources listed in the tools section (particularly the Monitoring Ideas Library) need to be kept current.

Development of Mechanisms to Roll Up Information Provided by Individual Enterprises to More Aggregate Levels

The Demonstrating Value Initiative provides direction to help social enterprises develop monitoring and reporting systems using a common conceptual model. It also helps social enterprises to ask certain questions (about their performance and impact) and guides them to specific monitoring approaches and indicators that can be applied to respond to these questions (and which are unique to enterprises that work in different mission areas). At the same time, the Investor Lens template guides investors to request similar information from social enterprises.

   All of these elements will contribute to better sector data and information that can more readily be used for research and policy development. Additional work is needed to develop processes and tools that can aggregate data within and across organizations, and combine them with other data that are being developed on social, cultural, and environmental outcomes (for instance, community indicator projects like Vital Signs).

Exploration of the Relevance of the Demonstrating Value Framework beyond Social Enterprises

While the Demonstrating Value Framework was developed specifically for social enterprise, in presenting the framework we received many comments that it would be useful for other types of organizations, such as non-profit and public agencies or for-profit businesses. It would be valuable to explore the framework's relevance to these other organizations in more detail, including examining how the individual tools could be used or adapted, and whether other tools would need to be developed to make it relevant to these other actors in the social economy.

Conclusion

Between 2005 and 2009, the Demonstrating Value Initiative brought together a wide range of organizations involved in the social enterprise sector to address how the sector as a whole can move towards better practices in gathering and using information for understanding performance, impact, and value. This collaborative process represents an important contribution to the social accounting field, not only in the framework and tools that were developed but also in the method used for exploring and addressing accounting issues in the sector with different stakeholders. By bringing diverse stakeholders together and identifying the common objective of developing a strong social enterprise sector, it was more possible to look critically at the development and effective use of information from a systems perspective and to identify practical solutions for improving the quality and use of information within and between organizations. Key within this process was the recognition that, in order to move towards better information, it is critical to equip social enterprises with the tools and resources they need to tell their stories, empowering them with the process for defining, developing, and using information from which all stakeholders benefit.

APPENDIX 6.1: INITIATIVE PARTICIPANTS

Organization Name	Website
Social Enterprise Participants	
Compagnie F Café, Compagnie F, Entrepreneurship pour femmes	http://www.compagnie-f.org/
Eva's Phoenix Print Shop, Eva's Phoenix*	http://phoenixprintshop.ca/
Inner City Development	http://www.icdevelopment.ca
Landscaping with Heart, Coast Mental Health Foundation*	http://www.coastfoundation.com/CSEF/landscaping.html
Lawn and Garden Smart, Evergreen Foundation*	Company is no longer in operation.
My Sister's Closet, Battered Women's Support Services *	http://www.bwss.org/workers-activists/bwss-retail-program/

Organization Name	Website
Social Enterprise Participants	
Potluck Café and Catering, Potluck Café Society*	http://www.potluckcatering.com/
Raven Recycling*	http://www.ravenrecycling.org
StarWorks Packaging and Assembly, Developmental Disabilities Association	http://www.starworks.ca/
The Right Stuff, Greater Trail Community Skills Centre	http://www.communityskillscentre.com
Vancouver Island Providence Community Association	http://www.providence.bc.ca
British Columbia Technology Social Venture Partners (BC STVP)	http://www.bctsvp.com
Xa:ytem Interpretive Centre Sto:lo Heritage Trust Society*	http://www.xaytem.ca/
Investor Participants	
Coast Capital Savings Credit Union	http://www.coastcapitalsavings.com
Ecotrust Canada	http://www.ecotrust.ca
Edmonton Social Enterprise Fund (Edmonton Community Foundation/ City of Edmonton)	http://www.socialenterprisefund.ca
enterprising non-profits	http://www.enterprisingnonprofits.ca
Ontario Trillium Foundation	http://www.trilliumfoundation.org
Renewal2 Investment Fund, Renewal Partners	http://www.renewal2.ca
Réseau d'investissement social du Québec (RISQ)	http://www.fonds-risq.qc.ca/
Social Capital Partners	http://www.socialcapitalpartners.ca
Toronto Enterprise Fund	http://www.torontoenterprisefund.ca
Vancity (Vancity Credit Union and Vancity Community Foundation)	http://www.vancity.com
Western Economic Diversification Canada	http://www.wd.gc.ca

* These social enterprises piloted the framework.

NOTES

1 While no comprehensive data exist that specifically attest to the size of the social enterprise sector in Canada, activity around social enterprise is visibly growing. Examples include:
   - enterprising non-profits (enp), a technical assistance funding program, has grown from forty applications in 2003 to 122 applications in 2008, and has recently expanded to Toronto. (It is also exploring further expansion in Ontario and into Alberta, Saskatchewan, and Manitoba.)
   - The City of Edmonton and the Edmonton Community Foundation recently launched the Social Enterprise Fund.
   - A recent Summit on Social Enterprise in BC attracted 150 guests who were involved in or supporting mature social enterprises.
   - In stakeholder interviews in the development phase of the project, the nine investors contacted reported that they wanted to increase their level of investment in social enterprise.

2 For instance, the Rockefeller Impact Investing Collaborative (RIIC) recently reviewed impact measurement practices by "impact investors" (venture capitalists who want their investment to result in positive social impact as well as a financial return) and made recommendations for how these should be advanced. See Olsen and Galimidi (2008). This also has figured strongly in the development of public social enterprise support in the United Kingdom. See Office of the Third Sector (2006).

3 Individuals who have led or who are currently leading SROI related initiatives. This includes the Rockefeller Foundation, Hewlett Foundation, New Economics Foundation, SVT Consulting, London Business School, Glasses for Humanity, Scholten and Franssen, and Jed Emerson (independent).

4 La chaire de recherche du Canada en économie sociale (CRCÉS); L'Alliance de recherche universités -communautés en économie sociale (ARUC-ÉS); Réseau québécois de recherche partenariale en économie sociale (RQRP-ÉS). This is not a comprehensive list of all research organizations in Quebec involved in social economy research.

5 The categories were as follows: 1. Social Enterprise Management's Track Record; 2. Governance; 3. Human Resources; 4. Status; 5. Rationale for the Business and Concept Viability; 6. Social/Environmental Mission – General; 7. Social/Environmental Mission – Employment Enterprises; 8. Links to the Community; 9. Financial Status; 10. Quality of Assets; 11. Operations.

6 A management committee was developed to provide management guidance to the project lead who had been hired to develop the project. An

advisory committee was also established to guide the initiative with academic and professional expertise in social accounting, evaluation, Social Return on Investment (SROI) methods, cost-benefit analysis, and social enterprise development. The committee worked with the project lead to provide critical review and comment on specific outputs of the initiative.

REFERENCES

Armstrong, K. (2006). *Social enterprise impact assessment project stakeholder interviews.* Vancouver: Demonstrating Value Initiative, Vancity Community Foundation.

Broadhead, T. (2004, February). Grantmaking Leadership. Keynote address presented at Excellence in Grantmaking Workshop for Grantmakers and Funding Organizations at Calgary, AB. Retrieved January 10, 2007, from: http://www.mcconnellfoundation.ca/media/pdf/en/Grantmaking_Leadership.pdf

Clark, C., Rosenzweig, W., Long, D., & Olsen, S. (2004). Double bottom line project report: assessing social impact in double bottom line ventures methods catalogue. Berkeley, CA: Center for Responsible Business, University of California. Retrieved January 10, 2007, from: www.community-wealth.org/_pdfs/articles-publications/social/paper-rosenzweig.pdf

Earl, S., Carden, F., & Smutylo, F. (2001). *Outcome mapping: Building learning and reflection into development programs.* Ottawa: International Development Research Centre.

Emerson, J., Wachowicz, J., & Chun, S. (2000). Social return on investment: Exploring aspects of value creation in the non-profit sector. San Francisco: The Roberts Enterprise Development Fund. Retrieved January 10, 2007, from: www.redf.org/download/boxset/REDF_Vol2_8.pdf

Fry, L., Haklay, M., & Esterhuizen, L. (2007). Evaluating the impact of social entrepreneurs: From deductive to inductive methods. Presented at the Voluntary Sector Studies Network (VSSN) Conference 2007, Warwick, 5–6 September.

Global Leaders for Tomorrow. (2003). *Philanthropy measures up: Benchmarking philanthropy report.* Geneva, Switzerland: World Economic Forum.

Goldman Sachs Foundation and the Rockefeller Foundation. (2003). Social impact assessment: A discussion among grantmakers. New York. Retrieved January 10, 2007, from: www.riseproject.org/Social%20Impact%20Assessment.pdf

Hebb, T., Wortsman, A., Mendell, M., Neamtan, N., & Rouzier, R. (2006). *Financing social economy enterprises.* Ottawa: Carleton Centre for Community Innovation.

Human Resources and Social Development Canada (HRSDC). (2006). *Findings from human resources and social development Canada's cross-country policy dialogue on the social economy*. Ottawa: Human Resources and Social Development Canada.

Keystone. (2008). *Learning with constituents: A guide to identifying, documenting and analyzing evidence of impact (planned and unplanned), and learning from this in dialogue with constituents*. London: Keystone.

Kramer, M.R. (2005). *Measuring innovation: Evaluation in the field of social enterprise*. Prepared for the Skoll Foundation by Foundation Strategy Group.

Kramer, M.R., Graves, R., Hirschhorn, J., & Fiske, L. (2007). *From insight to action: New directions in foundation evaluation*. Boston: Foundation Strategy Group.

Nicholls, J. (2007). *Why measuring and communicating social value can help social enterprise become more competitive*. London: Cabinet Office, Office of the Third Sector.

Office of the Third Sector. (2006). *Social enterprise action plan: Scaling new heights*. London: U.K. Cabinet Office.

Olsen, S., & Galimidi, B. (2008). *Impact measurement approaches: Recommendations to impact investors*. Social Venture Technology Group. San Francisco: The Rockefeller Foundation.

Paton, R. (2003). *Managing and measuring social enterprises*. London: Sage Publications.

Réseau d'investissement social du Québec (RISQ). (2005). *Guide for analysis of social economy enterprises (Guide d'analyse des entreprises d'économie sociale)*. Montreal: RISQ.

Scholten, P., Nicholls, J., Olsen, S., & Galimidi, B. (2006). *Social return on investment: A guide to SROI analysis*. Amstelveen, Netherlands: Lenthe Publishers.

Shah, H. (2003). "Needs analysis: key findings quality and impact project." Draft. Social Enterprise Partnership (GB) Ltd. Led by New Economics Foundation, London, UK.

Snibbe, A.C. (2006). Drowning in data. *Stanford Innovation Review*, 9–45.

Social Enterprise Partnership (GB) Ltd. (2004). *Briefing note quality and impact project*. London: Led by New Economics Foundation.

Social Enterprise Partnership (GB) Ltd. (2003). *Needs analysis – key findings quality and impact project*. London: Led by New Economics Foundation.

Standing Committee on Human Resources, Social Development and the Status of Persons with Disabilities. (2006). Evidence Number 39, Unedited Copy.

Twersky, F., & B.T.W. Consultants. (2002). *An information oasis*. San Francisco: REDF.

7 Measuring the Performance of Convention and Visitors Bureaus

TIMOTHY J. TYRRELL AND ROBERT J. JOHNSTON

Convention and Visitors Bureaus (CVBs) are nonprofit organizations initially created to represent tourism accommodations for the purpose of generating overnight tourist visits to the area (Gretzel et al., 2006). In their original roles, they provided information about a destination's lodging, dining, attractions, events, arts, culture, history, and recreational opportunities to visitors and potential visitors. This role was summarized by Gartrell (1988): "CVBs have one fundamental mission: to solicit and service conventions and other related group business and to engage in visitor promotions, which generate overnight stays for a destination, thereby enhancing and developing the economic fabric of the community" (p. 10).

CVBs in the United States are considered a special type of Destination Marketing Organization (DMO). As such, they are expected to play multiple roles and coordinate a wide range of activities within the destination (Wang, 2008). These may include operating one or more visitor centres, managing a convention centre, and conducting tourism sales marketing programs. According to a 2007 survey by Destination Management Association International (DMAI), the world's largest association of destination marketing organizations, DMOs spend almost half (48 per cent) of their budget on sales and marketing efforts, with media advertising the top activity (18 per cent of total expenses). The remainder is spent on personnel (39 per cent) and administrative expenses (13 per cent) (DMAI, 2007). Although they provide information to tourists directly and planned packages to conference attendees indirectly through meeting planners, the CVB's traditional clients have been tourism industry members. The CVB board of directors, unpaid and without shares of ownership in the CVB, are typically elected by the CVB membership and primarily beholden to the tourism industry.

The role of CVBs is expanding. As populations have grown and stakeholders have become more numerous, CVBs have gradually transitioned to institutions that influence and organize destination governance (Beritelli, Bieger, & Laesser, 2007, p. 106), typically "through a process of collaboration, cooperation and leadership and through finding a common understanding" (Padurean, 2010, p. 198). That is, they have adopted a broader set of responsibilities that includes a more central governance role. As the CVB's role has expanded, it has taken on the tasks of policymaking, quality control, safety, security, and a myriad of other services to visitors and residents. Reflecting this change, since the 1990s the term "Destination Marketing Organization" has gradually been replaced by "Destination Management Organization" (Perdue, Tyrrell, & Uysal, 2010). Initially, this change was paired with an increased public relations emphasis on contributions by the DMO to the qualities of host communities as destinations for tourists. Increasingly, however, DMOs – as recipients of public funds – are expected to demonstrate their contributions to communities as places where people live, thereby enhancing social welfare.

These changes are now reflected in the official positions of organizations representing DMOs and CVBs. For example, the Destination Marketing Association International (DMAI), whose mission is to "enhance the professionalism, effectiveness, and image of destination marketing organizations worldwide" (DMAI, 2010, p. 1), acknowledged the importance of the wider range of community stakeholders at its 2008 DMAI Annual conference. This included a "New Strategic Map" for Destination Marketing which included "a reconceptualization – or at least a clarification – of the potential role and contribution of DMOs to the destinations they serve." Two of its eight conference themes emphasized this changing mission:

> The Quest for Relevance – DMOs continue to face confusion and uncertainty on the part of their local governments, stakeholders and partners regarding their role and the value the DMO offers. DMOs must be a part of the strategic conversation that drives important decisions about the development of the community.
>
> Mixed Signals from Government – Governments are increasingly imposing taxes, laws and other restrictions upon travel-related commerce.

DMOs must advocate shared solutions that balance economic, ecological, social and political benefits for all involved. (DMAI, 2008, p. 3)

Meeting these ambitious goals will require CVB performance measurements that do more than justify operating performance. The success of CVBs has traditionally been measured by visitor expenditures generated by their operations. While visitor expenditures have been critical to the growth of the industry, performance measures based on *gross* industry revenues do not reflect profits earned, nor the full breadth of the consequences of CVB activities, particularly given the broader roles of CVBs as community-development and destination governance organizations. In addition to traditional measures of performance, the new, broader expectations of CVBs requires that performance be evaluated using broader *net* measures of social, economic, and environmental performance, preferably denominated in comparable units so that tradeoffs may be quantified. The lack of a broadly accepted mechanism to simultaneously evaluate these divergent areas of performance has led CVBs and others to adopt measures that do not allow for a meaningful comparison of progress in different areas.

The relevance of effective performance metrics extends beyond the perceived success and continued public support for CVBs. Effective governance must be capable of adapting to changes in complex social systems (Ostrom, 1999). Adaptation, in turn, requires accurate feedback to governing agents about the consequences of their behaviour in the context of the behaviour of others (Holland, 1995). An iterative cycle of feedback and adaptation drives change in social systems. The efficiency of the system, however, requires meaningful, comprehensive feedback. Hence, as CVBs increasingly adopt broader governance roles, their ability to advance (rather than hinder) social development depends on a useful way to gauge and contrast performance in economic, social, and environmental arenas.

Responding to this need, this chapter introduces a social accounting model using *total value* as a basis for evaluating the performance of the CVB, where these values are measured from the perspectives of tourists, the tourism industry and host community residents. The proposed model is grounded in a theoretical model and empirical data that establish a systematic linkage between each performance measure and benefits to each stakeholder group. Measures such as the ones proposed here can provide important information not captured by traditional measures to the CVB, tourism industry planners, and community poli-cymakers. In addition, results can be used for documenting local prog-ress towards sustainability goals of the tourism industry and its CVB.

The CVB as a Non-profit Organization

The large majority of CVBs are independent not-for-profits: 56 per cent of DMOs surveyed by DMAI are 501(c)(6) business leagues; 19 per cent are government agencies; 8 per cent are 501(c)(3) religious, charitable, educational organizations; and 5 per cent are a chamber of commerce or a division of a chamber (DMAI, 2007).[1] The tax exemption for busi-ness leagues has existed since 1913, with substantive changes in 1928 and 1954 (Brittain & Crotty, 1976, p. 629). The current Section 501(c)(6) of the Internal Revenue Code IRS Code (IRS, 2010) gives tax exemptions to business leagues and chambers of commerce that are not organized for profit. These organizations are not mandated to provide public services directly to residents, but rather, "a business league's activities must be devoted to improving business conditions of one or more lines of busi-ness" where "the term *line of business* generally refers either to an entire industry or to all components of an industry within a geographic area." CVBs are generally regarded as a type of chamber of commerce where "the principal distinction between a business league and a chamber of commerce is that the former must promote the common business inter-ests of persons within a line of business, while the latter must promote the common business interests of persons within a community or simi-larly defined geographic area" (Hopkins, 2006, p. 50).

CVBs and chambers of commerce generally fall under NTEE codes S01 and S30[2] within 501(c)(6) Community Improvement & Capacity Building.

> Alliances & Advocacy Organizations, whose activities focus on influenc-ing public policy within the Community Improvement, Capacity Building major group area. This category includes a variety of activities from public education and influencing public opinion to lobbying national and state legislatures. (NTEE code S01)
>
> Economic Development: Organizations, whose primary purpose is to stimulate the economy, expand employment opportunities, encourage the establishment and growth of commerce and industry and otherwise en-hance the economic development of the community. (NTEE code S30)

A business league does not have to pay income taxes, may be given preferential postage rates, is allowed to accumulate income from members for improvements, and may avoid state tax audits. On the other hand, it is open to scrutiny by the IRS (Brittain & Crotty, 1976, p. 641). "Nonprofit corporate law provides that the business league organization is 'managed by or under the direction of' the board of directors, without saying much at all about the board's core functions (or the functions of officers, or the relationship between the board and management)" (Brody, 2007, p. 523). "(T)he law generally leaves governance issues to the organization, viewing the extent of the members' rights (if any) as part of what they have agreed to join" (Brody, 2002, p. 856).

"The purpose of (the (c)(6)) exemption is to encourage the development of business leagues to promote the public welfare by improving the business conditions of an industry" (Brittain & Crotty, 1976, p. 628). However, "(t)he policy reasons underlying (the (c)(6)) exemption have not been well articulated ... it may be presumed that Congress believed – and continues to believe – that these organizations provide sufficient community and public benefits to warrant exemption" (Hopkins, 2006, p. 9).

On the one hand, 501 (c)(6) organizations cannot be expected to abandon their purpose: "While the borders between the nonprofit sector and both the business and governmental sectors have always been blurry, the fact that a nonprofit organization has received either corporate status or tax exemption does not render it a state actor" (Brody, 2002, p. 889). "On the other hand, in the past, the IRS has denied tax exempt status to organizations whose primary purpose was to advertise for its members (1943, 1948), conduct a cooperative multiple listing service for its members (1963), and conduct a telegraphic delivery service and clearing house for its members (1942)"(Brittain & Crotty, 1976, p. 640).

While the duties of the nonprofit organization require that it serve the "public purpose" or "quasi public purpose" (Brittain & Crotty, 1976, p. 634), the question, "Who is this public?" remains unanswered. "A nonprofit organization frequently has multiple 'stakeholders,' all of whom seek to speak for the organization and its purposes" (Brody, 2007, p. 526). Since even the purposes of a charitable nonprofit organization may not coincide with "the public interest" (Brody, 2007, p. 526), it is not unreasonable to suspect that the purposes of the CVB may not always align with those of its principal stakeholders: tourists, tourism businesses, and the host community's population.[3]

Traditional CVB Performance Measures

The purpose of the CVB Performance Reporting Handbook developed by DMAI in 2005 (a revision was released in May 2011)[4] is "to guide the CVB through the process necessary to implement actionable and credible performance reporting." It cautions the reader that "(t)hroughout the implementation process, two questions should be asked on a regular basis: 'Are we measuring the *right things*?' and 'Are we measuring the *things right*?'"

The handbook ultimately "recommends that CVBs use standard business ROI approaches to quantify its [*sic*] financial impact on its [*sic*] local community for convention and leisure" (DMAI, 2005, p. 40). ROI (Return on Investment) formulas are described for each of the four primary functions of the CVB (convention sales, travel trade, marketing and communication, and visitor information centre) with measured *return* illustrated by visitor spending and measured *investment* illustrated by the functional expenditures that generate that spending.[5]

$$\frac{\text{Visitor spending Generated by the CVBs Efforts}}{\text{Total CVB operating costs}} = \text{ROI(Gross,Market,Overall)}$$

This measures *gross, market-valued, overall benefits* generated by the CVB in relation to CVB operating costs. The text indicates that there may be variations on measures of *return* and *investment*:

> For a CVB, the amount of return is typically what the CVB returned to the destination (visitor spending, economic impact, tax dollars), *clearly and significantly generated* through its sales and marketing efforts. The amount of investment can also vary, based on which stakeholder is requesting the information. (p. 40)

These measures, while reflecting dollar flows at least arguably generated by CVB investments, do not reflect the *net benefit*[6] that CVB activities provide to the public. Put another way, while ROI may be a *right way* to measure narrowly defined economic impacts of a CVB, the list of *right things* needs to be expanded and at least partially redefined if the CVB is to become a "part of the strategic conversation that drives important decisions about the development of the community" (DMAI, 2008, p. 3). When considering both *return* and *investment*, each should reflect a more comprehensive, *total value*[7] perspective including environmental, social, and economic benefits and costs to each stakeholder. The purpose of this chapter is to provide a theoretical basis for performance measures based on *total values*. For simplicity, we consider benefits realized by three major stakeholders: the tourism industry, tourists, and local residents.

Total Value CVB Performance Measures

It is well established that social welfare (benefits) is generated both by market goods and services, and by goods, services, and community quality of life amenities that are not exchanged in organized markets. The latter are often grouped under the broad heading of nonmarket goods (Freeman, 2003; Holland et al., 2010). Accordingly, CVBs can influence community welfare through changes in market outcomes (e.g., tourist expenditures) as well as nonmarket outcomes (e.g., environmental quality, local arts and culture). Two related approaches to measuring value – or the return of social investments in a CVB – are the *market value* approach and the *total value* approach. For a broad discussion of the difference between market and total value approaches to policy analysis, see Holland et al. (2010, chapter 2). Simply put, the former measures the impacts only as they are realized in measurable market transactions; benefits or costs realized outside of traditional markets are ignored. The latter approach includes the broader perspective proposed here, measuring benefits or costs whether or not they involve market activities. Unlike traditional measures of CVB performance, appropriately valued market and nonmarket outcomes generally differ across stakeholder groups, reflecting the different net benefits the CVB activities provide to each group. The proposed total value, net benefit measures, in contrast, seek to measure influences on stakeholders' welfare that account for combined net market and nonmarket benefits to each stakeholder separately.

What should be included in total value, net benefit performance measures? Traditional ROI measures used by CVBs, as shown above in the DMAI handbook, illustrate the application of a relatively narrowly defined market-valued, gross benefits approach. As such, they overlook large areas of potential benefit, and possibly cost, related to CVB activities, and are poor measures of the benefits received by CVB stake-holders. Visitor spending, for example, does not reflect a net value to anyone, not even to the industry, and is a poor basis for a performance measure. Recognizing the shortcomings of existing performance measures, the following sections propose alternative measures that might be used to quantify the net benefits of CVB activities.

Net Benefits to the Tourism Industry

Tourist expenditures (average or total) are a typical measure of the market value of tourist visits to a particular destination. This is an important measure of gross returns that drives tourism industry investments in the community, under the assumption that increased sales revenues will translate into increased profits. The net benefits to the tourism industry are profits, however, not gross revenues. A corresponding net measure of industry returns would therefore subtract from these gross benefits the costs of production required to serve visitors. Accordingly, the net benefits to industry that should be included in the CVB net performance measure for this stakeholder group are profits (benefits minus costs) that are "clearly and significantly generated" by the activities of the CVB.[8] Nonmarket benefits such as the value of a better business environment could also be added to profits if measureable. The ROI to the public related to tourism industry benefits would be the ratio of those net benefits to the investment made by the community in the CVB. This investment could be measured by revenues and in-kind contributions, such as membership dues and the lodgings taxes collected, plus the value of volunteer hours and in-kind contributions made to the CVB. Alternatively, we could measure the investment by the operating costs of the CVB plus any nonmarket costs to the public. While such details could be specified in any comprehensive guide to performance measure calculation, the general concept is straightforward. In its simplest form the tourism industry ROI would be:

$$\frac{\text{Industry Profits Generated by CVBs Efforts}}{\text{Total CVB Operating Costs}} = \text{ROI (Net, Total, Industry)}$$

This reflects the net value to the tourism industry generated by CVB efforts, divided by the CVB's operating costs.

Net Benefits to the Tourists

Tourism marketers are familiar with the concepts of "value proposition" and "perceived performance" from the tourist's perspective. While tourism businesses seek to maximize profits, tourists have different goals (e.g., McLellan, 1996; Uysal, 2003; Sirgy, 2010). The market expenditures related to a tourist visit is the amount that is spent before, during, and after the days spent in the destination. The net total value of a tourist visit, in contrast, reflects the total perceived customer value of the visit (quantified in money terms) minus tourist expenditures. Economists often refer to this value as consumer surplus. That is, visitor expenditures do not reflect a "value" to tourist visitors, but rather a cost that is necessary in order to receive a valued tourism experience. The consumer surplus value generated by the CVB's efforts is not limited to surplus received by newly attracted visitors, but includes the extra enjoyment generated for all visitors to the destination clearly and significantly influenced by CVB's efforts. The denominator of the ROI calculation is again the investment made by the public, measured here simply by the operating costs of the CVB.

$$\frac{\text{Tourist Surplus Generated by CVBs Efforts}}{\text{Total CVB Operating Costs}} = \text{ROI (Net, Total, Tourists)}$$

This ROI ratio measures *Net, Total* benefits to *Tourists* in relation to total investments made by the community. The details of calculating tourists' consumer surplus could follow established methods as described by Freeman (2003) and Hanley and Barbier (2009), among others.

Net Benefits to Residents

The performance of the CVB from the perspective of community residents depends not only on the CVB's direct influence on residents but also its indirect influence through the impact of visitors and visitor industry activities.[9] Total values of these returns (benefits and costs) are reflected in the changes in social, cultural, and environmental aspects of the daily lives and well-being of residents (e.g., Akis et al., 1996; Mason & Cheyne, 2000; Mbaiwa, 2005). Because they include many nonmarket benefits and costs, these values must frequently be estimated as subjectively determined willingness to pay (WTP) rather than actual amounts paid.[10] Among the many nonmarket valuation methods, stated preference methods are best suited to quantifying the many nonmarket values (positive or negative) to local residents associated with tourism activities; these involve analysis of responses to survey questions that reveal information about values and WTP (Freeman, 2003; Hanley & Barbier, 2009). These values are often challenging to estimate – stated preference surveys require substantial attention to development and testing in order to provide valid results, particularly considering the many paths through which tourism activities may directly or indirectly influence local quality of life. However, since this ROI measure gauges the degree to which the CVB serves the general public, it may also be the most important performance measure of the three. Returns or benefits to local residents will include both market and nonmarket values. Market values of benefits generated by CVB (wages, salaries, and business profits) may, however, be offset by market and nonmarket costs. Nonmarket costs, for example, might include costs (losses in social welfare) related to the environmental damage caused by tourism activities.

Considering all of these market and nonmarket values (positive or negative), the ROI related to local resident impact is given by:

$$\frac{\text{Total Residential Value Generated by CVBs Efforts}}{\text{Total CVB Operating Costs}} = \text{ROI (Net, Total, Residents)}$$

This ROI ratio measures *Net, Total* benefits to *Residents* in relation to the total investments made by the community in the operations of the CVB.

Aggregate Net Benefits

The aggregate net benefits generated by the CVB can be measured by the sum of net benefits over the three stakeholder groups. Furthermore, the aggregate ROI can be measured by the ratio of that sum to total public investment.

$$\frac{\text{Industry Profits} + \text{Tourist Surplus} + \text{Residential Value Generated by CVBs Efforts}}{\text{Total CVB Operating Costs}}$$
$$= \text{ROI (Net, Total, All Stakeholders)}$$

This represents an ROI measure that reflects a more comprehensive perspective on the total net values generated by CVB activities. The ability to disaggregate this measure into effects on industry, tourists, and residents, moreover, provides an ability to assess who benefits most through investments in the CVB, and where improvements might be needed.

Example of Total Value Performance Measures

To illustrate the application of these proposed performance measures, consider the total values of changes held by three stakeholder groups caused by the activities of a hypothetical CVB. The illustration draws on an example used in the DMAI *Performance Reporting Handbook* (DMAI, 2005, p. 45), extended to include costs and nonmarket benefits. As stated in the DMAI example, "The Harmony Convention & Visitors Bureau's operating costs in 2003 were $4.0 million … [and it] was able to identify $150.5 million in visitor spending that was clearly and significantly generated by its sales and marketing efforts."

The Return on Total Operating Costs, the overall measure of financial performance by the Harmony CVB per dollar spent, is computed as[11]

$$\frac{\text{Visitor Spending Generated by the CVBs Efforts}}{\text{Total CVB Operating Costs}} = \frac{\$150.5 \text{ million}}{\$4.0 \text{ million}} = 37.6$$

This calculation is based on visitor spending, a gross market value of performance. It does not reflect the costs to CVB stakeholders, nor does it account for nonmarket values. As noted above, this measure does not reflect net benefits realized by any group served by the CVB.

To extend the example, let us assume that the average cost of goods and services sold by the industry (including taxes paid) are 95 per cent of revenues ($143 million), and that nonmarket benefits to the industry and nonmarket costs of CVB operations are as yet not quantified. So, the Harmony CVB is generating 1.9 dollars in tourism industry profits for every dollar of public investment.

$$\frac{\text{Industry Profits}}{\text{Total CVB Operating Costs}} = \frac{150.5 - 143.0}{4.0} = \frac{7.5}{4.0} = 1.9 = \text{ROI (Net, Total, Industry)}$$

The Harmony CVB should be proud of its service to the local indus-try, report it widely to gain industry support, and even consider raising membership dues. Nonmarket benefits to local business owners might increase the return and ROI, but nonmarket investment in volunteer hours gifted and in-kind services contributed would increase the public investment estimate, reducing the ROI. Such items will require special analysis[12] but should be kept in the ledger as recognition of their exis-tence and as a place saver for future economic research results.

Extending the example again, let us assume that the total value of visitor trips to Harmony is 10 per cent more than visitor expenditures and all trip expenditures are made in Harmony.[13] That is, tourist sur-plus of new visitors generated by CVB activities is 10 per cent of $150.5 million ($15 million). In actual applications this number could be calcu-lated using surveys of tourist visitors combined with economic valua-tion methods (Freeman, 2003; Hanley & Barbier, 2009; Holland et al., 2010). Furthermore, assume that the Harmony CVB has contributed to an increase of $2 million in tourist surplus to all visitors because of activities, which have improved the overall social and environmental amenities of the destination. Thus the total surplus to tourists gener-ated by the Harmony CVB is $17 million and the ROI to tourists from the public investment is 4.3. This ROI should serve as a measure of the satisfaction of visitors as it is influenced by the CVB operations. This measure could be linked to a detailed analysis of visitor satisfaction and tourism product quality in order to direct the CVB in its destina-tion development efforts.

$$\frac{\text{Tourist Surplus}}{\text{Total CVB Operating Costs}} = \frac{15.0+2.0}{4.0} = \frac{17.0}{4.0} = 4.3 = \text{ROI (Net, Total, Tourists)}$$

The third stakeholder in the performance of the Harmony CVB is the general public. Market values of returns to local residents will include only the portion of Harmony CVB-generated profits and wages that are paid to locals above the profits and wages that they might have earned elsewhere.[14] Let us assume that wages are 30 per cent of total visitor expenditures, 50 per cent of new wages and profits are returned to Harmony residents, and that opportunity costs are 90 per cent of both wages and profits.[15] This means that wages return $2.3 million to local residents ($150.5*0.3*0.5*0.1) and profits return $0.4 million ($150.5*(1–0.95)*0.5*0.1) in wage benefits to local residents.[16]

Other market-valued returns to residents include changes to the cost of living as influenced by local price increases or changes in property and sales taxes that result from activities of the Harmony CVB. Here we assume that 1 per cent of new local visitor expenditures, or $1.5 million, indirectly substitute for local property taxes in the cost of town services.[17]

Nonmarket returns to residents are an important addition to the market-valued returns.[18] Let us assume that the Harmony CVB actively preserves and enhances the cultural, historical, and natural resource amenities of the community as a destination.[19] Such investments benefit residents as well as tourists. Let us assume that according to a study made at a local university, Harmony residents benefit from these improvements just as they would have from a $1 million reduction in local taxes.[20] Let us also assume that the Harmony CVB directly and indirectly supports educational programs to industry employees valued at $1 million to local employees.[21] However, social costs to tourism development activities should be expected. Let us assume that Harmony streets and shopping areas are congested and certain public spaces reach capacity before local demands are met because of the large number of new visitors attracted. For this example, the cost of congestion to residents caused by the influx of visitors is valued at –$1.0 million. The total value of the return to the general public is therefore +$5.1 million and the ROI to local Harmony residents is 1.3. This suggests that residents are gaining the least of all stakeholders per dollar of public investment in the CVB. This might suggest that the Harmony CVB should expand its cultural and heritage preservation programs and local hiring practices, and seek to reduce the congestion caused by its new visitors.

$$\frac{\text{Total Residential Value}}{\text{Total CVB Operating Costs}} = \frac{2.3+.4+1.5+1+1-1}{4.0} = \frac{5.1}{4.0} = 1.3$$
$$= \text{ROI (Net, Total, Residents)}$$

Consequently the total ROI for the Harmony CVB can be given by:

$$\frac{\text{Industry Profits+Tourist Surplus+Residential Value}}{\text{Total CVB Operating Costs}} = \frac{7.5+17+5.1}{4.0}$$
$$= 7.4 = \text{ROI (Net, Total, All Stakeholders)}$$

This last result describes the overall performance of the CVB for the public based on net total values for each stakeholder. It can: (1) capture the impact of a wide range of CVB activities, (2) account for the many dimensions of market and nonmarket values, (3) value these outcomes according to different stakeholders, and (4) present results in a way that can be understood by non-expert policy makers.[22] While this is not the only way that a performance measure might be structured to reflect broader social values, it demonstrates a relatively straightforward mechanism through which the standard ROI concept could be adapted to reflect new, broader expectations of CVBs within the communities they serve.

Conclusions

There is currently a disconnect between the broader social contributions increasingly expected of CVBs and the narrow focus of current CVB performance measures. Simple financial measures and economic indicators are no longer sufficient.[23] This chapter proposes a new perspective towards CVB performance reporting based on measurements of total net benefits to different stakeholder groups. This is presented as a novel way to measure the performance of CVBs from a more comprehensive social value perspective. A simple example illustrates how ROI measures may be calculated and used to assess performance. This example demonstrates how the proposed performance measures reveal different conclusions about performance for each of three stakeholder groups, and suggests ways in which adjusted performance measures can both quantify overall performance and identify areas for potential improvement.

The proposed methods are not the only ways that one might adapt CVB performance measures to provide a more comprehensive and appropriate perspective on social contributions. Moreover, adoption of the proposed measures would require greater attention to performance reporting than is currently required for the calculation of measures based solely on simple economic and financial indicators. The proposed measures require applications of empirical methods that – while well-established in economic research – are largely unfamiliar to CVB staff. Hence, transition to the proposed measures would not be without cost or effort. In return, the resulting measures would provide much greater utility and information.

The proposed measures can be used to evaluate new CVB projects as well as changes in existing businesses' activities. They can also be used to focus the attention of tourism professionals and community leaders on private-public collaborations. Travel industry businesses and CVBs rarely report or get credit for many of their social and environmental contributions, often because they are not easily measured. These measures will allow the CVB and tourism businesses to document their contributions to community qualities of life and progress towards "sustainable tourism" goals for each stakeholder group,[24] while permitting stakeholders to hold the CVB responsible for negative consequences of uncontrolled tourism growth. Overall, it is our hope that the development and application of such improved performance measures will make a valuable contribution to the "strategic conversation that drives important decisions about the development of the community" (DMAI, 2008, p. 3).

NOTES

1 It is interesting that unlike a 501(c)(3) organization, a 501(c)(6) organization may "engage in an unlimited amount of lobbying provided that the lobbying is related to the organization's exempt purpose" (Reilly & Allen, 2003, p. 2).

2 The National Taxonomy of Exempt Entities system is used by the IRS to classify non-profit organizations.

3 There are of course other stakeholders, some of whom might be subcategories of the three: for example, vendors, labour unions, government agencies, tourism industry employees, and investors.

4 The new version is based on the 2005 edition with new definitions and metrics for digital marketing (DMAI, 2011).

5 Ratios have long been used to measure corporate social performance (Dierkes & Preston, 1977, p. 14) and to measure portions of total effects in Social Accounting Matrices (Defourny & Thorbecke, 1984, p. 32). The ratio of outgoing resources to incoming resources (Social Return on Investment) has been well established as a measure of an organization's productivity and stewardship of resources (Richmond, Mook, & Quarter, 2003, p. 311).

6 The difference between a gross benefit measure and a net benefit measure is that the former reflects benefits only, without accounting for any related costs. The latter reflects gross benefits minus costs.

7 The term "value" is used here as defined in economics. As described by Bockstael et al. (2000), "in economics, [value relates] to human welfare. So, the economic value of [something] relates only to the contribution it makes

to human welfare, where human welfare is measured in terms of each individual's own assessment of his or her well-being." Economic values reflect the well-being of one or more individuals, such that the economic
value of a good or service is defined by the amount of compensation (positive or negative) that an individual would need to receive in order to be
as well off (by her own reckoning of well-being) as she would have been
without that good or service. This is often termed willingness to pay, or
WTP (Holland et al., 2010).

8 These could be estimated as the product of the average industry profit rate
and sales revenues clearly and significantly generated by the activities of
the CVB.

9 Although CVBs are assuming greater responsibilities for destination governance, they have little direct control over most of the products they
represent or the packages offered by intermediaries (Pike, 2004, p. 4).
Therefore, their influence on the community is largely felt indirectly
through tourism industry member activities.

10 Willingness to pay reflects the maximum amount (typically of money) that
an individual would be willing to give up in order to obtain something
(e.g., a good or service), rather than go without that thing.

11 In the DMAI handbook example, visitor spending and operating costs
were broken out by four functional areas: convention sales, travel trade,
marketing and communication, and visitor information centre. For our
purposes we are considering only the CVB's total performance.

12 Fortunately, economics provides established theories and mechanisms that
allow the evaluation of total values through individuals' willingness to
pay (WTP) (Freeman, 2003). This allows broader impacts on environmental, social, and economics outcomes to be quantified – and related tradeoffs
assessed – using the same types of money measures traditionally used to
measure market impacts.

13 Such estimates can be made from specially designed visitor surveys. Bhat
(2003), for example, estimated current consumer surplus for trips to the
Florida Keys to be $463 per trip, compared to total trip expenditures of
$900 per person per day.

14 The benefits are the incremental wages and profits – the totals minus their
opportunity costs.

15 Opportunity costs are analogous to costs of production for industry and
depend on the alternatives that are available to workers and investors. One
indication of the lack of opportunities for workers is the level of underemployment. A recent Gallup poll suggests underemployment reached 20 per
cent in 2010 (http://www.gallup.com/poll/126821/underemployment-hits-
20-mid-march.aspx).

16 See Boardman et al. (2006) for a broader discussion of the calculation of such wage benefits.

17 Evidence of this was found in Tyrrell and Johnston (2009).

18 Our analysis does not distinguish between nonmarket use values (such as the examples used in the text) and nonmarket nonuse values (option values for things that might be used one day, plus existence values for things that are beneficial in that they exist, even if they may not be used).

19 The Scottsdale CVB (Arizona), for example, has raised money to build a Desert Discovery Center that will educate residents and visitors about protecting the desert. The Blackstone Valley Tourism Council (Rhode Island) has invested heavily in the restoration of the Blackstone River from Providence, Rhode Island, to Worcester, Massachusetts.

20 Estimates can be made using standard approaches. Ecosystem Valuation (http://www.ecosystemvaluation.org) is a website that describes how to value changes in environmental quality. Navrud and Ready (2003) describe a measurement of the value of cultural heritage.

21 The Greater Phoenix CVB sponsored the BEST College program that funds a college internship program. Some local restaurants provide employment and training to newly released prisoners and half-way house residents.

22 "An analysis is useless, no matter how well it is conducted and regardless of how accurate its findings, if policy makers cannot both understand and explain the results" (Nagel & Teasley, 1998, p. 509).

23 In 2004 Diener and Seligman proposed that rigorous measurement should be a primary policy imperative and that "well-being needs to be assessed more directly, because there are distressingly large, measurable slippages between economic indicators and well-being" (p. 1).

24 The tourist is also more interested than ever before in the effects of his/her footprint on the local culture and environment. A TIA and National Geographic Society (2003) survey found that 61 per cent of American travellers prefer a destination that has protected its unique natural, historic, and cultural sites.

REFERENCES

Akis, S., Peristianis, N., & Warner, J. (1996). Resident attitudes to tourism development: The case of Cyprus. *Tourism Management, 17*(7), 481–94. http://dx.doi.org/10.1016/S0261-5177(96)00066-0

Beritelli, P., Bieger, T., & Laesser, C. (2007). Destination governance: Using corporate governance theories as a foundation for effective destination management. *Journal of Travel Research, 46*(1), 96–107. http://dx.doi. org/10.1177/0047287507302385

Bhat, M.G. (2003). Application of non-market valuation to the Florida Keys marine reserve management. *Journal of Environmental Management, 67*(4), 315–25. http://dx.doi.org/10.1016/S0301-4797(02)00207-4 Medline:12710920

Boardman, A.E., Greenberg, D.H., Vining, A.R., & Weimer, D.L. (2006). *Cost-benefit analysis: Concepts and practice* (3rd ed.). Upper Saddle River, NJ: Prentice Hall.

Bockstael, N.E., Freeman, A.M., III, Kopp, R.J., Portney, P.R., & Smith, V.K. (2000). On measuring economic values for nature. *Environmental Science & Technology, 34*(8), 1384–89. http://dx.doi.org/10.1021/es9906731

Brittain, V.K., & Crotty, R.W. (1976). Creation of tax-exempt business leagues: For the Section 501(c)(6) "First-Timer." *Washburn Law Journal, 16*, 628–54.

Brody, E. (2007). The Board of Nonprofit Organizations: Puzzling through the gaps between law and practice. *Fordham Law Review, 76*(2), 521–66.

Brody, E. (2002). Entrance, voice and exit: The constitutional bounds of the right of association. *U.C. Davis Law Review, 35*(4), 821–902.

Defourny, J., & Thorbecke, E. (1984). Structural path analysis and multiplier decomposition within a social accounting matrix framework. *Economic Journal, 94*(373), 111–36. http://dx.doi.org/10.2307/2232220

Destination Marketing Association International (DMAI). (2005). *Standard CVB performance reporting: A handbook for CVBs*. Washington, DC: Destination Marketing Association International. Retrieved February 11, 2011, from: http://www.destinationmarketing.org/images/pdf/PerformanceReporting-Handbook_2005.pdf

Destination Marketing Association International. (2007). *Profile of a destination marketing organization*. Washington, DC: Destination Marketing Association International. Retrieved February 11, 2011, from: http://www.destination-marketing.org/images/pdf/DMO_Profile_2007.pdf

Destination Marketing Association International (DMAI). (2008). *Placemaking and tourism*. Conference Program, Las Vegas, NV, July 27. Washington, DC: Destination Marketing Association International.

Destination Marketing Association International (DMAI). (2010). *Introduction*. Washington, DC: Destination Marketing Association International. Retrieved February 11, 2011 from: http://www.destinationmarketing.org/destination_professionals/page.asp?pid=20

Destination Marketing Association International (DMAI). (2011). Standard DMO performance reporting: A handbook for destination marketing organizations (DMOs). Washington, DC: Destination Marketing Association International. Retrieved February 11, 2011, from:

http://webportal.destinationmarketing.org/Purchase/ProductDetail.
aspx?Product_code=bf2fa3e4-d2a1-e011-a887-0022191972a4

Diener, E., & Seligman, M.E.P. (2004). Beyond money: Toward an economy of
well-being. *Psychological Science in the Public Interest, 5*(1), 1–31. http://dx.doi.
org/10.1111/j.0963-7214.2004.00501001.x

Dierkes, M., & Preston, L.E. (1977). Corporate social accounting reporting for the physical environment: A critical review and implementation
proposal. *Accounting, Organizations and Society, 2*(1), 3–22. http://dx.doi.
org/10.1016/0361-3682(77)90003-4

Freeman, A.M., III. (2003). *The Measurement of environmental and resource values:
Theory and methods.* Washington, DC: Resources for the Future.

Gartrell, R.B. (1988). *Destination marketing for convention and visitor bureaus.*
Dubuque: Kendall/Hunt Publishing Company.

Gretzel, U., Fesenmaier, D.R., Formica, S., & O'Leary, J. (2006). Search-
ing for the future: Challenges faced by destination marketing organizations. *Journal of Travel Research, 45*(2), 116–26. http://dx.doi.
org/10.1177/0047287506291598

Hanley, N., & Barbier, E.B. (2009). *Pricing nature: Cost benefit analysis and environmental policy.* Cheltenham, UK: Edward Elgar.

Holland, J.H. (1995). *Hidden order: How adaptation builds complexity.* Reading,
MA: Addison-Wesley.

Holland, D.S., Sanchirico, J., Johnston, R.J., & Joglekar, D. (2010). *Economic
analysis for ecosystem based management: Applications to marine and coastal environments.* Washington, DC: RFF Press.

Hopkins, B. (2006). *The tax law of associations.* New York: John Wiley & Sons.

Mason, P., & Cheyne, J. (2000). Residents' attitudes to proposed tourism
development. *Annals of Tourism Research, 27*(2), 391–411. http://dx.doi.
org/10.1016/S0160-7383(99)00084-5

Mbaiwa, J. (2005). The Socio-cultural impacts of tourism development in the
Okavango Delta, Botswana. *Journal of Tourism and Cultural Change, 2*(3),
163–85. http://dx.doi.org/10.1080/14766820508668662

McLellan, H. (1996). Evaluation in a situated learning environment. In H.
McLellan (Ed.), *Situated learning perspectives* (pp. 101–12). Englewood Cliffs,
NJ: Educational Technology Publications.

Nagel, S.S., & Teasley, C.E. (1998). Diverse perspectives for public policy. In J.
Rabin, W. Bartly Hildreth, & G. Miller (Eds.), *Handbook of public administration* (pp. 507–34). New York: Marcel Dekker.

National Geographic Society. (2003). *Travel watch. National Geographic traveler.*
Washington, DC: National Geographic Society.

Navrud, S., & Ready, R.C. (2003). *Valuing cultural heritage: Applying environmental valuation techniques to historic buildings, monuments and artifacts.*

Retrieved February 11, 2011, from: http://eh.net/book_reviews/valuing-cultural-heritage-applying-environmental-valuation-techniques-historic-building

Ostrom, E. (1999). Coping with the tragedy of the commons. *Annual Review of Political Science*, 2(1), 493–535. http://dx.doi.org/10.1146/annurev.polisci.2.1.493

Padurean, L. (2010). Implementing destination governance. In *Proceedings Think Tank X: Networking for sustainable tourism* (pp. 193–201). Vienna, Austria: MODUL University. Retrieved February 11, 2011, from: http://www.besteducationnetwork.org/ttx/pdf/Padurean.pdf

Perdue, R., Tyrrell, T.J., & Uysal, M. (2010). Understanding the value of tourism: A conceptual divergence. In D.G. Pearce & R.W. Butler (Eds.), *Tourism research: A 20–20 vision* (pp. 123–32). Oxford: Goodfellow.

Pike, S. (2004). *Destination marketing organizations*. New York: Elsevier.

Reilly, J.F., & Allen, B.A. (2003). Political campaign and lobbying activities of IRS 501 (c)(4) (c)(5), and (c)(6) organizations. *Exempt organizations – Technical instruction program for FY 2003*. Washington, DC: U.S. IRS. Retrieved February 11, 2011, from: www.irs.gov/pub/irs-tege/eotopicl03.pdf

Richmond, B.J., Mook, L., & Quarter, J. (2003). Social accounting for nonprofits: Two models. *Nonprofit Management & Leadership*, 13(4), 308–24. http://dx.doi.org/10.1002/nml.2

Sirgy, M.J. (2010). Toward a quality of life theory of leisure travel satisfaction. *Journal of Travel Research*, 49(2), 246–60. http://dx.doi.org/10.1177/0047287509337416

Tyrrell, T.J., & Johnston, R.J. (2009). An econometric analysis of the effects of tourism growth on municipal revenues and expenditures. *Tourism Economics*, 15(4), 771–83. http://dx.doi.org/10.5367/000000009789955134

Uysal, M. (2003). Satisfaction components in outdoor recreation and tourism settings. *E-Review of Tourism Research* 1. Retrieved February 11, 2011, from: *http://ertr.tamu.edu*

Internal Revenue Service (IRS). (2010). *Nonprofits*. Washington, DC: U.S. Internal Revenue Service. Retrieved February 11, 2011, from: http://www.irs.gov/charities/nonprofits/article/0,id=96107,00.html

Wang, Y. (2008). Collaborative destination marketing: Roles and strategies of Convention and Visitors Bureaus. *Journal of Vacation Marketing*, 14(3), 191–209. http://dx.doi.org/10.1177/1356766708090582

PART III

Moving Forward

8 Environmental, Ethical Trade, and Fair Trade Purchasing Policies: Some Challenges of Promoting Sustainability in Canadian Universities

J.J. MCMURTRY, JACQUELINE MEDALYE,
AND DARRYL REED[1]

The social missions of universities are generally associated with their three core functions: teaching, research, and service. In undertaking these tasks, members of the university community have historically engaged in a variety of practices (e.g., boycotts and divestment) that have intentionally sought to address pressing issues of social justice (e.g., the feminist and civil rights movements and anti-apartheid activism).

As the notion of "sustainable development" came to prominence in the 1980s, it is not at all surprising that universities were considered potentially key to its promotion very early on. While universities have generally come to embrace this role publicly, critics have argued that they have not always backed up their stated commitments, much less committed themselves to measuring their impact on sustainability. This lack of commitment to (and reporting on) sustainability issues not only relates to the core functions of the university, but also its auxiliary activities, such as investment and procurement policies.

This chapter examines the latter topic. It does so by examining the discourse and practice relating to the adoption of sustainable purchasing policies. The reason for this approach is that while few universities have adopted explicit social accounting practices, a significant number have adopted (or have considered adopting) purchasing policies that include items that are typically considered under a social accounting framework. To the degree that the latter have hard standards, they potentially provide some account of impact on university procurement practices, depending, of course, on the degree to which the policies are effectively implemented. In this chapter, we draw upon survey data and follow-up interviews with university procurement managers. We investigate both the extent to which Canadian universities have adopted sustainable purchasing policies (including ethical trade and fair trade policies) and the reasons underlying their decision to do so (or not), along with the experiences that they have had in trying to implement such policies. The chapter concludes with key findings and directions for future research, including some discussion of the importance of universities adopting social accounting measures.

Introduction – Universities and Sustainability

The Discourse on Sustainability

Sustainable development and the more general idea of sustainability are highly contested concepts. For our purposes, three events linked to the emergence and rise to prominence of the notion of sustainable development are key to understanding the nature of the disputes in question.[2] The first of these was the publication of the World Conservation Strategy (WCS) in 1980 (IUCN, 1980). Based on a discourse dating back to the early 1970s, this publication was primarily responsible for introducing the concept of "sustainable development." The second major event was the publication of the report of the World Commission on Environment and Development (WCED). More commonly known as the Brundtland Report – after the head of the Commission, former Norwegian Prime Minister Gro Harlem Brundtland – this document has provided the most widely cited definition of sustainable development: "development that meets the needs of the present without compromising the ability of future generations to meet their own needs" (WCED, 1987, p. 43). The third key development was the United Nations Conference on Environment and Development (UNCED) in 1992. More commonly known as the Earth Summit or the Rio Summit – after the host city – this event was at the time the largest ever meeting of heads of states in the world. It gave unprecedented publicity to the issues of the environment and development and popularized the term "sustainable development" to such an extent that its use is now *de rigueur* among NGOs, governmental bodies, other public institutions, and even the private sector.

What is significant about these three different events for our concerns is the fact that they represent three very different approaches to sustainable development: a conservation-centred, equity-centred, and growth-centred approach respectively (Reed, 2002). Each of these models offers distinct understandings of the notions of sustainability and sustainable development, the extent of the current crisis and its causes, and the strategies that should be pursued and the actors who should have the prime responsibility for promoting sustainable development. In the case of the WCS, sustainability is conceived of in terms of the physical environment, with conservation and the "sustenance" of ecosystems being the goal. The roots of the dire current problems can be traced back to industrialization (and overconsumption), especially as countries in the South seek to imitate the development paths of the North. Governments and development agencies are primarily responsible for developing "conservation-centered" strategies (including small scale and subsistence projects that draw upon traditional knowledge) in which socio-economic development is subjugated to the primary goal of conservation (Adams, 1990).

For the WCED, by contrast, the notion of sustainable development is decidedly more human-centred, with a focus on equity in the current North–South relations as well as our relationship to future generations. The current developmental, environmental, and security crises are understood as a reflection of the failure of states to ensure a just distribution of the world's resources; a resolution of the situation requires not an end to growth, but a redistribution in the rates of growth (and consumption) between North and South and structural change in the global economy, including more stringent international regulation. Finally, while there were sharply differing opinions represented at the Rio Summit, the final documents conceived of sustainable development primarily in terms of the ability to maintain growth levels in both developing and developed countries, with environmental degradation subordinated to economic growth. Current problems were understood as significant but manageable through education and technological development. Strategies consisted predominantly of multilateral agreements (e.g., the Kyoto agreement) and a reliance on self-regulation by business, along with approaches to ensuring bio-diversity and ecosystems that did not impinge in significant ways on the ability of businesses to continue to exploit the natural environment (e.g., setting off small pristine areas or maintaining the gene pool through the collection of specimens to preserved in gene banks) (Kirby et al., 1995).

While the discourse on sustainability has continued to evolve since the Rio Summit, the contested nature of the discourse has remained a constant. In many subsequent documents, however, such disagreements have been downplayed or papered over (e.g., by the use of

formal definitions of sustainability, such as that offered by the Brundtland Commission) to ensure a broad, though not very deep, consensus.
One place in which this has occurred is in documents relating to the
role of universities in promoting sustainability.

Declarations on Universities and Sustainability

The role of universities in promoting environmental sustainability, especially through their teaching function, has been recognized by multilateral bodies for some time. In 1972, for example, the United Nations
Conference on the Human Environment, sponsored by the United
Nations Educational, Scientific and Cultural Organization, issued the
Stockholm Declaration (UNESCO, 1972). Although it did not focus on
the practice of universities, the Stockholm Declaration is commonly
cited as the first document to highlight the importance of universities
in promoting sustainability. It is the Tbilisi Declaration, however, coming out of the 1977 Intergovernmental Conference on Environmental
Education, sponsored by UNESCO and United Nations Environment
Program (UNEP), which marks for many the starting point for formal
international environmental education initiatives (UNESCO-UNEP,
1977). A decade and a half later, the key document to come out of the
Rio Summit, Agenda 21, would base itself in the Tbilisi Declaration in
reaffirming the importance of the teaching role of universities in the
promotion of environmental education (Calder & Clugston, 2003a).

For their part, universities have gradually come to acknowledge the
variety of roles that they could and should play in the promotion of
sustainability, especially over the last two decades. Several international initiatives have been particularly influential. First, in 1990 the
president of Tufts University convened an international conference of
university leaders, which issued the Talloires Declaration. Proclaiming
that "universities' heads must provide leadership and support to mobilize internal and external challenges so that their institutions respond to
this urgent challenge," the document laid out a ten-point program and
challenged other institutions to join and work together for environmental sustainability (UNESCO, 1990, p. 2).[3]

The Talloires Declaration would serve as a spur to others. The Association of the University Leaders for a Sustainable Future (ULSF), a
U.S.-based organization, would come on board as the official registrar
for the Talloires Declaration. Not long after Talloires, the Conference of
European Rectors (CRE) – acting in response to the invitation issued

in chapter 36 of Agenda 21, but also referencing Tailloires – issued its own statement on sustainability (Copernicus Charter, 1994). It also initiated the Copernicus-Campus network, which would become an independent network in 1999. In 2002, the ULSF and Copernicus-Campus joined together with the International Association of Universities (IAU) and UNESCO to form the Global Higher Education for Sustainability Partnership (GHESP), a relationship which would last for five years before being disbanded (Wright, 2002; Calder & Clugston, 2003a).

Canadian universities have also taken up the call to sustainability, both individually and collectively. The initial step in developing inter-university collaboration within Canada was a conference on University Action for Sustainable Development organized in Halifax in 1991. Called in part as a response to the Talloires Declaration, participants reflected on the implications of Talloires for Canadian universities as well as the broader question of how universities can improve the capacity of countries to address issues of development and the environment. The resulting Halifax Declaration (Lester Person Institute for International Development, 1992) called upon universities to rethink how their environmental policies and practices could better contribute to sustainable development at local, national, and international levels. One of the novel aspects of the Halifax document was its Action Plan, which provided Canadian universities with a framework for action, including a series of short-term and long-term goals (Wright, 2002).

The Practice(s) of Sustainability in Universities

There are a variety of ways to delineate the roles and/or functions through which universities might contribute to the promotion of sustainable development (Clugston & Calder, 1999). For our purposes, it is sufficient to delineate two (broadly defined) primary roles of universities – teaching and research – along with two other areas of activity, operations and procurement, which are essential to fulfilling the primary roles. As noted above, teaching is the most strongly emphasized role of universities in international documents on sustainability. Chapter 36 of Agenda 21, for example, lays out a broad agenda by inviting universities and other educational institutions to reorient education towards sustainable development, increase public awareness, and promote training (UNCED, 1992). National and international documents issued by universities themselves, such as Talloires and the Halifax Declaration, further specify possible teaching functions, including activities such as incorporating sustainability issues across the curriculum, developing new programs of study, encouraging student environmental activism, engaging in public outreach, and so on (Calder & Clugston, 2003b).

While not mentioned by Agenda 21, research represents another key manner in which universities can contribute to sustainable development. Research into sustainability needs to incorporate fundamental and applied approaches as well as interdisciplinary perspectives and methods in order to contribute fully and effectively. Closely associated with the research function of universities are two other activities, public policy engagement and the commercialization of research. While public policy has long been viewed as an arena for engagement by universities, the issue of commercialization, especially the participation of large corporations with government and universities in triple-helix models, has become quite controversial. Critics are skeptical as to whether such involvement with the private sector, especially large corporations, is more likely to contribute to or discourage sustainable development (Reed, 2004). Such skepticism has led to calls for alternative triple-helix models, in which governments and universities collaborate with local social economy partners who have a proven history of concern for sustainable development (MacLeod, McFarlane, & Davis, 1997).

As mentioned above, in fulfilling their teaching and research functions, universities impact the environment and the prospects for sustainable development in two major ways. On the one hand, they have a direct impact on the environment through their physical operations, including such areas of policy and practice as building design and maintenance, energy consumption, land use, and transportation. The issue of operations has been a central concern during efforts to "green the university," and the site of a wide range of initiatives, many of which involve university members with participatory research and hands-on educational opportunities (Wright, 2010). A key issue that tends to arise is how universities are to manage their operations. More specifically, the question is whether they need to adopt environmental management systems, and if so, whether it is adequate to adopt approaches developed with corporate actors in mind (Bekessy, Samson, & Clarkson, 2007).

On the other hand, universities have a slightly less direct, but equally if not more significant impact on sustainability through their purchases of goods and services. There have been increasing demands on universities not only to purchase and offer for sale more environmentally friendly products (paper products, branded goods, food, etc.), but also to ensure full life cycle management of such products (e.g., through recycling, waste reduction and diversion programs). A key indicator of this pressure is the development of online evaluation methods, such as the Sustainable Endowment Institute's "College Sustainability Report Card" (http://www.greenreportcard.org/). In addition, universities have also come under pressure from ethical trade and fair trade movements to ensure that select products offered for sale (sportswear and other branded products, coffee, chocolate, etc.) are produced under conditions that are fair to workers and small producers (Ross, 2006). Universities in particular countries, under pressure from student activists, have taken the lead in meeting such standards. The two major U.S.-based labour rights certifying bodies, the Fair Labor Association (FLA) and the Workers Rights Consortium (WRC), have 208 (http://www.fairlabor.org) and 186 (http://www.workersrights.org) affiliated universities and colleges in the U.S. and Canada, respectively (this includes some overlap in membership among the two bodies). Meanwhile, the United Kingdom has taken the lead in the development of "fair trade universities," with more than 120 academic institutions of higher education meeting the standards for this designation (http://www.fairtrade.org.uk).

Accounting for Underperformance

While a significant proportion of institutions of higher education have publicly affirmed their commitment to promoting sustainability, progress towards this goal has been slow and uneven. As a number of studies have pointed out, signing declarations has not resulted in the creation of sustainable universities (Corcoran, Calder, & Clugston 2002; Bekessy, Samson, & Clarkson, 2007). In the case of Canadian universities, Wright (2002) reported that a decade after the launch of the Halifax Declaration, most of the signatories had not implemented it, while those that did had usually only incorporated the value statements into their own documents without adopting the action plan as the basis of their own university policy. In the literature, a variety of factors are mentioned that might account for the failure of universities in Canada and abroad to effectively take up the sustainability agenda (including the failure to adopt sustainable purchasing policies).

First, there is the question of *planning*. A number of authors point out that many universities have not generally planned for sustainability

(Sharp, 2002; Bekessy, Samson, & Clarkson, 2007). Rather, they have tended to rely upon raising awareness and a "club based" approach to change in which small groups (especially student groups) are encouraged to address specific aspects of sustainability and/or develop pilot or demonstration projects. While such an approach, critics argue, might achieve individual successes (e.g., establishing a recycling program or the erection of an individual green building), it does not provide a viable means for addressing the larger problems at hand (e.g., ensuring that all buildings meet appropriate environmental standards).

Second, there is the issue of *resources*, especially financial resources. Studies frequently point out that specific programs suffer from under-financing. Generally, the underlying cause of the lack of funding is not directly attributed, but the impression is sometimes given that it represents a lack of commitment on the part of universities to promoting sustainability (Thompson & Green, 2005). For their part, university presidents (in Canada, at least) also tend to see underfunding as the primary constraint on the promotion of sustainable universities, but they assert that the ultimate problem of underfunding comes from a lack of public financing for universities (as opposed to a lack of commitment on their part to sustainability) (Wright, 2010).

Third, there is the nature of the *structures* of contemporary universities. A number of authors have argued that, despite their pretensions to rationality, there are a variety of features of universities that make organizational learning difficult, and thereby inhibit the promotion of the transformational change that is required to address issues of sustainability effectively (Clugston & Calder, 1999; Sharp, 2002). More specifically, it is argued that the complexity of the institutions (and the environmental imperative itself), recent periods of extensive growth in universities, mental models of the organization (which hide dysfunctional behaviour), system archetypes (such as the myth of rationality), academic silos, and shifting coalitions make it extremely difficult for sustainability committees to achieve consensus on goals and possible solutions. It is this situation, Sharp argues, that leads to the tendency for universities "to shift their focus from broad reaching systemic transformation to well-bounded projects with lower levels of participation" (2002, p. 130).

Issues of *agency* represent another factor in accounting for underperformance. Several groups of actors are cited as being particularly relevant in this regard. First, while senior administrators are generally acknowledged as being key actors for successful implementation of sustainability initiatives, they are frequently seen as failing to provide effective leadership (Thompson & Green, 2005). Second, students –

because they often know very little about how university administrations work, generally feel disempowered, and spend only a few years on campus – tend to pursue smaller, more tangible projects (where a victory seems more feasible), rather than working for more systemic change (Sharp, 2002). Third, active resistance to sustainability initiatives is sometimes cited as a problem. Though the source of such resistance is not always clearly identified, the administrative staff would seem to be one group susceptible to such a charge (Wright, 2010). In addition to failings on the part of particular groups, some authors have pointed to the need for groups of actors to work together as an essential condition for effecting change (Sharp, 2002).

Ideology represents a fifth factor that can come into play with public sector institutions. Murray (2001) has pointed out, for example, that there has been a general tendency for public sector institutions to adopt management approaches (strategic management, purchasing policies, etc.) from the private sector. Transferral of private sector approaches in areas such as procurement, which do not take into account the different goals, mandates, and constraints of public sector institutions, can prove to be sub-optimal and even dysfunctional. Public sector institutions, Murray argues, must develop their own approach to developing procurement policies.

Finally, the *vision* or conceptualization of sustainability itself may be a limiting factor in its effective promotion. Newport, Chesnes, and Lindner (2003), for example, have argued that there has been a tendency to overemphasize the environment and to think of sustainability exclusively in terms of the "greening of universities," thereby failing to incorporate issues of economic development and social equity adequately. The problem here, the authors contend, is twofold. Not only is an underdeveloped notion of sustainability being pursued, but pragmatically, it will be difficult to promote sustainability unless you also appeal to the constituencies concerned about economic development and social equity.

Study on Universities and Purchasing Policies

The Purpose and Design of the Study

There were two broad purposes of this enquiry. The first (more descriptive) goal was to examine the current state of affairs related to efforts by Canadian universities to promote sustainable development. The second (more analytical) task was to provide an account of this state of affairs. For practical reasons, the authors have had to narrow their gaze to focus on a particular function – purchasing policies – through which universities might contribute to sustainable development, rather than examine their practices as a whole. Thus, this study focuses on the role of universities as consumers of goods and resources, and the formal or informal processes by which they construct purchasing policies geared towards "sustainability." More specifically, the authors decided to investigate whether, in addition to having general purchasing policies (focusing on issues such as conflict of interest, transparency, etc.), universities had developed any of three different types of purchasing policies that might contribute to sustainability: "green" or environmental sustainability policies, ethical trade policies, or fair trade policies.

In examining this issue, the analytic goal has been to determine which factors have influenced decisions regarding the adoption and implementation of policies. The design of the survey reflects this intent. With respect to vision, for example, the distinction between the different types of policy (environmental, ethical trade and fair trade) helps to indicate how a university's understanding of sustainability can influence the scope of issues taken up under the aegis of sustainability (specifically, whether it primarily focuses on environmental issues or whether it aligns more closely with a broader understanding of sustainable development that includes issues of social justice and development, such as concern for workers' rights and the plight of small producers in the South). Also integrated into the design of the survey were questions regarding the dynamics of the process of adopting and implementing purchasing policies, including: which types of actors were supportive/ not supportive and most influential (at different stages) in decisions regarding the development and implementation of policies; what type of organizational structures and strategies facilitated the adoption of policies; what types of justifications were given for (not) adopting given policies and implementation strategies; and what role resource considerations played in decision-making. These various types of questions were intended to address the roles, as discussed above, that issues of agency, ideology, structure, planning, and resources might play in the adoption and implementation of sustainable purchasing policies.

Method

In this section we will discuss the phases of the research project, the research design, and the challenges of implementing the study. Our research consisted of five phases, including a literature review, research design, survey distribution, data collection, and follow-up interviews.

1) Literature Review

We began the study with a comprehensive literature review on the subjects of environmental, ethical trade, and fair trade purchasing policies in Canada, the United States, and Europe. Key sources of literature, including academic journals, books, and conference presentations, were collected and analysed. In addition, background literature produced by advocacy groups, think tanks, and representative associations in the fair trade and ethical trade movements were reviewed and studied. The purpose of the literature review was to identify the gaps in knowledge surrounding the processes and challenges of developing and deploying green, ethical, and fair trade purchasing policies in public institutions. This work yielded the background knowledge necessary for formulating the guiding research questions and also served to structure the initial key informant interviews.

2) Research Design

The formation of the survey instrument began with preliminary telephone interviews with key contacts at Canadian universities and representative associations in order to identify crucial issues, concerns, and questions surrounding ethical and fair trade purchasing policies. These informants were selected based on their interest in the research project as well as their experience in the field of procurement and purchasing. The incentive provided for participation in the key informant interviews was a promise to share the findings of the study with participants through formal publication of the study's findings. Initially, ten key informants were interviewed by the lead researchers. These initial interviews were conducted in order to design the study. The key informant interviews were conducted by telephone and lasted for approximately twenty minutes. Informants were asked five questions in order to prompt a discussion around the key issues that related to the formation, implementation, and monitoring of fair and ethical purchasing policies, as well as to derive a sense of what knowledge gaps exist.

After compiling the data derived from the interviews into themes, the research team proceeded to design the research study. In order to ensure a breadth of feedback, it was decided that an online survey targeted at Canadian post-secondary institutions would be best suited for wide-spread data collection. The key informant interviews revealed that "sustainable purchasing" policies, primarily understood as involving environmental issues, were important for the target group and in some instances were seen as overlapping with issues of ethical trade and fair trade. For this reason, the study was broadened to include three types of alternative purchasing policies – environmental (or green), ethical trade, and fair trade – and reformulated in terms of the larger, overarching conception of sustainability. These three types of "alternative" purchasing policies, which focus on issues of sustainability, stand in contrast to more conventional, or general, purchasing policies which address issues of procedural fairness (such as competitive bidding procedures, conflicts of interest, etc.).

The three researchers collectively designed a preliminary online survey (which was to be administered through Survey Monkey). They tested the survey on four subjects who were selected on a random basis from the key informant set. The test group was given a month to provide comments on the survey design, logic, and content. After review of the comments, the final survey was narrowed to a set of forty-nine questions and to an approximate completion time of fifteen to twenty-five minutes.

The survey was divided into the following sections: Information and Consent, Demographic Information, General Purchasing Policies, Environmentally Sustainable (Green) Purchasing Policies, Ethical Trade (Labour Standards) Purchasing Policies, and Fair Trade Purchasing Policies. The survey instrument was programmed with conditional logic, and the software catered the questions to the different circumstances of each institution based on the previous answer. For example, for those institutions without green, fair trade, or ethical purchasing policies, the survey would switch to questions regarding the possibility of developing these purchasing policies or the difficulties encountered in attempting to adopt such policies.

3) Survey Distribution

The university sample was derived manually through online research. Universities were identified based on the list publicly provided by the Association of Universities and Colleges of Canada, and one of the researchers proceeded to locate the contact information of the purchasing or procurement manager at each institution by visiting their websites and directories. The direct email addresses of ninety purchasing managers or purchasing departments were located. Where no purchasing or procurement office was available, an email contact for the finance department or general inquiries was located. This yielded forty email addresses. The result was a comprehensive sample of 130 subjects representing universities and colleges across all Canadian provinces and territories.

An invitation (in both English and French) to participate in the online survey was sent by email to 130 post-secondary education institutions in Canada. The survey instrument was available in English and French online at Survey Monkey and began collecting data in February 2009. Respondents were invited to participate in the survey three times over the course of four months.

4) Data Collection

Overall, the survey collected data for six months, and yielded twenty-five responses in English and three in French, representing a 21.54 per cent response rate. Only degree-granting universities responded to the survey. If we factor out community colleges (none of which responded), then the response rate calculated on the basis of the eighty-nine degree-granting universities rises to 29.21 per cent.[4] If we approach our data from the perspective of the size of the universities we sampled as measured by their total population of full-time and part-time undergraduate and graduate students (631,345),[5] our university sample represents 40.76 per cent of the total university student population of Canada.[6] For our analysis, we broke down our university sample into "large universities" (25,000 or more students), "small universities" (less than 25,000 students), and "recently established universities" (universities that were formerly community colleges and have recently been given degree-granting status by their provincial governments).[7] Table 8.1 shows that our sample represents 76.47 per cent of all large Canadian universities, 16.67 per cent of small universities, and 33.33 per cent of recently established universities. Table 8.2 shows the regional breakdown of our sample: 20 per cent of universities in the Atlantic provinces, 29.41 per cent of Quebec's universities, 56.52 per cent of Ontario's, 14.28 per cent of universities in the Prairie provinces, and 26.67 per cent of universities in British Columbia.

A statistical summary and breakdown of the responses was compiled by Survey Monkey and was available in aggregate or on a per-response basis for review by the research team. These statistical aggregates were reviewed and analysed for the purpose of revealing the findings. Additionally, individual responses, especially where comments were provided, were reviewed by the research team in order to identify the qualitative nuances not captured by the statistical aggregates.

5) Follow-Up Interviews

A final round of interviews was conducted by a research assistant with a selected group of nine informants in order to obtain further insight into their responses and to confirm the survey findings. Representatives from four large, two small, and three recently established universities from across Canada were interviewed. The informants were selected on the basis of: (a) their indication on the initial survey that they would be willing to participate in a follow-up interview, and (b) obtaining a representative range of institutions at different stages in the process of developing sustainable purchasing policies. The interviews were conducted by phone and generally lasted around thirty minutes. The questions varied, depending on the stage of purchasing policy development, but all focused on the following issues: who initiates policies, what conditions induce policies, what are the perceived and real barriers to policies, and where is information on policies sourced by purchasing managers.

Research Challenges

The study confronted several challenges throughout the duration of the research, especially as a result of the reliance on cost-effective online and email technologies. The first relates to reaching the target research subjects. Due to the impersonal nature of email invitations, it is unknown whether target subjects received the request to participate in the study. It is plausible that some requests for participation were labelled as spam and automatically diverted to the trash folders of recipient email boxes. Moreover, where a personal email was not available for a purchasing or procurement department at the university, it is difficult to know whether the survey invitation reached the intended target subject. It is difficult to assess how response rates may have been affected by these factors.

Another challenge relates to the ability of target subjects to answer survey questions covering all three research themes (i.e., sustainability, ethical trade, and fair trade purchasing). Due to the organization of institutional structures across universities, different departments may have responsibility for different areas covered by the survey (e.g., one may be responsible for sustainability while another is responsible for general procurement). In such circumstances, the survey could only have been effectively filled out with participation and coordination across departments. A lack of such coordination may have prevented the survey from being filled out by the intended subjects and/or could have resulted in certain sections of the form not being adequately completed. Moreover, respondents may not have been part of the institution long enough to comment on all three themes. For example, sustainability procurement initiatives in some universities began as early as fifteen years ago and staff involved in the process of establishing the policy may no longer be employed at the institution or department in question. Without personal knowledge of the history, a limited ability on the part of respondents to tap into institutional memory could have significantly affected the completeness and accuracy of responses. This point was alluded to by several of our follow-up interviewees who had arrived at their jobs as procurement managers after policies were already in place. Furthermore, a lack of knowledge about some areas may have discouraged subjects from completing or submitting the survey, thus lowering the response rate.

In addition, the timing of the survey and the cycle of the academic year raises another potential implementation challenge. This is unlikely to have played a significant role, however, as the survey was distributed in February 2009 and was available for completion for six months (and several reminders were sent out). This means that, even taking into account vacation time and particular planning cycles, in the vast majority of cases administrative staff would have had some time available to fill out the survey.

Finally, we will mention the length of the survey, which may have impacted the response rate. The forty-nine questions were extensive and could have presented an overwhelming task to subjects lacking the background knowledge, institutional memory, or the time to complete the survey. Some questions may have required respondents to engage in an extended hunt for information that was not readily available. This may have affected response rates and the number of "unable to comment" or "not applicable" or "do not know" responses.

Results

The results of our research are presented below.[8] The results are broken down according to the four different types of purchasing policies distinguished in the survey.

Table 8.1. Purchasing Policies at Canadian Universities and Colleges

	Total #	Responses	General Policy	Green Policy	Ethical Trade Policy	Fair Trade Policy	MSN[9]	Talloires Signee[10]
Large Universities	17	13	11	6	6	1	9	2
Small Universities	54	9	9	1	5	3	3	1
Recently Established Universities	18	6	6	4	1	0	1	0
Totals	89	28	26	11	12	4	13	3

Table 8.2. Geographic Distribution of Purchasing Policies

	Total #	Responses	General Policy	Green Policy	Ethical Trade Policy	Fair Trade Policy	MSN
AtlanticProvinces	20	4	4	1	0	0	1
Quebec	17	5	4	2	2	0	0
Ontario	23	13	13	4	7	3	10
Prairie Provinces	14	2	1	2	1	0	1
British Columbia	15	4	4	2	2	1	1
Territories	0	0	NA	NA	NA	NA	NA
Totals	89	28	26	11	12	4	13

General Purchasing Policies

While the broad concern of this study was on sustainable purchasing policies, to get some baseline data, questions about general purchasing policies were also posed. The vast majority of the respondents, 93 per cent, reported having a general purchasing policy. These policies typically included provisions involving competitive bidding processes, conflicts of interest, acting in good faith, and fair and impartial award recommendations.

It was not possible to determine directly through the survey the considerations that went into the development of the general policies. The general components of the policies, however, tend to reflect standard assumptions (in neo-classical economics and related management traditions) about the purposes of general procurement policies. These include the assumptions that goods should be procured at the lowest cost possible and that procedural norms in accord with the logic of competitive markets are necessary for ensuring this goal. While in principle, the tradition of neo-classical economics acknowledges that the costs of externalities need to be taken into consideration, in practice this stipulation is generally not incorporated into cost calculations.

Green Purchasing Policies

While the vast majority of universities that responded to the survey had a general purchasing policy, less than half, 42 per cent, reported having a green purchasing policy.[11] Moreover, subsequent interviews and analysis of the actual policies revealed that in the majority of these cases, there was not actually an explicit policy on environmental sustainability. It appears that there was some significant confusion between the notion of having a green policy and incorporating some environmental concerns into a more general purchasing policy (or adopting some green *practices*). For example, when pressed on this issue, one respondent articulated it this way: "We have a component of sustainable purchasing in our policy" (Interview 1). Moreover, in the cases in which green policies were in place, they tended to focus on a limited range of products (e.g., paper products, computers, printers, photocopiers, lighting) and issues (e.g., energy consumption). Such an approach might be characterized as a policy of convenience or a low-hanging fruit approach, rather than a systematic effort to address issues of environmental sustainability.

While only a minority reported having a policy, the issue of green policies seems to be very much a topic of discussion in universities. Overall, almost 90 per cent of the respondents indicated that they are considering or have considered adopting green policies. Moreover, in follow-up interviews, purchasing managers were eager to indicate that, although their institution had not yet adopted a sustainability policy, they did have a draft of a policy or were in the process of developing one. However, there seemed to be a lot of ambiguous space between having a policy and being in the process of developing one. One interviewee encapsulated this grey area between intention and concrete policy well: "[We] do have the policies but we have not expanded on them, they are part of the evaluation process but I see that they need to go further" (Interview 2).

An interesting point that arose in a number of the follow-up interviews with universities that had not adopted an official policy was the fact that in most of these institutions, there has been some institutional reorganization around green issues, including the creation of official administrative "champions" of (environmental) sustainability. A number of universities reported hiring a "green coordinator" (Interview 2), "sustainability manager" (Interview 3), or a "sustainability officer" (Interview 5), either to coordinate green policies across the university, to work under the procurement manager, or to work under facilities management in collaboration with the procurement office.

In terms of their perception of the agents involved in driving discussion around policies, all managers indicated that students constituted the key group in raising issues of environmental sustainability. Faculty members were also cited by many respondents as having played a role, but their participation does not seem to have been as prominent. In follow-up interviews, the support of faculty members was often seen to be ancillary and limited to individuals or small groups. One follow-up interview participant, for example, expressed the situation this way:

> The big push comes from a student group; a group called ... They are the sustainability group from the students. There is also a faculty member well known for his environmental considerations and he is a resource as an expert. (Interview 3)

While students, and to a much lesser degree individual faculty members, were seen as key to raising the issue of green policies and pressuring for their adoption, other internal (to the university) and external stakeholders seemed to have played little or no role. In terms of internal stakeholders, for example, staff and faculty unions seem to have been almost entirely absent from the process in most instances. It is also interesting to note that the purchasing policy managers did not generally see themselves as playing (or having the right to play) a role in policy development, despite the fact that they were often key channels of information on decisions regarding the adoption of policies. Some, however, did express a willingness to be more involved.

With regards to external stakeholders, while community organizations are sometimes mentioned, their influence seems to have been minor. The one major external stakeholder that is an exception to this trend is government, which was perceived by two-thirds of the respondents as having a positive impact on their decision to adopt green policies. Government, of course, has the ability to influence university policy in very pragmatic ways through its role as the primary funder and regulator of institutions of higher education. One respondent summed up what was seen as the key role of government in the following manner:

> The largest [external] group [for influencing green purchasing policies at universities] is the public sector through the department of finance of the Ontario government. Their objective is to try to get all those organizations that are partially funded by the Ontario government, which includes educational facilities, hospitals, municipalities, etc., to implement these policies. (Interview 7)[12]

While students are seen as the key initiators in raising green issues, and government is acknowledged as playing a key role in influencing the environment in which decisions to adopt policies are made, policy managers generally perceived senior university administrators as being the key actors in determining whether a green policy was actually adopted or not. A key question then becomes which factors in particular induce administrators to decide to adopt green policies.

From the perspective of the purchasing managers, senior administrators who were "champions" were key to the expeditious adoption of the policies. However, managers did not typically experience university administrators as showing great vision and leadership when it came to the cause of sustainability, at least in terms of initiating policies. In most instances, senior administrators did not emerge as champions of green policies without pressure from below. (Board members were perceived to be even less supportive of green policies.)

When the issue of adopting a green policy was raised, managers saw senior administrators primarily concerned with the costs involved. In this regard, managers perceived resource limitations to be a determining factor in administrators' decisions to adopt purchasing policies or not, where resources were primarily understood in terms of the short-term cost implications of paying more for "green" products. Here, the attitudes of senior administrators often stood in contrast with the self-reported views of many of the managers themselves. One purchasing policy manager, for example, commented that sustainable policies are simply "the right thing to do" (Interview 9), while another said they must be enacted for "the good of mother earth" (Interview 5).

Moreover, administrators tended to assume, at least initially, that there would be significant costs for adopting policies. In this regard, they typically lagged behind purchasing managers, who were much more likely to perceive (through their own practice, talking with product representatives and colleagues from other universities, etc.) that there could actually be significant cost savings in the long run by adopting green purchasing policies (at least in some key areas).[13]

While an absence of vision and leadership on the part of senior administrators was seen as an important constraint on efforts to adopt green policies, purchasing managers also pointed to the complexity of university structures, which tend to result in a lack of effective coordination, information sharing and planning amongst different divisions and departments of universities. The degree to which problems of complexity influenced the information available to senior administrators in their decision-making processes was not clear from the data. This would partly depend on the degree to which senior administrators relied upon staff in particular departments to supply data (or whether they incorporated research findings from faculty, outside consultants, etc.) and how they, in turn, procured their information.

While our data do not provide much detail with regard to the former issue, with respect to the latter it was clear that purchasing policy managers relied heavily upon three main sources for their information regarding the issues of environmental sustainability (e.g., the "environmental" quality of green products, their availability, their costs, etc.). A large majority (88 per cent) of respondents reported relying upon certification programs (e.g., Energy Star) for information. A substantial number (63 per cent), however, also indicated that they relied upon suppliers for information. One respondent expressed the situation this way: "I get information from bulletins and websites ... suppliers are our knowledge base" (Interview 2). As we expand on below, colleagues in other universities represented the third key source of information.

Once policies had been implemented, purchasing policy managers perceived that stakeholders were generally satisfied with the results, and some even expressed the opinion that the standards adopted should be more stringent. Nearly half reported that there were significant problems with the implementation of the program, but most did not report any major difficulties with suppliers, nor were there major cost implications. Despite their overall satisfaction with their policies, it was not immediately clear how effective the policies were in their actual environmental impact, or in their precise long-term costs. A major concern here is the fact, as noted above, that many managers continued to rely heavily on suppliers for information about the environmental quality of the products, along with certification labels.

It should be noted that in implementing policies, managers also have another key source of information: their peers. They rely heavily on the opinions of other university managers and the experiences that they have had with suppliers when making their own decisions around sustainability.[14] A key location for this information exchange is at the annual or semi-annual meetings of procurement managers – a point that was made strongly by a number of the respondents to the follow-up interviews. One manager noted that "sustainability is at the agenda of every one of those meetings" (Interview 2). Another commented, "Yes, we talk almost daily [with other university purchasing departments]. We also have two meetings during the year where we discuss new things coming up or any problems with ethical purchasing, we also find out about different suppliers" (Interview 5). The quality of the information that was shared among managers with respect to the environmental quality of products was not entirely clear, however.

Ethical Trade Purchasing Policies

The reported prevalence of ethical trade purchasing policies (48 per cent) was similar to that of green purchasing policies (42 per cent). (See Table 8.3.) The number of those reported to be developing a policy were slightly less, however. The total number claiming to have or be considering an ethical trade policy amounted to 65 per cent (as compared to 90 per cent of those who had or considered adopting a green policy).

Table 8.3. Ethical Trade Policies in Canadian Universities and Colleges

	Total #	Responses	Self-Reporting	MSN Report	WRC Membership	FLA Membership
Large Universities	17	13	6	9	5	4
Small Universities	54	9	5	3	2	0
Recently Established Universities	18	6	1	1	0	0
Totals	89	28	12	13	7	4

As in the case of green policies, the accuracy of these numbers is open to question. A report from the MSN, for example, points out that only nineteen Canadian universities (or 21.35 per cent of all Canadian universities) have explicit ethical trade policies (MSN, 2008; see also MSN, 2004). Interestingly, our data also revealed that, while fourteen of the nineteen universities appearing in the MSN report as having "no sweat" licensing policies were in our sample, four of these institutions from our sample did not self-report having any ethical trade purchasing policy. Analysis of the data and subsequent interviews revealed that a major reason for these discrepancies was that the managers tended to use different terms and to conflate ethical trade and environmentally sustainable (green) policies. Furthermore, as with green policies, there was some confusion between having official policies and the inclusion of some wording in more general purchasing policies.

As for the actors who are driving discussions on ethical trade policies, managers again agreed that it was students who were the main protagonists. One respondent, for example, having been asked who initiated the ethical trade policy, answered, "It was basically students" (Interview 5). Another replied, "Generally it has been the student body [that motivated changing ethical trade policies]" (Interview 1). While the University of Toronto was the first to adopt a "sweat free" purchasing code after a much-publicized student sit-in of the president's office by its Students Against Sweatshops group in 2000 (Bégin, Wolff, & Atkinson, 2005), since then, another seventeen Canadian universities have adopted such a policy, with student activism or sit-ins playing key roles in a number of these cases (Wells, n.d.). Further corroborating these perceptions by purchasing managers is the fact that at least sixteen of the twenty student-run Public Interest Research Groups (PIRGs) currently active in Canadian universities have or recently had working groups dedicated to issues such as sustainable and green campuses, fair trade, and ethical and "sweat free" trade.[15] In addition, at least two student conferences have been held recently dealing with issues of fair trade and ethical purchasing at Canadian universities.[16] Wells (n.d.) writes: "Through sit-ins, rallies, teach-ins, anti-sweat fashion shows, hunger strikes, occupations, political theatre and other forms of education, publicity and protest, students have been demanding the adoption of ethical buying policies throughout Canada, Australia, the US, and much of Europe" (p. 1; see also Wells, 2004).

Again, as in the case of green policies, faculty members were seen as playing a significant role, but ancillary to students. Also similar to the aforementioned policies was the fact that pressure from campus-based unions was not seen as particularly important in driving ethical trade policies. This situation seems perhaps even more surprising in this context given formal expressions of solidarity between unions and labour activists on such issues (Wells, 2004). Also interesting was the fact that – more than was the case in green purchasing policies – pressure from other stakeholder groups and influence from the practices of other universities were seen as contributing significantly to the adoption of these policies. This may be a result of the specific nature of the "branded goods" that are typically the products that fall under such policies (e.g., spirit wear, sports uniforms and sports equipment). These goods have a higher public profile, as do many of the companies that tend to supply them to universities, and the conditions of their production have been the object of investigations by different non-state labelling bodies as well as labour rights organizations (O'Rourke, 2003; Einwohner & Spencer, 2005; Schaller, 2007).[17]

The dynamics involved in terms of getting university administrators to agree to ethical trade policies seem to have been different than in the case of green policies. Again, ethical purchasing policies were not typically perceived as being high on the priority lists of senior administrators. On the other hand, the stakes involved in adopting them were also not as high (as this represented a very narrow range of goods in relatively small quantities). In practice, this meant that while leadership among senior administrators on this issue (i.e., the incorporation of labour standards as part of a social justice component of the university's mission) was often lacking, this did not necessarily inhibit the adoption of a "no sweat" policy as administrators seemed to be willing to consider policies on the basis of relatively straightforward calculations involving costs. Thus, in this case having a "champion" among the administration was generally less important than the fact that there were few cost implications to adopting the policy (as well as some potential reputational costs from not doing so).

As such, the key limiting factor which seemed to have influenced the openness of administrators to adopting ethical trade policies the most was the issue of resources. In terms of costs, some purchasing managers did identify higher prices of "no sweat" products and the fees involved in working with certification bodies as potential considerations. They also expressed two other concerns. One of these was the availability of "sweat free" products. This was more of a concern for the managers themselves, rather than senior administrators, and one usually expressed with regard to whether this would cause any problems with their existing suppliers. The second concern, which managers saw as more important for administrators, was reputational costs: that is, how the impact of not adopting a policy might affect the reputation of the institution (especially if neighbouring institutions had done so).

Again, the issue of costing is not entirely separate from the related issues of structure and ideology. In terms of ideology, it is important to note that managers and administrators tended to assume traditional cost accounting practices rather than adopting social accounting approaches, which could have contributed to a stronger case for implementing an ethical trade policy. With respect to structure, the complexity of the university as an institution is not so much of an issue here as is the manner in which the institutions tend to collect information. Again, even more so than in the case of green policies, there was a strong tendency on the part of managers to rely on information that comes directly from suppliers, rather than certifying bodies such as the FLA and WRC.

Once universities implemented ethical trade policies, the experience of purchasing managers was universally positive. The cost implications of adopting the policies were seen to be minor, few or no problems arose with suppliers and there were positive benefits in terms of institutional reputation. For the most part, the managers did not express any particular concerns about monitoring. Some noted that their institutions had set up stakeholder committees for oversight of the policy. One respondent, for example, explained that "for some of the tenders and for most of the major contracts ... [these are] done by committee with students, grad students, faculty reps included in an evaluation committee to make sure the products that are bought are ethical" (Interview 2). It seemed that in other universities, however, managers retained oversight of the policies and often continued to rely on suppliers themselves for monitoring information rather than certifying bodies.

Fair Trade Purchasing Policies

Although there is already a strong fair trade university network in the UK with established standards for membership, in North America this network has been slower to develop. This may help to account for the fact that only five universities reported having a fair trade policy. However, another 50 per cent of the respondents indicated that they are considering developing a policy. Among those that claimed to have a fair trade policy, only two used FLO certification as the standard of fair trade (two others mentioned using other labels). Again, there seemed to be some confusion between having a fair trade policy and incorporating practices.

The dynamics with respect to developing fair trade policies seemed to mirror closely those in the development of ethical trade policies. Students were the primary initiators of fair trade policies, though they tended to work more closely with other internal and external stakeholders. In at least one instance, at McMaster University, this included working closely with senior administrators (Wells, n.d.). Cost considerations and the ability to monitor were the primary concerns that were raised. Among the few universities that had implemented policies (which involved only the requirement of offering fair trade tea and coffee options),[18] the response from stakeholders as reported by managers was universally positive and there were few or no cost considerations or implementation problems that arose.

Summary of Results

The key findings of the research can be summarized as follows:

1. Internal stakeholder (especially student and faculty) pressure is a necessary but not sufficient condition for the development of sustainable purchasing policies.
2. Administrators play a key role in implementing sustainable purchasing policies as "champions," but often need to be convinced (by pressure from below or by cost-benefit analysis) to implement these policies.
3. External community perception can be a consideration but typically does not drive the implementation of sustainable purchasing policies.
4. Ease and effectiveness of monitoring and short-term cost considerations are seen as major hurdles by administration, while procurement managers see long-term cost savings and environmental reasons for implementing such policies.
5. Awareness of sustainable purchasing in all three of its forms is generally high among procurement managers (though detailed understanding may be lacking).
6. Procurement manager networks and suppliers' documents contribute significantly to managers' awareness of issues and their decisions about what products best conform to the university's standards and values.
7. Purchasing managers are supportive of sustainable/ethical trade/fair trade purchasing policies as they believe that they are the "right thing to do."

However, all of the managers felt that they were restricted in their ability to promote policies or to make significant changes in practice without authorization from above. This sense of powerlessness seemed to be felt more strongly in the recently established universities.

8. A key driver of university sustainability policies (although not ethical trade or fair trade) are top-down initiatives from provincial governments for greening the public sector.

9. Coalitions of internal stakeholders can be effective in initiating and implementing sustainable purchasing policies. Such coalitions seem to become more prominent as sustainable purchasing policies become more inclusive of equity and development concerns.

Discussion

In our findings, while some patterns in the adoption of policies were discerned, we were not able to demonstrate statistically significant correlations or support strong causal accounts based upon more qualitative data. In terms of patterns of adopting policies, there was a clear difference in participation rates with respect to different types of purchasing policies (see Tables 8.1 and 8.2) according to university size and location, but not any consistent pattern across all policy types. Ethical trade policies, for example, were adopted almost exclusively by established institutions, with only one recently established university having an ethical trade policy. It was also the case that the larger, more established universities tended to be members in the FLA and WRC. Similarly, none of the recently established universities had a fair trade policy. Geographically, relatively more Ontario universities tended to have ethical or fair trade policies. On the other hand, the newly established universities reported a higher rate of green policies than the smaller established universities.

One consistent pattern that does seem to emerge relates to the order in which universities have adopted policies. Almost all universities had general purchasing policies and had adopted these first. Next, the universities tended to adopt green policies and/or ethical trade policies. Fair trade policies tended to be the last to be adopted. The reasons for this pattern seem to reflect the historical circumstances of the promotion of these policies, especially in the United States. Thus, for example, while the first fair trade certification body was developed in 1988, in Canada there was no national certification body until 1995 and in the

U.S. not until 1997. The first fair trade universities were recognized in the UK only in 2002. By contrast, after the FLA was initiated by the Clinton administration, it spread rapidly among American universities throughout the 1990s and a strong student movement grew, led in part by United Students against Sweatshops (Moore, 2000; Featherstone, 2002; O'Rourke, 2003).

Perhaps the more important issue relating to the adoption of policies that the study was not able to address adequately was the internal dynamics involved in the decisions on the part of universities to adopt policies or not. Our study has highlighted above some of the factors that can inhibit the promotion of purchasing policies (e.g., resource deficits, ideology, structure), but listing factors does not provide an explanation. The latter requires some account of agency. As we noted above, while a range of agents may be involved in advocating for policies, it is ultimately senior administrators that must be brought on board for policies to emerge. Thus, a causal explanation for the pattern of adoption of purchasing policies must be based upon the decision-making processes of senior administrators.

One of the most common factors that purchasing managers cited with respect to the decisions to adopt sustainable purchasing policies was the catalytic role of key actors. Such key actors were commonly referred to as "champions" or as exercising "leadership." A number of different actors were sometimes cited as being "champions," including faculty members, staff members whose job involved implementing purchasing policies ("official champions") and senior administrators. While the role of the latter group was most commonly seen as the key to shepherding a purchasing policy through, no clear patterns came through from the survey and follow-up interviews as to the nature of the motivation of such actors or the actions in which they engaged. The one fact that was clear from the data was that it was typically pressure from students, who tended to initiate discussion around policies, especially in the case of ethical trade and fair trade policies.[19]

It was not evident, however, in this context of pressure from below, how "champions" arose to take up the cause of "sustainability." It is not clear whether such champions were primarily motivated by personal convictions or whether they were more concerned about protecting or promoting the good of the institution. Similarly, it was not clear whether such champions led by taking risky decisions or by promoting learning and developing consensus. Thus, while most respondents saw individual leadership as an important factor in facilitating the development of policies, our data did not provide sufficient information to distinguish any clear patterns regarding the nature of leadership and the role that it played in policy formation.

The flip side of questioning the agency of senior administrators is whether different structures or practices (including the implementation of social accounting) might diminish the importance of administrators or, perhaps more likely, facilitate their making decisions to support the establishment of sustainable purchasing policies. Purchasing managers tend to feel that the main blockage in adopting and implementing sustainable, ethical, or fair trade policies by their universities is the lack of coordination amongst different divisions and departments. With clearer channels of communication, policies that administrators see as compelling (due to cost-effectiveness and key stakeholder support) could be generated.

Policy Recommendations

There are a number of policy recommendations that flow from this study (and the related literature and practice on Canadian universities). We have organized these around the basic categories, which were seen in the literature as inhibiting the development of successful sustainable purchasing policies.

Vision: Many senior university administrators formally subscribe to a vision of sustainability for their institutions (e.g., in the form of the Talloires Declaration) and it is unlikely that anyone would oppose such visions. Moreover, many universities have sought to embody this vision in the core activities of the university, teaching (e.g., in programs in environmental studies, social justice studies, and business and the environment) and research (e.g., establishing research institute on sustainability and international development). Universities typically have not integrated a vision of sustainability as well in the operations side of their mandate, including in their purchasing policies. Here there is a need for senior administrators to see sustainability not as an "add on" to their core mission, but as an integral part of their mandate. What this means, more specifically, is directing the university's concern about teaching and research (and policy development) not just outwards, but also inwards towards the university's own practices in a systematic fashion. The university needs to see itself (its structures, its practices, and its policies) as an essential site of research, education, practical innovation, and engagement on sustainability.

Agency: When confronted with demands for more sustainable policies and practices, universities often respond defensively. Students, in particular, often feel that they are ignored, patronized, and/or deflected when they raise concerns about the need for systematic attention to broadly understood issues of sustainability. Other members of the university community might feel that their skills and expertise are not being sought out and taken advantage of for the promotion of sustainability on campus. This includes faculty members (many of whom are recognized experts and may even consult with other institutions on such issues) as well as purchasing managers (who typically feel that their position is limited to implementing policies rather than playing a more active role in the development of policy). There is also a range of external actors who are actively involved in issues of sustainability and who are interested in engaging with universities in the development of more sustainable practices and polices. Senior administrators need to create an environment and structures that encourage and facilitate engagement by a full range of stakeholders in the development and implementation of sustainability policies.

Structure: Universities have, in a sense, a bifurcated structure. On the one hand, the core academic mission is based on the practice of collegial governance, which involves democratic representation by key stakeholder groups (e.g., faculty, administration, and students). On the other, the university's administration operates on a structure more akin to a state or corporate bureaucracy, in which there is a clear top-down chain of command from the president and senior administrators (who are subject to board oversight) through various operational units and departments. A basic concern about the university's administrative structure in relationship to sustainable purchasing policies is that its complex nature does not allow for effective collaboration in the development and implementation of purchasing policies. Part of the problem here may be the top-down logic inherent in this part of the university's bureaucratic structure. It is possible that a more effective approach to developing and implementing sustainable purchasing policies is to draw upon the more collegial approach to governance that characterizes the academic mission of the university. This approach may more effectively encourage stakeholder participation, break down academic and administrative silos, encourage the sharing of information and learning, and promote more experimentation and innovation. Senior administrators should promote experiments with more collegial and participatory approaches to policy development and implementation, whose decisions may still be subject to approval by senior administrators and the board of governors.

Resources: Despite being subjected to budget cuts and rising costs, universities are immeasurably rich in terms of the resources, especially the human resources, that they have available. Internal human resources include students, faculty, staff, administrative personnel, and board members. External human resources, who are frequently happy to partner with universities in different ways, include government, other institutions of higher education, NGOs, social economy actors, community organizations, and more. As noted above, universities need to engage a full range of stakeholders in the development and implementation of purchasing policies. To do this effectively and systematically, senior administrators need to encourage participation in ways that overlap with the core missions of the university: teaching and research. Many students are taking courses and entire programs of study that specifically address issues of sustainability, while many faculty members and research institutes dedicate significant parts of their time and resources to research issues of sustainable development and promote more effective policies and practices. Arrangements need to be developed, promoted, and institutionalized that enable students to pursue their academic interests in issues of sustainability in ways that contribute to the development and implementation of sustainable purchasing policies (e.g., the promotion of student-run businesses or practicum courses within the university). External stakeholders (e.g., NGOs, social economy enterprises, or community organizations) may be effective and essential partners in promoting such student involvement. Similarly, the university needs to encourage participation by faculty members more systematically, not only as researchers on sustainability, but as experts in policy development and implementation strategies.

Ideology: While universities are the social institutions par excellence at generating knowledge, as institutions they can become ensnared in the trap of uncritically accepting dominant theoretical traditions of inquiry. When developing purchasing policies, universities need to critically reflect on the understanding of sustainability that shapes their policies, and the practices and institutions that they use to measure, monitor, and implement such policies, rather than unreflectively accepting dominant approaches. In the case of the understanding of sustainability, universities need to challenge a dominant trend, which conceives of sustainability primarily in environmental terms, or considers sustainability strictly against financial costs, at the expensive of social sustainability. There is substantial evidence from development studies and related fields that there is a strong internal connection between the pursuit of environmental and social sustainability, not only at the level of normative theory, but in the development of effective strategies (Cavenaugh & Mander, 2004; Loxley, Silver, & Sexsmith, 2007; Noya & Clarence, 2009; Mook & Sumner, 2010). In terms of practices for measuring and monitoring the success of sustainability programs, universities need to move beyond conventional cost accounting approaches and employ social and environmental accounting practices. One way of working towards developing these practices might include a national consortium of universities engaging in sustainable purchasing. For example, the MSN recommends establishing "a national consortium of No Sweat universities" that could work collaboratively on concerns, issues, and benchmarks towards implementing sustainability (MSN, 2004, p. 8). Finally, with respect to institutions, universities need to consider whether alternative economic firms (e.g., co-operatives or social enterprises with formal missions that commit them to social purposes such as sustainable development) might prove to be more appropriate suppliers than conventional firms, whose primary commitment is earning profits for their shareholders.

Conclusion

The research outlined above is an important step in connecting the theoretical discussion of sustainability and sustainable development at universities with the on-the-ground practice of purchasing. It attempts to connect the mission of universities to the practices that exist alongside it. The primary purpose of the research is not to judge universities in Canada on their sustainable purchasing policy development, but rather to outline the issues contained and often obscured in these two sets of practices. It also details the processes through which purchasing policies are developed, and identifies the key actors in developing such policies. Finally, it attempts to explicate the key perceived and real limits to developing more nuanced practices of sustainable purchasing at universities in the Canadian context.

The authors are aware that further research is important for corroborating and developing some of these findings, as well as promoting more effective implementation of policies. While some such areas were noted above, as part of the conclusion to this chapter and the collection, special mention needs to be made here of the potential importance of social (or sustainable) accounting in facilitating the adoption of purchasing policies in public institutions, especially universities. There are three contributions in particular that need to be investigated.

First, there seems to be significant potential for social accounting to make explicit the nature and extent of the contributions of university purchasing policies towards promoting sustainability. The specific contributions that universities make to promoting sustainability can be, on the one hand, more facilitative in nature. This would involve providing a market for those offering more sustainably made products. This can be done by universities either directly purchasing more sustainable products or requiring vendors operating on their campuses to make such products available. On the other hand, universities can be more directly involved by actively developing programs to support their purchasing policies (e.g., composting and recycling programs) as well as actively supporting firms which are providing more sustainable products (e.g., through research and education). This latter approach may involve universities deploying their research and teaching functions in support of their purchasing policies. This may happen coincidently (through decisions by individual researchers and teachers) and/or may be more actively encouraged by universities (through more formal relationships with business and community partners). A variety of quantitative and qualitative social accounting methods could be used to measure such contributions by universities.

Second, universities can potentially make use of such social accounting practices to engage with different stakeholder groups in ways that provide benefits to the university and/or encourage the promotion of purchasing policies. One key group is students, who may be particular interested in sustainability profiles when choosing a university. A further consideration for students might be the degree to which their studies (and research possibilities) can be related to the further improvement of the university's sustainability record. Similar considerations may be important for universities in attracting new professors. Another key stakeholder group that may be interested in social accounting measures generated by universities is government. To the degree that governments are interested in the improving the sustainability performance of public institutions (as in the case of Ontario and Nova Scotia), then social accounting measures can be very important for universities in demonstrating that universities are not only formally complying with policies, but are actually generating social and environmental value. Similarly, more sustainable practices by universities can benefit local communities and business stakeholders.

Third, social accounting can potentially facilitate the adoption and extension of purchasing policies. By more accurately indicating the true costs and benefits involved in adopting policies, social accounting provides champions within the university with arguments to overcome opposition from skeptics. Moreover, social accounting might be able to facilitate learning among managers and administrators, which in turn might encourage more extensive use of such programs and more active participation by a wide variety of stakeholders.

While there would seem to be a logical link between public purchasing policies (in public institutions such as universities) and social accounting, relatively little work seems to have been done so far on the extent to which they are actually used in complementary ways in practice. In this chapter, we have almost exclusively focused on the functioning of public purchasing policies and have only been able to drawn upon our results to raise the question of their link as an important and exciting topic for future investigation.

NOTES

1 The authors would like to acknowledge the significant assistance that they received in writing this chapter from Jean-Frederic Lemay (who provided invaluable help in translating the survey, interview questions, etc.) and Marcelo Vieta (who conducted follow-up interviews and assisted in various other tasks).

2 The Stockholm Declaration (UNESCO, 1972) was in fact the first effort in the international community to focus on the environment. It was to be a pivotal point in the history of debates on sustainable development, because at this conference the G77 refused to accept any environmental declaration in which the environment took precedence over development priorities. Stockholm made the environment a legitimate cause for international attention, but also set forward an agenda whereby development and environmental protection would necessarily be linked.

3 The number of signatories had grown to over 275 by 2000 and currently includes 417 institutions of higher education. See http://www.ulsf.org/programs_talloires_signatories.html.

4 Total population of Canadian degree-granting institutions was compiled by consolidating data from the Association of Canadian Universities and

Colleges (AUCC, 2009), the *Globe and Mail*'s 2009 "University Report Card" (Canadian University Report Card, 2010), *Maclean's* magazine's "Rankings" (Dwyer 2009), and the Canadian Association of University Business Officers' "Financial Information of Universities and Colleges" (CAUBO, 2009).

5 Association of Universities and Colleges of Canada (http://www.aucc.ca/policy/quick-facts_e.html).

6 As of 2009 there were 1,549,000 full-time and part-time undergraduate and graduate students. Association of Universities and Colleges of Canada (http://www.aucc.ca/policy/quick-facts_e.html).

7 While our distinction between "large" and "small" universities is synthetic and the 25,000-student mark somewhat arbitrary, we are following here the practice of the *Globe and Mail*'s "University Report Card" in distinguishing the size of universities. Unlike the *Globe and Mail*, for simplicity we included "medium" universities (12,500 to 25,000 students) in the "small" university category.

8 Respondents to both the broad questionnaire and follow-up interviews were promised anonymity. Respondents from our interviews are cited as Interview 1, Interview 2, Interview 3, etc.

9 Universities listed in the Maquila Solidarity Network's (MSN) "No Sweat Policy" report as having implemented ethical purchasing policies or practices banning the purchasing of products from companies that engage in "sweat shop" production practices (http://en.maquilasolidarity.org/no-sweat/action) (MSN 2008).

10 According to the latest list of signatories as posted on the Talloires Network Members website, as of October 2010 (http://www.aucc.ca/policy/quick-facts_e.html). Three of the five Canadian universities that are signatories were part of our sample.

11 We excluded food services from the survey for pragmatic reasons. This area is generally dealt with by a different department, a fact which would likely have compromised the accuracy of the data and the response rate.

12 In Ontario this also includes the Green Energy Act (2009). In Nova Scotia it includes commitments by public institutions to follow the Electronic Stewardship Plan, whereby there is a fee charged when electronic equipment is purchased to be applied to the subsequent costs of recycling these products at the end of their life and placing them into the proper waste stream.

13 This was a palpable frustration with the procurement managers we interviewed. Managers felt their universities could show real savings benefits from buying green if they had better ways of tracking long-term costs. Our

purchasing manager interviewees, on the whole, felt that universities are too wrapped up in short-term cost considerations, which consequently shut out many green products.

14 The role of other universities in information exchange is not surprising given the fact that purchasing has become increasingly formalized in the university context. For example, in Nova Scotia, universities tender products together in what is called the "Interuniversity Services" program. In British Columbia, the provincial purchasing association, "The University and Colleges Purchasing Program," and the regional "Western University Purchasing Association" play major roles in helping choose which sustainable products to purchase. This exchange of information is predominantly centred on the green or recycled content of printing or electronic products, rather than the application of broad sustainability programs within the university. Meetings (and networks emerging out) of the Canadian Association of University Business Officers (CAUBO) also, according to our interviewees, were forums for exchanging information on products on a national basis.

15 From our own survey of PIRG websites.

16 For example, the Canadian Students Against Sweatshops held a national conference in 2006, while in 2008 ten Canadian universities and three colleges participated in the Canadian Students Fair Trade Network's "Ethical Purchasing Policies: Activist School" at Trent University.

17 See, for example, the numerous sector and company-specific reports for firms supplying goods to universities available at the Workers' Rights Consortium (2007), the Fair Labor Association (2010), and the Ethical Trade Initiative (2010). Other labour-rights organizations of note actively monitoring key products and companies' labour practices include the Worldwide Responsible Apparel Production certification program, Social Accountability International and its SA8000 certification, and the Fair Wear Foundation.

18 According to the Fairtrade Foundation, over 120 universities and colleges in the UK have gone fair trade since 2003 (Fairtrade Foundation, 2010). Several universities in the U.S. have gone to 100 per cent Fair Trade, while over 300 campuses in the U.S. now sell fair trade coffee (Fridell, 2007, p. 75; United Students for Fair Trade, 2008). In Canada, while many universities have fair trade coffee options, the University of British Columbia decided in 2007 to sell only fair trade coffee after consulting with a fourth-year science class that conducted a project on the issue ("UBC Moves to Fair Trade, 'Ethical' Coffee," 2007). Public institutions' procurement policies in

both the U.S. and Canada, however, lag far behind their European counter-parts (Fridell, 2007, p. 75).

19 In the case of green issues, public policy seems to play a stronger role in the initiation of policies. This appeared to be the case in Nova Scotia and Ontario where there was pressure placed on universities to adopt provincial government sustainability policies.

REFERENCES

Adams, W.M. (1990). *Green development*. London: Routledge.

Association of University and Colleges of Canada (AUCC). (2009). Fall 2009 preliminary full-time and part-time enrolment at AUCC member institutions. Association of University and Colleges of Canada. Retrieved September 30, 2010, from: http://www.aucc.ca/publications/stats/enrol_e.html

Bégin, G., Wolff, J., & Atkinson, J. (2005). Turning up the heat: A step-by-step guide to foster the Atlantic Canadian no-sweat movement. No-Sweat Coalition, Mount Allison University. Retrieved September 15, 2010, from: http://www.mta.ca/clubs/nosweat/turning_up_the_heat.doc

Bekessy, S.A., Samson, K., & Clarkson, R.E. (2007). The failure of non-binding declarations to achieve university sustainability: A need for accountability. *International Journal of Sustainability in Higher Education, 8*(3), 301–16. http://dx.doi.org/10.1108/14676370710817165

Calder, W., & Clugston, R. (2003a). International efforts to promote higher education for sustainable development. *Planning for Higher Education* (March-May): 34–8.

Calder, W., & Clugston, R. (2003b). Progress towards sustainability in higher education. *Environmental Law Reporter, 33*(1), 10003–22.

Canadian University Report Card. (2010). Your guide to Canadian universities. *Globe and Mail*. Retrieved October 13, 2010, from: http://www.globe-campus.ca/in-the-news/article/your-guide-to-canadian-universities/

CAUBO. (2009). Financial information of universities and colleges. Canadian Association of University Business Officers. Retrieved October 13, 2010, from: http://www.caubo.ca/fedora/repository/caubo:1341/OBJ/CAUBO_2008_2009_FINANCIAL_INFORMATION_OF_UNIVERSITIES_AND_COLLEGES.pdf

Cavenaugh, J., & Mander, J. (2004). *Alternatives to economic globalization: A better world is possible: A report of the International Forum on Globalization*. San Francisco: Berrett-Koehler Publishers.

Clugston, R., & Calder, W. (1999). Critical dimensions of sustainability in higher education. In W.L. Filho (Ed.), *Sustainability and university/Life: Environmental education, communication and sustainability* (pp. 31–46). Berlin: Peter Lang.

Corcoran, P.B., Calder, W., & Clugston, M.R. (2002). Introduction: higher education for sustainable development. *Higher Education Policy, 15*(2), 99–103. http://dx.doi.org/10.1016/S0952-8733(02)00009-0

Charter, C. (1994). *The University Charter of Sustainable Development of the Conference of European Rectors (CRE)*. Geneva: CRE-Copernicus Charter.

Dwyer, M. (2009, November 5). Our 19th annual rankings. *Mcleans*. Retrieved 7 October 2010, from: http://oncampus.macleans.ca/education/2009/11/05/our-19th-annual-rankings/

Einwohner, R.L., & Spencer, J.W. (2005). That's how we do things here: Local culture and the construction of sweatshops and anti-sweatshop activism in two campus communities. *Sociological Inquiry, 75*(2), 249–72. http://dx.doi.org/10.1111/j.1475-682X.2005.00121.x

Ethical Trade Initiative. (2010). The ETI blog. Retrieved October 25, 2010, from: http://www.ethicaltrade.org/news-and-events/blog/

Fair Labor Association. (2010). News releases and statements. Retrieved October 25, 2010, from: http://www.fairlabor.org/news_releases_a1.html

Fairtrade Foundation. (2010). About fairtrade universities and colleges. Retrieved October 15, 2010, from: http://www.fairtrade.org.uk/get_involved/campaigns/fairtrade_universities/about_fairtrade_universities.aspx

Featherstone, L. (2002). *Students against sweatshops*. London: Verso.

Fridell, G. (2007). *Fair trade coffee: The prospects and pitfalls of market-driven social justice*. Toronto: University of Toronto Press.

IUCN (World Conservation Union). (1980). *World conservation strategy: Living resource conservation for sustainable development*. Gland, Switzerland: IUCN, UNEP, and WWF.

Kirby, J., O'Keefe, P., & Timberlake, L. (1995). Sustainable development: An introduction. In J. Kirby, P. O'Keefe, & L. Timberlake (Eds.), *The earthscan reader in sustainable development* (pp. 1–14). London: Earthscan.

Lester Person Institute for International Development. (1992). *Creating a common future: Proceedings of the Conference for University Action for Sustainable Development*. Halifax: Atlantic Nova Print.

Loxley, J., Silver, J., & Sexsmith, K. (2007). *Doing community economic development*. Halifax: Fernwood Press and Canadian Centre for Policy Alternatives.

MacLeod, G., McFarlane, B., & Davis, C.H. (1997). The knowledge economy and the social economy: University support for community enterprise development as a strategy for economic regeneration in distressed regions in

Canada and Mexico. *International Journal of Social Economics*, 24(11), 1302–24. http://dx.doi.org/10.1108/03068299710764297

Mook, L., & Sumner, J. (2010). Social accounting for sustainability in the social economy. In J.J. McMurtry (Ed.), *Living economics: Canadian perspectives on the social economy, co-operatives, and community economic development* (pp. 155–78). Toronto: Edmond Montgomery Publications.

Moore, D. (2000, October 6). Speaking with a unified voice: Student consumers make targeted change. *Carnegie Council*. Retrieved October 20, 2010, from: http://www.carnegiecouncil.org/resources/publications/dialogue/2_04/articles/893.html/:pf_printable

MSN. (2004). *No sweat review: Phase 1 report*. Maquila Solidarity Network on behalf of the Ethical Trade Action Group. Retrieved October 2, 2010, from: http://www.trademarks.utoronto.ca/downloads/nsreviewpub.pdf

MSN. (2008). Canadian universities with "no sweat" licensing policies. Maquila Solidarity Network. Retrieved October 2, 2010, from: http://en.maquilasolidarity.org/node/517

Murray, J.G. (2001). Improving purchasing's contribution – The purchasing strategy of buying council. *International Journal of Public Sector Management*, 14(5), 391–410. http://dx.doi.org/10.1108/EUM0000000005567

Newport, D., Chesnes, T., & Lindner, A. (2003). The environmental sustainability problem: Ensuring that sustainability stands on three legs. *International Journal of Sustainability in Higher Education*, 4(4), 357–63. http://dx.doi.org/10.1108/14676370310497570

Noya, A., & Clarence, E. (2009). Putting community capacity building in context. In G. Craig, A. Noya, & E. Clarence (Eds.), *Community capacity building: Creating a better future together* (pp. 15–35). Paris: Organization of Economic Co-operation and Development (OECD).

O'Rourke, D. (2003). Outsourcing regulation: Analyzing nongovernmental systems of labor standards and monitoring. *Policy Studies Journal: The Journal of the Policy Studies Organization*, 31(1), 1–29. http://dx.doi.org/10.1111/1541-0072.00001

Reed, D. (2002). Resource extraction industries in developing countries. *Journal of Business Ethics*, 39(3), 199–226. http://dx.doi.org/10.1023/A:1016538006160

Reed, D. (2004). Universities and the promotion of corporate responsibility: Reinterpreting the liberal arts tradition. *Journal of Academic Ethics*, 2(1), 3–41. http://dx.doi.org/10.1023/B:JAET.0000039006.33143.02

Ross, R. (2006). No sweat: Hard lessons from garment industry history. *Dissent* (Fall): 50–6.

Schaller, S. (2007). *The democratic legitimacy of private governance: An analysis of the Ethical Trade Initiative. University of Duisburg*. Essen: Institute for Development and Peace.

Sharp, L. (2002). Green campuses: The road from little victories to systemic transformation. *International Journal of Sustainability in Higher Education*, 3(2), 128–45. http://dx.doi.org/10.1108/14676370210422357

Thompson, R., & Green, W. (2005). When sustainability is not a Priority: An analysis of trends and strategies. *International Journal of Sustainability in Higher Education*, 6(1), 7–17. http://dx.doi.org/10.1108/14676370510573104

UBC Moves to Fair Trade "Ethical" Coffee. (2007, March 8). *The Vancouver Sun*. Retrieved October 17, 2010, from: http://www.canada.com/vancouversun/news/story.html?id=e2a19f13-5b0c-4470-becb-5cc29dc6084f&k=49118

United Nations Conference on Environment and Development (UNCED). (1992). *Agenda 21, the United Nations Programme of Action from Rio*. New York: UN Department of Public Information.

United Nations Educational, Scientific and Cultural Organization (UNESCO). (1972). *The Stockholm Declaration*. Stockholm: UNESCO.

United Nations Educational, Scientific and Cultural Organization (UNESCO). (1990). *The Talloires Declaration*. Gland, Switzerland: UNESCO.

United Nations Educational, Scientific and Cultural Organization – United Nations Environment Programme (UNESCO-UNEP). (1977). *The Tblisi Declaration*. Moscow: UNESCO-UNEP.

United Students for Fair Trade. (2008). About us guide. Retrieved October 9, 2010, from: http://www.usft.org/fairtrade/files/u1/Aboutus.pdf

Wells, D. (n.d.). No sweat a success with ethical purchasing. Canadian Association of University Teachers (CAUT). Retrieved October 5, 2010, from: http://www.crimt.org/Publications/CAUT_WELLS.pdf

Wells, D. (2004). How ethical are ethical purchasing policies? *Journal of Academic Ethics*, 2(1), 119–40. http://dx.doi.org/10.1023/B:JAET.0000039011.17896.05

World Commission on Environment and Development (WCED). (1987). *Our common future*. Oxford: Oxford University Press.

Workers' Rights Consortium. (2007). Search the factory disclosure database. Retrieved October 25, 2010, from: http://www.workersrights.org/search/

Wright, T.S.A. (2002). Definitions and frameworks for environmental sustainability in higher education. *International Journal of Sustainability in Higher Education*, 3(3), 203–20. http://dx.doi.org/10.1108/14676370210434679

Wright, T.S.A. (2010). University presidents' conceptualizations of sustainability in higher education. *International Journal of Sustainability in Higher Education*, 11(1), 61–73. http://dx.doi.org/10.1108/14676371011010057

9 The Role of Intermediaries in Social Accounting: Insights from Effective Transparency Systems

KATHERINE RUFF

Social accounting, since its earliest conceptualizations, has carried with it the pragmatic challenges of application to a specific organization within a specific temporal and social context, as well as the lofty aspirations of one day existing as a widely adopted accountability tool that could better align capital markets with sustainability goals by integrating social and environmental impacts into hitherto purely financial performance assessments. Social accounting stems from a body of critical accounting literature highlighting the deficiencies caused by externalities to financial accounting and the effect they have on the decisions we make as a society (see chapter 1 for a longer discussion of the origins of social accounting).

More recently, social accounting has received renewed attention within social capital markets. High-involvement philanthrocapitalists and impact investors in pursuit of blended value (Emerson, 2003) have been frustrated by the market inefficiency and weak transparency that arises from systemic information asymmetries (Emerson & Spitzer, 2007). This has renewed interest in a common social accounting system shared by all social economy organizations under the premise that more accurate, more consistent, and more comparable social accounting would improve the functioning of social capital markets and allocate more money to organizations creating social value.

Extant literature provides sobering discussions of the drawbacks of and hindrances to a shared social accounting system. Social impact is a complex construct, not easily observed or quantified. Representing numerically something so intangible, value-laden, and multifaceted is difficult. Simplifying social results into something more easily reported creates its own dysfunctions such as gaming, perverse incentives, mission drift, donor control, and corruption of the measures themselves (Paton, 2003; DiMaggio, 2001; Ostrander, 2007).

In social accounting there is an inherent tension between uniformity and flexibility. Uniformity offers the common measures and formats that would allow users – social investors, volunteers, ethical shoppers, and so on – to compare the results of several organizations in order to decide where to invest their time and money. This is needed to improve social capital markets, but comes at a risk of perverse incentives and other dysfunctions. Flexibility offers measures and formats tailored to each organization. Tailored approaches tend to trigger fewer dysfunctions, but they have limited meaning outside the organization.

An effective social accounting system needs both. It must be flexible enough to be adapted to each organization's specific context so that it conveys performance information that is most relevant. And it must be uniform enough to be useful to stakeholders who are making decisions about the nature of their relationship with the organization: it must be simple, concise, and comparable across time and organizations.

In the last decade, research into transparency systems and standard setting systems has revealed that the tensions faced by social accounting have been faced and overcome before, albeit in somewhat different contexts. Tentative theories are being developed to answer the question of how effective measurement and reporting systems are created and sustained. These theories open new avenues of research for those interested in accounting for social value. Research can go beyond the why and why not, and move into the how. How might social economy organizations reconcile the need for flexibility and uniformity? How can social accounting be both embedded within an organization and in the public domain? How can a common standard be created from the myriad of performance measurement tools and approaches currently in practice?

This chapter will focus on one element that has emerged out of studies on transparency systems and standard-setting: the role of intermediaries in creating and sustaining a complex compromise between flexibility and uniformity. It begins with a case study of the creation of Anglo-American financial accounting, a case chosen because of the similarities to social accounting and because it is by far the best studied and most understood of the cases. The roles of intermediaries are discussed in relation to the case and other standards and transparency systems. It ends with some concluding remarks on social accounting.

The Birth of Financial Accounting

Financial accounting with which we are familiar today appears straightforward compared with the quagmire of social performance measures. In non-profit literature, profit has been described as "simple" (Herman & Renz, 1999, p. 109), "tangible" (Gutierrez-Nieto & Serrano-Cinca, 2007, p. 450), and "objective" (Shoham, Ruvio, Vigoda-Gadot, & Schwabsky, 2006, p. 466).[1] So widely accepted are the basic elements of financial accounting that they have the appearance of an objectively observable truth. But accounting constructs reality as much as it represents reality. Mouck (2004) likens accounting to football. Having invented the game, it is clear how to keep score, but the score cannot exist without the rules, and the rules were imagined into existence. He writes, "Within the context of a given set of rules, certain financial accounting representations may be considered epistemologically objective even though there is no epistemologically objective basis for the rules themselves" (p. 528). Before financial accounting rules were established there was no common way to measure and report financial results (Lee, 1975). A common understanding of profit had to be created. The rules of the game had to be imagined into existence.

Impossible Beginnings

While accounting is arguably as old as trade itself, financial accounting, the preparation of accounts for shareholders and other stakeholders, did not exist until the Industrial Revolution (1770–1850), when changes in how businesses were owned and capitalized spawned changes in how transparent companies needed to be.

In the 1700s, securities were floated with a mere sentence. Investors had no means of independent analysis or verification, nor did they expect it or seek it. After a few bubbles crashed and a few fraudulent offerings were exposed, public attitudes towards corporate secrecy began to change. By the mid-1800s, some newspapers and politicians were proposing that companies be required to disclose factual, objective financial statements (Maltby, 1998; Hawkins, 1963). Most of this discussion was in London, which was the centre of the Anglo-Saxon financial world at the time.

When the 1854 Mercantile Laws Commission (MLC) sought testimony on proposed compulsory disclosures, businessmen responded that such a requirement would be foolhardy, if not impossible. Many mentioned something to the effect that there is no certain way to measure a company's financial results. Just as new forms of ownership had changed public attitude towards corporate secrecy, new forms of business – larger and more complex than those prior to industrialization – had put new demands on how businesses conceptualized and measured their performance. Things we take for granted today – like depreciation expense and distinguishing revenue from capital – were nascent concepts. Accounting was in a period of innovation. There were few rigid rules or even general guidelines. Lord Curriehill described "the impracticability of ascertaining correctly, at any time, the amount or even the existence of profits" (MLC, 1854, p. 14).

A number of testimonies argued that even if companies could disclose financial information in some standard form, doing so would be detrimental to the public precisely because there was so much variation in how companies calculated their numbers. Lord Overstone and William G. Prescott testified that presenting company performance with the appearance of hard numbers was misleading to the reader. They wrote, "if the tendency of such [financial] statements shall be to generate confidence, which would not otherwise exist on the part of the public, we think such publication may probably do more harm than good" (MLC, 1854, p. 98). Others were concerned that the only effect of disclosures would be to encourage gaming. James Clark of the Chamber of Commerce of Glasgow testified, "Making things pleasant in the way of accounts is known to be a facile art, level to very mean capacities, and the stimulus of a very strong desire on the part of limited partners to retrieve losses would elevate this art into a science" (MLC, 1854, p. 107). And there was concern that compulsory disclosures would systematically prejudice some types of companies. Opponents of mandatory disclosure were particularly concerned for the most and least profitable companies, as well as new and young companies, because readers of the statements would not understand the effects of different operating circumstances (Jones & Aiken, 1994).

How did financial accounting move from "the impracticability of ascertaining the amount or even existence of profit" to descriptions like "simple," "objective," and "tangible"?

An Elusive Truth

The obvious solution didn't work. If the barrier to better financial disclosures was too much variety in accounting methods, it would seem reasonable to conclude that developing uniform accounting methods would resolve the problem. This 1894 *New York Times* editorial captures the prevailing sentiment that businesses "[be] compelled by law to observe a uniform method in rendering its periodical statements of earnings and expenses ... [thus] tell the whole truth about earnings and expenses, and not cover up important shortages or improper expenditures by 'bunching' the figures or by resorting to tricky methods of bookkeeping" (*New York Times*, 21 October 1894; emphasis added).

Britain, the U.S., and Canada each experimented with versions of uniform accounts in the late nineteenth and early twentieth centuries. Generally speaking, these were a series of very detailed reporting frameworks prescribed by governments for the major industries of the time – railways, utilities, insurance companies. They brought modest improvements to disclosures (Edwards, 1989, p. 168; Blough, 1939, p. 267; Hawkins, 1986), but it proved difficult to regulate true uniformity. Weldon Powell, the first Chair of the Accounting Principles Board, reflecting back on an era of uniformity, commented that despite

> a great measure of uniformity in the conditions, under which [regulated industries] operate, the products or service they sell, the customers they serve, the means they employ in distributing their output ... circumstances uniform accounting would be expected to be at its most effective ... even here it is not fully achieved. (Powell, 1965, p. 679)

Moreover, the very aim of uniform accounts was called into question. By the 1930s, railways and utilities had waned as the engines of the economy, and a new diversity of manufacturing businesses were emerging. Accountants, who by this time had assembled themselves into a well-organized profession, argued that flexibility was a desirable and necessary component of transparency (Keller, 1965). Truth, they said, cannot be separated from the specific context of a specific transaction. To be truthful, accounting treatment must reflect a business' strategy, industry, market, geography, and so on, which means the invariant rules that were meant to create perfect uniformity were creating one type of truth – a uniform, but abstract one – even as they undermined another truth, a relevant one.

A Surprising Result

What surprises many people who are not themselves accountants is that the concerns presented to the Mercantile Laws Commission of 1854 persist today. The financial statements of companies are not absolute truths, nor do the numbers within them represent any objective reality (MacIntosh & Shearer, 2000). Small changes in seemingly minor details of accounting can substantially alter a company's reported profits. Financial reports aren't comparable, and certainly not in a simplistic line-by-line fashion. If anyone were to do a simplistic comparison it would systematically disadvantage some industries over others. Concerns about gaming and perverse incentives rise when investors emphasize a particular metric. The problems of 1854 persist, but transparency is drastically improved.

Rather than striving for perfect uniformity in how each account was rendered, but without giving up on investor demands for more reliable, comparable financial disclosures, accounting bodies in the U.S., Canada, and Britain focused on developing common report formats and consistent material disclosures (Zeff, 1972a; Murphy, 1993). With this approach, companies aren't required to adhere to a single correct method of accounting, but they are required to disclose their major accounting policies. Parameters around these methods are such that while there is no one uniform way to calculate profits, there are correct and incorrect ways. The systems evolved slightly differently in the three countries, but all use this bounded flexibility coupled with consistent, material disclosure. Modern financial disclosures, complying with Generally Accepted Accounting Principles (GAAP) or International Accounting Standards (IAS), are the result of a well-struck and continuously evolving balance between uniformity and flexibility (Zeff, 1972a, b).

Financial Accounting Then, Social Accounting Now

The early development of financial accounting is a particularly relevant case for social accounting because of the similarity of the fields prior to development, the similarity of users, and the similarity of the subject the transparency system recounts.

Today, social accounting – and, more broadly, performance reporting among social economy organizations – is characterized by innovation. It has borne witness to the development of outcome reporting (known variously as theory of change or logical framework analysis), stakeholder-engagement methodologies (rapid rural appraisal, social audit), expanded value-added statements (Quarter, Mook, & Richmond, 2002), and social return on investment (SROI). These innovations build tools and measures around new concepts like double bottom-line, stakeholders, valuation of volunteers, and social return – each a part of the new sophistication of operating a social economy enterprise. Innovation currently happens within an organization, or between the funding and funded organization and, although effective methods are rapidly imitated, there is also frequent adaptation. As Brown and Hicks (chapter 4 of this volume) illustrate with Co-op Atlantic adapting the Co-operative Audit Scorecard to be "rooted more clearly in the ICA co-operative principles and values," social economy organizations borrow successful ideas, but do not implement them without thought to their own needs and constraints. Performance measurement approaches mutate with each implementation, as was the case with industrial-era accounting.

The form, content, and frequency of social reports vary greatly within the social economy and are typically developed for each major funder. Normally, relevance and accuracy are priorities high above comparability. Some foundations or grant-making organizations seek comparability among the projects they fund, which is another form of relevance from the perspective of the grant-making organization. Social economy organizations typically provide their most thoughtful performance measurements to the narrowest of audiences: their large donors (Cutt & Murray, 2000; Fine, Thayer, & Coghlan, 2000). For most non-profits, charities, and social enterprises, the social results made available to the general public, on websites or in annual reports, are greatly simplified and unwaveringly positive. It is marketing, not accounting. So, too, at one time, was financial reporting. Like the eighteenth-century investor, today's average donor is given little opportunity for independent assessment of results.

A major concern raised by opponents of standardized financial disclosures was that subjecting financial reports to external review would cause gaming, motivate deceptive book-keeping, and create an unfair bias against certain companies. This is perhaps the most oft-mentioned criticism of any common system for accounting for social value. DiMaggio calls this the "Flamingo Problem":

> Like Alice [in Wonderland's] flamingo mallets, performance indicators often develop lives of their own, and their meanings change as they are measured. This problem is ubiquitous and well documented … the reporting organizations are given incentive to attend to the outcome being measured … it is equally probable that the organization will figure out how to game the system. (DiMaggio, 2001, p. 259)

When organizations attend to the outcome, myopia and suboptimization arise. When organizations focus their attention on performing well on near-term tangible measures, selected impacts are maximized in a way that does not maximize total impact (Smith, 1996). When organizations game the system, measures and reports become dissociated from performance. Either organizations go about their business and continue to spin what Paton (2003, p. 29) describes as the public tale of progress and achievement, or they get caught up in their own game and become what Chambers (1996, p. 211) refers to as the "deceiving and self-deceiving NGO." The threat that a common social accounting system does more harm than good echoes concerns from businessmen in the 1850s that common financial disclosures would be impossible and probably foolhardy.

And yet, 120 years after the Mercantile Laws Commissions, Powell wrote, "comparability of the published financial statements of given business from period to period has been effectively achieved in practice during the past 30 years ..." (Powell, 1965, p. 683). Given the common challenges at the outset, it is worth looking at how financial accounting developed in the hopes that one day someone might look at a social economy enterprise's social results and presume that the measuring and reporting of them has always been straightforward.

Creating a Shared Framework

There are a number of factors that have been identified as influential in the creation of financial accounting. Economic development, political climate, and globalization influenced the behaviour of accounting professionals, created enabling environments, and spurred (as well as at times deterred) companies to adhere to recommended accounting practice (Hawkins, 1986; Edwards, 1989). Certain charismatic and visionary individuals have been identified as important changemakers (Bocqueraz & Walton, 2006; Richardson, 2000). The emergence of stock exchanges and the financial press helped to create a demand for greater disclosures (Hawkins, 1986; Basikin & Miranti, 1999). Government regulation was also a factor. Tax policy had a harmonizing effect on accounting methods. Company law and securities regulation set minimum disclosure levels (McWatters, 1998; Edwards, 1989; Arnold & Matthews, 2002). In the U.S., a series of accounting-related lawsuits were a major impetus for the creation of GAAP as corporations sought a formal definition of accepted accounting practice in order to defend themselves against further lawsuits. All of these factors played important roles in shaping financial accounting.

This chapter will focus on another factor that has been identified as critical to the development of financial accounting. It is a factor that is also identified as critical to the development of other standards, as varied as technical standards on screw threads and total quality management, and other transparency systems, from public school report cards to nutritional labelling on food: the presence of strong intermediaries.

Role of Intermediaries

Intermediaries have played a critical role in the development of standards and transparency systems. Intermediaries have helped to build consensus on what the standard ought to be, advance and maintain the standard, and manage the complexity of information disclosed. By studying how accounting standards and other transparency systems have emerged in the past, and what attributes those that remain share, we can start to develop some hypotheses about how a shared social accounting system might be created.

An intermediary is any organization or individual involved in the production or consumption of transparency information, but is neither the original producer nor the final consumer. Accounting associations, standard-setting organizations, and agencies rating ethical mutual funds are all intermediaries.

A standard defines a level of quality that can be attained. Fair trade certification is an example of a standard. A consumer is able to know only one piece of information – that the item in question met the standard. A transparency system facilitates the disclosure of a range of factual information about a company's products and practices (Fung, Weil, Graham, & Fagotto, 2004). Nutritional labelling and financial reporting are examples of transparency systems. Transparency systems tend not to set an explicit ideal level of performance, but rather provide a range of information to enable users to make decisions in their lives as consumers, parents, investors, donors, and volunteers. In financial reporting there is a standard for the accounting itself – an auditor verifies that it is probable that the accounts have been prepared according to the standard, and there is a transparency system for the performance of the company.

Most methods of accounting for the social results of social economy organizations share this split – they strive to have a common method for measuring and reporting (the standard) in order to disclose a range of pertinent information about the organization (the transparency system) so that others can draw their own conclusions. To understand how a social accounting system may develop, we must understand the development of both standards and transparency systems.

An Institutional Identity

Literature on standard-setting has emphasized the importance of the entity that houses and shepards the standard. It is a common, but not ubiquitous, element of standards that they are developed by an organization with an inclusive governance structure. This provides adherents shared control of the standard (Sahlin-Andersson, 2000). Historically it has also facilitated the consolidation of competing standards through the consolidation of competing standard-setting organizations (Hallström, 2004).

The emergence of professional associations of accountants was important to the development of an accounting standard. Over time, these associations drew the development of accounting out of companies where it was developed to meet the specific needs of each company, into the professional associations where accounting was developed as a standard (West, 1996). Accounting became the expertise of accountants, developed independent of any single application. There were many accounting associations, each with slightly different variations of accounting. As some associations emerged as leaders, so too did their variants of accounting (Richardson, 1986, 1987; Loeb & Miranti, 2004).

Corporate sustainability reporting used to be something each company designed for itself. Now there are several available standards. The sustainability reporting standard that is enjoying the widest adoption, the Global Reporting Initiative (GRI) (Hess, 2008; KPMG, 2008) was developed by an organization that sees itself as a "multi-stakeholder network," in which organizations have the opportunity to share in the control of the standard (GRI, 2011). Similarly, the first standard for socially responsible behaviour, the ISO 26000– Social responsibility, was developed by the largest working group in the history of the International Standards Organization, with 450 participating experts and 210 observers from 99 ISO member countries and 42 liaison organizations (ISO, 2011). Standards need institutional identities. Many such institutions are ones in which the users of the standard have some influence.

Based on these experiences, one might hypothesize that social accounting initiatives with an institutional form, like the Demonstrating Values Project (chapter 6 of this volume), are more likely to gain broad adoption than those without an institutional form, and that adoption might be increased if that institution used a broad stakeholder approach to govern development of the standard.

From De Facto to De Jure Standards

In financial accounting standards and technical standards can be observed a progression from de facto standards (those that emerge on their own through imitation, diffusion, and other market forces), to de jure standards (those that are deliberately created and then recommended to the market), and, finally, to regulation.

Early accounting associations, still establishing their legitimacy, limited themselves to documenting the accounting norms that were already in practice. Later, once the standard-setting role was formalized, associations systematically advanced the standard and recommended specific practice. In a final stage, national laws regulated financial disclosure by referencing the standards of the accounting profession.

Furutsen (2002) observes this progression with the ISO 9000 – a quality management standard, where the first de jure standards were largely an articulation of the de facto norms. Once the standard had sufficient adoption, subsequent iterations advanced the de facto norm, into the de jure standard. In some countries the ISO 9000 has been incorporated into government regulation (Furutsen, 2002).

The Global Reporting Initiative similarly created a du jure standard from de facto norms and then increased the rigour of the standard. GRI has become part of regulations in Sweden, where the government requires state-owned companies to report their social performance using the GRI standard (Government of Sweden, 2007).

If a standard is to be sustained, it needs a critical mass of adherents. A de jure standard of an intermediary body is more likely to earn broader adoption if the standard departs very little from existing practice (Brunsson, Jacobsson & Associates 2002, pp. 149–150; Henning, 2000). If these cases are to be followed, any proposed social accounting standard should closely echo de facto norms, build a critical mass of adherents, and then, in conjunction with the broad base of stakeholders referred to above, advance a de jure standard.

Infomediation

In their study of twelve mature transparency systems in the United States, Fung, Weil, Graham, and Fagotto (2004) asked why some disclosure systems stagnate into costly, outdated, bureaucratic exercises, while others remain vibrant, responsive, and useful. They identified the presence of strong intermediaries as a key differentiator between effective and ineffective transparency systems. One role these strong intermediaries play is to distill complex information. The term used for information-distilling intermediaries is "infomediaries."

Good reporting increases accountability and transparency only if the reports are read, and read carefully. Financial statements reconcile uniformity and flexibility by putting the onus on the reader to recognize the significance of different accounting policies. The reports are prepared under the assumption that readers know how to read financial statements – something that many users do not know how to do. As W.Z. Ripley expressed it in an entertaining essay in the *Atlantic Monthly*, information should be disclosed in annual reports

> not because each shareholder, male or female, old or young, will even bother to remove the wrapping from the annual report in the post, but because specialists, analysts, bankers, and others will promptly disseminate the information, translating it into terms that will be intelligible to all. (Ripley, 1926)

The formation of professional associations of investment bankers and financial analysts followed close on the heels of the accounting associations (Fogarty & Rogers, 2004), beginning with the founding of the Investment Bankers Association of America in 1912. (The Toronto Society of Financial Analysts was founded in 1936; the Montreal Society was founded in 1950.) These societies created and flourished on a type of expert knowledge distinct from accounting: the analysis and interpretation of financial disclosures. Analysts have become an essential part of the financial transparency system.

Corporate sustainability is not much different. The GRI reporting standard is more complex than many investors are interested in reading. Analysts, like Jantzi Sustainalytics, have emerged. These analysts create products that guide ethical investors to the most socially responsible companies based on the expertise they have cultivated in reading and analysing the reports and comparing the sustainability of companies in different industries.

Social results are complex things to convey. Social accounting will be less prone to dysfunction if the results are disclosed in a manner that does justice to that complexity. In other transparency systems where the disclosures are complex, analysts have emerged to develop expertise in comparing dissimilar entities and distilling information.

Of all the intermediary roles in financial accounting, it is the auditor that has garnered the most attention outside of accounting (Power, 1997). The audit, and assurance in general, does not create transparency. Certainly, assurance can help to support a standard by corroborating, for each implementation, sufficient adherence to the standard. However, the auditor's statement is not a very powerful transparency tool. It says nothing about the company's performance. The auditor's role in creating accounting standards, and sustaining the transparency system, is less significant than the roles of professional bodies, standard-setting organizations, and analysts.

Uniformity and Flexibility

Intermediaries help standards strike and maintain a balance between uniformity and flexibility. The unintended consequences and corrupting nature of uniform top-down performance measures can be mitigated by introducing flexibility in the standard. Comparability can be brought to flexible stakeholder-driven methods by focusing on reporting formats and material disclosures. An ecosystem of intermediaries is needed to do this.

In highly structured (uniform) social performance measurement frameworks, social economy organizations are typically allowed only a numerical answer to indicators like "number of visitors" or "number of participants who attend the program." This leads to guesswork if the organization is not able to track the required performance data. For example, an open-air public art display may not be able to track the number of visitors. Structured frameworks can also yield misleading information if organizations interpret the performance metric differently. For example, one organization might consider those who attend 60 per cent of a program as having "attended" it, while another organization counts all those who showed up on day one. As was done with railway accounts, top-down prescribed indictors can strive for uniformity by creating an ever-expanding list of rules on increasingly minute details, or, as financial accounting eventually did, by inviting flexibility into the performance framework by allowing reporting organizations to interpret indicators in a way that is relevant to the organization, requiring disclosure of all material information about how the accounts were prepared. The latter puts an emphasis on the skills of the reader to make appropriate judgments. IRIS is an example of a social economy performance measurement taxonomy that has bounded flexibility. For example, social purpose businesses are able to choose the most appropriate expression of poverty line from among several options.

In constructionist (flexible) methods, organizations typically develop performance metrics organically based on consultations with stakeholders. There is no uniformity from year to year or organization to organization. These methods can increase comparability while still maintaining a bottom-up, highly tailored approach to social performance measurement by focusing on material disclosures, using a common reporting format and providing information on methods and assumptions. The SROI Network (2012)'s guide to social return on investment is an example of a stakeholder-engaged method that balances flexibility with comparability.

In both cases, balancing uniformity and flexibility requires an ecosystem of intermediaries to build, promote, and maintain the standard and to distill complex information.

There may be other benefits to creating a social accounting reporting standard. It has been argued, both in the case of technology-related standard-setting bodies (Murphy & Yates, 2009) and financial accounting (Waterhouse, 1982), that the creation of a single framework reduces costs. Where accountability tools must be developed uniquely for each transaction, there is the opportunity to save costs, collectively as a sector, by agreeing on one standard

Conclusion

This chapter has sought to advance three main points to the study of social accounting for social economy organizations. The first is that for social accounting to achieve widespread adoption, tensions between flexibility and uniformity must be resolved. Top-down, rigid reporting frameworks fail to achieve relevance to the broad spectrum of organizations, and they struggle to evolve with a dynamic world. Deeply contextualized reporting systems fail to achieve comparability, which impedes the degree to which donors embed the information in their decision-making processes. Both uniformity and flexibility are required for effective transparency.

The second point is that other transparency systems and standards, from nutritional labelling to the assurance of quality management, have had to reconcile similar tensions in the past, and from these experiences are emerging some tentative theories about how systems are implemented and sustained that can be useful to social accounting. At the very least, the history of financial accounting should call into question the notion that there is something unique about social accounting that defies standardization.

The third point is that intermediaries played a crucial role in the creation of an accounting standard and in sustaining the transparency system. This chapter has focused on (a) the development of accounting know-how in a shared space outside the contextualized application; (b) how institutionalization of the standard facilitated greater consolidation; and (c) the possibility of a link between the legitimacy of the standard-setting organization and the extent to which it can move beyond simply encoding norms to advancing practice through standards. On creating and sustaining an effective transparency system, this chapter paid attention to the role of analysts in advocating for clear and consistent disclosures, and the importance of expert, nuanced interpretation of complex performance reports in which complexity is a by-product of flexibility.

The development and functioning of financial accounting reveals both complex and dynamic socioeconomic systems. Those who beseech the social economy to settle on a standard promptly, arguing that the benefits of uniformity outweigh marginal improvements in methodology, have mistakenly understood a standard as an output that can be published in a book or rendered into a spreadsheet. In standards that sustain, there is a rich supporting socio-political and economic system. To achieve a standard social accounting system, we should develop not just the techniques and presentations undertaken by each social economy organization, but also the institutions and intermediaries that support the system.

NOTE

1 Given the contexts in which these references appeared, these authors were reasonable in their characterizations of profit.

REFERENCES

Arnold, A.J., & Matthews, D. (2002). Statutory and voluntary influences on corporate financial disclosures in the UK, 1920–50. *Accounting and Business Research*, 32(1), 3–16.

Barron, B., & Miranti, P.J., Jr. (1999). *A history of corporate finance*. Cambridge: Cambridge University Press.

Blough, C.G. (1939). Accounting principles interpreted in the light of recent developments. *Journal of Business of the University of Chicago, 12*(3), 265–79.http://dx.doi.org/10.1086/232525

Bocqueraz, C., & Walton, P. (2006). Creating a supranational institution: the role of the individual and the mood of the times. *Accounting History, 11*(3), 271–88.http://dx.doi.org/10.1177/1032373206065863

Brunsson, N., Jacobsson, B., & Associates. (2002). *A world of standards*. Oxford: Oxford University Press.http://dx.doi.org/10.1093/acprof:oso/9780199256952.001.0001

Chambers, R. (1996). The primacy of the personal. In M. Edward & D. Hulme (Eds.), *Beyond the magic bullet: NGO performance and accountability in the post cold war world* (pp. 241–53). Hartford, CT: Kumarian Press Books.

Cutt, J., & Murray, V. (2000). *Accountability and effectiveness evaluation in non-profit organizations*. London: Routledge.

DiMaggio, P. (2001). Measuring the impact of the nonprofit sector on society is probably impossible but possibly useful: A sociological perspective. In P. Flynn & V.A. Hodgkinson (Eds.), *Measuring the impact of the nonprofit sector* (pp. 249–72). New York: Klewer Academic.

Edwards, J.R. (1989). *The history of financial accounting*. London: Routledge.

Emerson, J. (2003). The blended value proposition: Integrating social and financial returns. *California Management Review, 45*(4), 35–51.

Emerson, J., & Spitzer, J. (2007). From fragmentation to function: Critical concepts and writings on social capital markets' structure, operation and innovation. Retrieved February 23, 2010, from: http://www.blendedvalue.org/media/pdf-capital-markets-fragmentation.pdf

Fine, A.H., Thayer, C.E., & Coghlan, A. (2000). Program evaluation practice in the nonprofit sector. *Nonprofit Management & Leadership, 10*(3), 331–39.http://dx.doi.org/10.1002/nml.10309

Fogarty, T., & Rogers, R. (2005). Financial analysts' reports: An extended institutional theory evaluation. *Accounting, Organizations and Society, 30*(4), 331–56.http://dx.doi.org/10.1016/j.aos.2004.06.003

Fung, A., Weil, D., Graham, M., & Fagotto, E. (2004). The political economy of transparency: What makes disclosure policies sustainable? Retrieved July 31, 2011, from: http://www.innovations.harvard.edu/cache/documents/67/6784.pdf

Furutsen, S. (2002). The knowledge base of standards. In N. Brunsson & B. Jacobsson, & Associates (Eds.). *A world of standards* (pp. 71–84). Oxford: Oxford University Press.

Global Reporting Initiative (GRI). (2011). What is GRI? Retrieved July 31, 2011, from: http://www.globalreporting.org/AboutGRI/WhatIsGRI/

Government of Sweden. (2007). Guidelines for external reporting by state-owned companies. Retrieved April 9, 2012, from: http://www.sweden.gov.se/sb/d/574/a/94125.

Gutierrez-Nieto, B., & Serrano-Cinca, C. (2007). Factors explaining the rating of microfinance institutions. *Nonprofit and Voluntary Sector Quarterly, 36*(3), 439–64.http://dx.doi.org/10.1177/0899764006296055

Hallström, K.T. (2004). *Organizing international standardization: ISO and the IASC in quest of authority.* Northampton, MA: Edward Elgar Publishing.

Hawkins, D.F. (1963). The development of modern financial reporting practices among American manufacturing corporations. *Business History Review, 37*(3), 135–68.http://dx.doi.org/10.2307/3112231

Hawkins, D.F. (1986). *Corporate financial disclosure: 1900–1933.* New York: Garland.

Henning, R. (2000). Selling Standards. In N. Brunsson, B. Jacobsson, & Associates. (Eds.), *A world of standards* (pp. 115–18). Oxford: Oxford University Press.

Herman, R., & Renz, D. (1999). Theses on nonprofit organizational effectiveness. *Nonprofit and Voluntary Sector Quarterly, 28*(2), 107–126.http://dx.doi.org/10.1177/0899764099282001

Hess, D. (2008). The three pillars of corporate social reporting as new governance regulation: Disclosure, dialogue and development. Available at: http://ssrn.com/abstract=1176882

International Organization for Standardization (ISO). (2011). ISO 26000 – Social Responsibility. Retrieved July 31, 2011, from: http://www.iso.org/iso/sr_iso26000_overview.htm

Jones, S., & Aiken, M. (1994). The significance of the profit and loss account in nineteenth-century Britain: A reassessment. *Abacus, 30*(2), 196–230.http://dx.doi.org/10.1111/j.1467-6281.1994.tb00350.x

Keller, T. (1965). Uniformity versus flexibility: A review of the rhetoric. *Law and Contemporary Problems, 30*(4), 637–41.http://dx.doi.org/10.2307/1190773

KPMG. (2008). International survey of corporate responsibility reporting. Retrieved July 31, 2011, from: http://www.kpmg.com/Global/en/IssuesAndInsights/ArticlesPublications

Lee, G. (1975). The concept of profit in British accounting, 1760–1900. *Business History Review, 49*(1), 6–36.

Loeb, E., & Miranti, P. (2004). *The institute of accounts: Nineteenth-century origins of accounting professionalism in the United States.* London: Routledge.

Macintosh, N., & Shearer, T. (2000). The accounting profession today: A post-structuralist critique. *Critical Perspectives on Accounting, 11*(5), 607–26.http://dx.doi.org/10.1006/cpac.2000.0407

Maltby, J. (1998). UK joint stock companies legislation 1844–1900: Accounting publicity and "mercantile caution." *Accounting History, 3*(1), 9–32.http://dx.doi.org/10.1177/103237329800300102

McWatters, C. (1998). Accounting thought, practice and legislation: Early Canadian evidence. *Accounting History, 3*(2), 103–42.[REMOVED HYPERLINK FIELD]http://dx.doi.org/10.1177/103237329800300205

Mercantile Laws Commission (MLC). (1854). *First report of the Royal Commission on the Mercantile Laws and Amendments to the Law of Partnership (MLC).* British Parliamentary Papers, Vol. XXVII.

Mouck, T. (2004). Institutional reality, financial reporting and the rules of the game. *Accounting, Organizations and Society, 29*(5–6), 525–41.http://dx.doi.org/10.1016/S0361-3682(03)00035-7

Murphy, G.J. (Ed.). (1993). *A History of Canadian accounting thought and practice.* New York: Garland Publishing.

Murphy, C., & Yates, J. (2009). *The International Organization for Standardization (ISO): Global governance through voluntary consensus.* Abingdon, Oxon: Routledge.

New York Times. (1894, October 21). Uniformity in railway accounts. Retrieved September 22, 2009, from: http://query.nytimes.com/mem/archive-free/pdf?res=9501E7D71531E033A25752C2A9669D94659ED7CF

Ostrander, S. (2007). The growth of donor control: Revisiting the social relations of philanthropy. *Nonprofit and Voluntary Sector Quarterly, 36*(2), 356–72.http://dx.doi.org/10.1177/0899764007300386

Paton, R. (2003). *Managing and measuring social enterprises.* London: Sage.

Powell, W. (1965). Putting uniformity in financial accounting into perspective. *Law and Contemporary Problems, 30*(4), 674–89.

Power, M. (1997). *The Audit Society: Rituals of verification.* Oxford: Oxford University Press.

Quarter, J., Mook, L., & Richmond, B.J. (2002). *What counts: Social accounting for nonprofits and cooperatives.* Upper Saddle River, NJ: Prentice Hall.

Richardson, A.J. (1986). Who audits? The emergence of hegemony in the Ontario accountancy profession. In G.J. Murphy (Ed.), (1993). *A History of Canadian accounting thought and practice* (pp. 209–50). New York: Garland Publishing.

Richardson, A.J. (1987). Professionalization and intra-professional competition in the Canadian accounting profession. In G.J. Murphy (Ed.), (1993). *A History of Canadian accounting thought and practice* (pp. 183–208). New York: Garland Publishing.

Richardson, A.J. (2000). Building the Canadian chartered accountancy profession: A biography of George Edwards, FCA, CBE, LLE, 1861–1947. *Accounting Historians Journal, 27*(2), 87–116.

Ripley, W.Z. (Sept. 26, 1926). Stop, look, listen. *The Atlantic Monthly*. Retrieved September 22, 2009, from: http://www.theatlantic.com/issues/26sep/ripley.htm

Sahlin-Andersson, K. (2000). Arenas as standardizers. In N. Brunsson & B. Jacobsson, & Associates (Eds.), *A world of standards* (pp. 101–14). Oxford: Oxford University Press.

Shoham, A., Ruvio, A., Vigoda-Gadot, E., & Schwabsky, N. (2006). Market orientations in the nonprofit and voluntary sector: A meta-analysis of their relationships with organizational performance. *Nonprofit and Voluntary Sector Quarterly, 35*(3), 453–76.http://dx.doi.org/10.1177/0899764006287671

Smith, P. (1996). *Measuring outcomes in the public sector*. Bristol, PA: Taylor & Francis.

SROI Network. (2012). *A guide to social return on investment*. Retrieved April 9, 2012, from: http://www.thesroinetwork.org/publications.

Waterhouse, J.H. (1982). A descriptive analysis of selected aspects of the Canadian accounting standard-setting process. In G.J. Murphy (Ed.) (1993). *A History of Canadian accounting thought and practice* (pp. 327–84). New York: Garland Publishing.

West, B. (1996). The professionalisation of accounting: A review of recent historical research and its implications. *Accounting History, 1*(1), 77–102.http://dx.doi.org/10.1177/103237329600100105

Zeff, S.A. (1972a). *Forging of accounting principles in five countries: A history and analysis of trends*. Champaign, IL: Stripes.

Zeff, S.A. (1972b). Chronology of significant developments in the establishment of accounting principles in the United States, 1926–1972. *Journal of Accounting Research, 10*(1), 217–27.http://dx.doi.org/10.2307/2490230

10 Social Accounting: Lessons Learned for the Road Ahead

LAURIE MOOK AND MIKULAS PSTROSS

The goal of this book was to provide an understanding of key issues and areas of activity in social accounting, especially relating to social economy organizations such as non-profit organizations, co-operatives, and social enterprises. The cases presented in this book are not constrained by traditional accounting rules and frameworks. We see innovation in many areas, such as the expansion of boundaries in terms of which entities are included in the accounts, which stakeholders are considered, alternative motivations for producing the accounts, and differences in specific content and methods.

In this book we show that social accounting is a tool that can be used in many ways. It can tell the performance of an organization and can provide an alternate way of seeing a particular reality. It can also be a driver of behaviour, unveil power structures, and facilitate learning about externalities and sustainability. Indeed, each of the presented cases provides distinct applications of letting economic, social, and environmental factors tell a different "story" than traditional accounting. This chapter highlights both the diversity and uniformity of these cases, and then proceeds to connect these experiences of social accounting with principles of democracy. It ends with implications and suggestions for educating a new generation of social accountants and organization leaders.

Diversity and Uniformity in Social Accounting

We have seen in the previous chapters that the term social accounting is an umbrella for a diverse spectrum of frameworks and their underlying theories in a number of international settings.[1] To illustrate the richness of how social accounting is used, we now look at some of the sources of this diversity (Gray, Owen, & Adams, 2010).[2]

1. What type of entity is accounted for?

Social accounting is usually an activity done by and for organizations. In the first chapter, the close link between social accounting and social economy organizations is discussed. Case studies in this book offer a more detailed description of these organizations: co-operatives in chapter 4, credit unions in chapter 5, and social enterprises in chapter 6. In addition, we show that trusts (chapter 2), Convention and Visitors Bureaus (chapter 7), universities (chapter 8), and standard-setting organizations (chapter 9) can also make use of social accounting.

At the same time, social accounting is not restricted to organizations. At one end of the spectrum, social accounting can be applied at the program level (chapter 1 and chapter 5). At the other end, social accounting practices are also applied to geographical regions (chapter 2), fair trade value chains (chapter 3), and neighbourhoods (chapter 1). Just as the links between economic, social, and environmental factors can be made explicit, so too can the interconnections between organizations in a community or regional setting.

2. Which stakeholders are considered?

Social accounting is not based on a one-directional flow of information from one entity to another. Rather, it can be thought of as a communicative process that requires openness and a willingness to be challenged from all parties involved. Depending on the context, different stakeholders take part in the social accounting process. In the hereby-presented case studies, the stakeholders included consumers, town residents, students, tourists, government institutions, immigrant businesspersons, at-risk populations such as the poor and the unemployed, members and leaders of co-operatives, and other representatives of social economy organizations.

3. What is the motivation for producing a social account?

There are numerous reasons why organizations and other entities engage in social accounting. The Falkland Heritage Trust (chapter 2) uses social accounting practices to promote an ethic of stewardship. The motivation of Assisi Organics (chapter 3) is to help the organization gain an understanding of the reputation of its local community, as well as of its customers and the fair trade system more generally. For the Consumer's Community Co-operative (chapter 4), the motivation is showing the co-operative difference as a value proposition. For Convention and Visitors Bureaus (chapter 7), being able to show the broader social contributions of Destination Management Organizations is important as they increasingly become recipients of public funds. For the Demonstrating Value Initiative (chapter 6), social accounting is a way of attracting stakeholders to the discussion table to create a viable reporting model that would satisfy enterprises and funders alike. The Alterna Savings Credit Union (chapter 5), by spreading the word about the benefits it brings, appeals to the government to provide more support to credit unions and caisses populaires in general, and also proves beneficial for the organization itself through increased loans and member recruitment. Social accounting is also proposed in chapter 8 to help universities remain true to their social mission and to be more responsive to their student body and other stakeholders as far as procurement policies are concerned.

4. What is the specific content of the accounts?

The content of the social account varies due to the unique missions of social economy actors. The Falkland Heritage Trust case study in chapter 2 proposes that the objects of account address biodiversity, cultural heritage, and systems of knowledge. Chapter 3 introduced the link between social accounting and fair trade as a tool to measure and track equitable shares of profit to be distributed among producers. The stories of the women and poor who found jobs as well as support through Assisi Organics might also be included in that organization's social account. Alterna Savings Credit Union in chapter 5 assesses the positive changes in its clients' financial situation. The Convention and Visitors Bureaus in chapter 7 might be interested in enumerating indirect financial gains that result from the Bureaus' operations and universities can give an account of their procurement policies. For the Consumer's Community Co-operative in chapter 4 and the Demonstrating Value Initiative in chapter 6, the content of social accounting can be centred on how social accounting tools and resources are being provided to other stakeholders and entities.

5. What are the broad objectives of the accounts?

Several concepts and principles have a distinct presence in the case studies. Chapter 2 brings forth the concepts of stewardship, sustainability, and environmental responsibility. Chapter 3 puts an emphasis on fair trade and innovation, while chapter 4 emphasizes stakeholder engagement, sustainability, and democratic governance, as does the Demonstrative Value Initiative in chapter 6. Social accounting orients the Alterna Savings Credit Union (chapter 5) with the concepts of social responsibility. The Convention and Visitors Bureaus are concerned with accountability, while the university procurement policies investigated in chapter 8 were examined for their orientation to sustainability, ethical trade, and environmental protection.

6. What methods/techniques were used to "do" social accounting?

Social accounting lends itself to a mix of qualitative and quantitative methods. Indeed, a variety of approaches were used in this book to develop and conduct social accounting, including organization document review, literature searches of academic articles, and exploration of the Internet for similar organizations. To gather data, mixed methods were often used, from surveys, logic model exercises, focus groups, interviews, and stakeholder dialogue to participatory action research. Reporting on results also took various forms. Some social accounting reporting was part of internal management processes, while in other cases it was intended to be disseminated to a wider external audience.

Social Accounting and Democracy

Although diverse in many ways, the cases in this volume also reveal an inherent connection and uniformity between social accounting and principles of transparency, accountability, and the participation of multiple stakeholders. As such, social accounting makes a contribution to the project of democracy.

By protecting individual and collective rights and freedoms, democratic societies expect no less from their citizens than to partake in collective governance. Such participation takes place on many levels, starting with one's freedom to voice opinions and criticize authorities; it continues with voting in free elections, being a member of a political party, or starting a non-profit organization. In reality, democracy can seldom fully live up to its ideals, because both individual and institutional flaws are sources of injustices. It is for this reason that Sartori (1987) speaks of democracy *as a project* trying to reach *what ought to be*, while still being situated in *what is*. However, by means of auto-corrective measures, the system as such can be regulated and flaws constantly corrected. Contrary to authoritarian regimes, where criticism is strongly prohibited, democratic institutions call for a focused analysis of the status quo and for learning from mistakes in order to improve the quality of democracy (Popper, 1964).

In such processes of piecemeal improvements on the road to democratic ideals, the principles of transparency and accountability play a key role. They both attest to the necessity of sharing information about the status quo so that the public can participate in democratic governance. The medieval Latin word *transparere* means "to show light through" (http://www.etymologyonline.com). In other words, transparency has to do with seeing. Accountability refers to the commitments of individuals and institutions to act in an ethical and predictable way (from the Old French *aconter* – "to count, to render account") (http://www.etymologyonline.com). We can simply say that accountability involves, among other things, making things transparent. Drawing this statement back to democracy, auto-corrective measures can best work when various aspects of democratic institutions are open to "observations" and the criticism that results from them. Thus the system provides an avenue for making improvements. However, transparency by itself does not guarantee better governance. What is needed is the combination of accountability of individuals, organizations, and groups, and a transparent discussion over how these agents influence the world, such as that found in social accounting.

Approaches to accountability can be reactive or proactive. Reactive responses often occur as a result of crises, shifting societal values and expectations, or obligations such as with grants and contracts. For example, outside stakeholders such as funders establish rules to monitor organizations and ensure that they are in compliance with those rules (Ebrahim, 2003). Each funder may have their own set of rules and reporting requirements. Conventional accounting is used as a way of tracking and monitoring how the organization spends the funds that have been entrusted to it.

Proactive responses to accountability are driven by the desire to influence and shape the environment in which the organization operates, and are more strategic. This may involve umbrella organizations in national-level policy debates to support or facilitate the pursuit of sector objectives, or may concern the development of long-term approaches to sustainability (Ebrahim, 2003; Gray, 2000; Mook & Sumner, 2010).

Social accounting is one approach that enables organizations to facilitate both reactive and proactive responses to accountability, through transparency and participation of stakeholders in dialogue and decision-making. In line with Popper's understanding of democracy, mentioned above, this includes identifying and learning from failures as much as successes (EWB, 2011). We now turn to the implications of this for educating a new generation of social accountants and social economy organization leaders.

Implications for Education

This edited volume proposes alternative accounting models that take into account variables often excluded from traditional financial statements. At the present time, this approach is being applied by a number of social economy organizations with very promising results. However, in the larger context of accounting practice, it is still a marginal and invisible initiative. The adoption of new accounting models is a complex process that takes time and effort, and needs to consider the realities of education, at both formal institutions and in the community.

Challenges for the Accountancy

In terms of accounting education, there are several challenges to be addressed. There is a general recognition among many accounting scholars and practicing accountants that current accounting education is outdated for the complexities of contemporary realities and in need of significant reform (Amernic & Craig, 2004; Boyce et al., 2012; Gray & Collison, 2002; Gray, Dillard, & Spence, 2009; Jones & Abrahams, 2007; Hazelton & Haigh, 2010; Mook et al., 2005). This is particularly relevant for socially minded organizations.

As Jones and Abrahams (2007, p. 17) point out, the role of accounting professionals needs to evolve from "information provision" to that of "extended information facilitation" requiring "forward thinkers, skilled strategists and team players." Indeed, there have been repeated calls for accounting curricula to go beyond a technical focus to one that allows for broader reflection on critical issues such as environmental reporting and sustainability (Bebbington, Brown, Frame, & Thomson, 2007; Boyce et al., 2012).

Related to this is the fact that accounting models in use today were developed for for-profit organizations, and may not be the best fit for organizations who do not have profit as their primary objective. As a result, accounting and management students have a low exposure to currently used alternative accounting models that go beyond the conventional financial statements. These models pay attention to externalities, the social construction of accounting models and practices, and the development of rigorous yet flexible accounting frameworks that reflect the realities of social economy organizations.

This is not without difficulties. Hazelton and Haigh (2010) attempted to incorporate a sustainability focus into accounting courses in a traditional accounting program in Australia at both the undergraduate and graduate level. Three challenges in particular stood out in their effort. First was the predominately vocational orientation of students. This tension relates to the second challenge, which was to find space in the curriculum, and this in turn relates to the third challenge, which is the traditional, technical focus of professional bodies for which students write their certification exams.

Amernic and Craig (2004, p. 343) also point out that it is important for accounting educators and students to recognize that accounting is "idiosyncratic, political, rhetorical, ideological and non-objective." As they elaborate,

> By ignoring the social perspective of accounting we are not playing "fair" with the students who "learn" accounting, and with the future generations of people who will bear the consequences of ill-informed accounting behavior by those students when they enter practice. (Amernic & Craig, 2004, p. 351)

Based on this assessment, they make three recommendations to accounting educators in order to promote independent thought in the field of accounting: curricular reform, engaging students with critical theory, and exposing students to the history of the field.

Similarly, there are few spaces for practitioners to share and learn about accounting innovations in their workplaces (Mook et al., 2005). It is important to encourage the formation of networks and spaces to dialogue and learn about these issues, develop curricula, and propose policy. Workshops and mentoring circles could also be developed for practicing accountants to provide support and resources for the adoption and use of alternative accounting practices. These workshops and support groups would provide a space for practitioners to upgrade their skills and share lessons, experiences, and practices. All of these recommendations serve to breathe new life into the field of accounting and inspire a new generation of accountants and organization leaders.

Beyond the Accountancy

This is not to say that social accounting should be relegated to the field of accounting. As Pinnington, Lerner, and Schugurensky (2009) found, non-professionals without training in accounting have been very successful in participatory budgeting and other aspects usually performed within the domain of accountants. Indeed, in an interesting controlled experiment performed by Riahi-Belkaoui (1999), students with no, low, and high accounting knowledge were asked to review several scenarios and evaluate the creation of wealth. Those students with low or high accounting knowledge were not able to get beyond measures of wealth as dictated by Generally Accepted Accounting Principle (GAAP), or in other words, profit. Those with no accounting knowledge came up with intuitive ways to measure wealth that totally eluded those constrained by their knowledge of accounting rules and regulations.

Competencies for Social Accounting

In 2011, the United Nations Decade in Education for Sustainable Development (2005–14) undertook a review of learning processes aligned with monitoring and evaluating sustainable development, and identified four that were key:

(1) processes of collaboration and dialogue (including multi-stakeholder and intercultural dialogue);
(2) processes that engage the "whole system";
(3) processes that innovate curriculum as well as teaching and learning experiences; and
(4) processes of active and participatory learning. (Tilbury, 2011, p. 39)

The report goes on to note that learners must have the ability to ask critical questions, clarify one's own values; envision more positive and sustainable futures; think systematically; respond through applied learning; and explore the dialectic between tradition and innovation (Tilbury, 2011).

These processes are also relevant for social accounting. The cases in this volume clearly point to the need for future social accountants and organization leaders to cultivate skills in collaboration, dialogue, creativity and innovation, systems-thinking, team work, active listening, stakeholder engagement, group decision-making, conflict management, qualitative and quantitative data gathering and analysis, story-telling, critical reflection, learning from failure, change management, strategic forecasting, and lifelong learning. Special attention should also be paid to mentoring, as a means of passing on social accounting skills to the next generation of scholars and practitioners, and creating an understanding of their purpose and meaning.

Conclusion

Social accounting provides tools for bringing to light the powerful, yet often hidden, dimensions of social economy organizations in communities around the world. Systematic analysis of the responsible involvement of organizations in the society's social fabric, coupled with discussions to which a diverse spectrum of stakeholders are invited, embody the lively and communicative aspects of civil society. As the authors of the chapters in this book have shown, social accounting draws its energy from elementary democratic principles – especially from accountability, transparency, and participation, which are inherent aspects of democratic institutions. At the same time, social accounting emphasizes the deeply rooted responsibility of individuals and organizations for the welfare of others and for the sustainable use of community resources.

The chapters in this volume have made a significant contribution to the field of social accounting by bringing together instrumental tools from mainstream and social accounting, theoretical insights from critical accounting, and the values and principles of sustainability. They have provided useful frameworks to put previously invisible organizational activities into a communicable format for accountants and stakeholders, a format that emphasizes the interrelationship between economic, social, and environmental factors. Challenges still remain, but the cases in this book demonstrate that another accounting is indeed possible.

NOTES

1 Readers will notice that the authors in this volume mention most of the following factors explicitly; however, some factors are implicit.
2 Gray et al. (2010, p. 5) provide 10 categories to consider: "The entity for which we account – it could be an organization, a group, an individual, a nation, a geographic region, or even a natural resource like water; The type of organizations for which we account whether private, public, NGO, social enterprise, large, medium or small; The subject matter of the account: employees, sustainability, social responsibility and so on; The stakeholders who need to be considered; The audience for the account including whether it is a public or private document; The content of the account (what is excluded from the account); The organization's motivation for producing a report (including intended impact – whether external or internal); The reliability of the account; The extent to which the account is governed by law, codes or guidelines; The preparer of the report – the accountable organization of an independent body."

REFERENCES

Amernic, J., & Craig, R. (2004). Reform of accounting education in the post-Enron era: Moving accounting "out of the shadows." *Abacus, 40*(3), 342–78. http://dx.doi.org/10.1111/j.1467-6281.2004.00162.x

Boyce, G., Greer, S., Blair, B., & Davids, C. (2012). Expanding the horizons of accounting education: Incorporating social and critical perspectives. *Accounting Education, 21*(1), 47–74. http://dx.doi.org/10.1080/09639284.2011.586771

Bebbington, J., Brown, J., Frame, B., & Thomson, I. (2007). Theorizing engagement: The potential of a critical dialogic approach. *Accounting, Auditing & Accountability Journal, 20*(3), 356–81.

Ebrahim, A. (2003). Accountability in practice: Mechanisms for NGOs. *World Development, 31*(5), 813–29. http://dx.doi.org/10.1016/S0305-750X(03)00014-7

Engineers Without Borders (EWB). (2011). Reports: Successes and failures. Retrieved on January 14, 2012, from: http://www.ewb.ca/reports/

Etymology Online. (2012). "Transparent," "Account." Retrieved on January 1, 2012, from: http://www.etymonline.com

Gray, R. (2000). Current developments and trends in social and environmental auditing, reporting and attestation: A review and comment. *International Journal of Auditing, 4*(3), 247–68. http://dx.doi.org/10.1111/1099-1123.00316

Gray, R., & Collison, D. (2002). Can't see the wood for the trees, can't see the trees for the numbers? Accounting education, sustainability and the public interest. *Critical Perspectives on Accounting, 13*(5–6), 797–836. http://dx.doi.org/10.1006/cpac.2002.0554

Gray, R., Dillard, J., & Spence, C. (2009). Social accounting research as if the world matters: An essay in postalgia and a new absurdism. *Public Management Review, 11*(5), 545–73. http://dx.doi.org/10.1080/14719030902798222

Gray, R., Owen, D., & Adams, C. (2010). Some theories for social accounting? A review essay and a tentative pedagogic categorisation of theorisations around social accounting. In M. Freedman & B. Jaggi (Eds.), *Sustainability, environmental performance, and disclosures* (pp. 1–54). Bingley: Emerald.

Hazelton, J., & Haigh, M. (2010). Incorporating sustainability into accounting curricula: Lessons learnt from an action research study. *Accounting Education, 19*(1–2), 159–78. http://dx.doi.org/10.1080/09639280802044451

Jones, G., & Abrahams, A. (2007). Education implications of the changing role of accountants: Perceptions of practitioners, academics and students. *The Quantitative Analysis of Teaching and Learning in Business, Economics and Commerce, Forum Proceedings* (pp. 89–105). Melbourne: The University of Melbourne.

Mook, L., Sousa, J., Elgie, S., & Quarter, J. (2005). Accounting for the value of volunteer contributions. *Nonprofit Management & Leadership, 15*(4), 401–15. http://dx.doi.org/10.1002/nml.79

Mook, L., & Sumner, J. (2010). Social accounting for sustainability in the social economy. In J.J. McMurtry (Ed.), *Living economics: Perspectives on Canada's social economy* (pp. 157–78). Toronto: Emond Montgomery.

Pinnington, E., Lerner, J., & Schugurensky, D. (2009). Participatory budgeting in North America: The case of Guelph, Canada. *Journal of Public Budgeting, Accounting & Financial Management, 21*(3), 455–84.

Popper, K.R. (1964). *The poverty of historicism.* New York: Harper & Row.

Riahi-Belkaoui, A. (1999). *Value added reporting and research: State of the art.* Westport, CT: Quorum Books.

Sartori, G. (1987). *The theory of democracy revisited.* Chatham, NJ: Chatham House Publishers.

Tilbury, D. (2011). *Education for sustainable development: An expert review of processes and learning.* Paris: UNESCO.